ON KAFKA'S CASTLE
A Study

Richard Sheppard

——

ON KAFKA'S
CASTLE
A Study

BARNES & NOBLE
BOOKS
10 East 53d St., New York 10022
(a division of Harper & Row Publishers, Inc.)

PUBLISHED IN THE U.S.A. 1973 BY
HARPER AND ROW PUBLISHERS, INC.
BARNES AND NOBLE IMPORT DIVISION

ISBN–06–496234–2

PRINTED IN GREAT BRITAIN BY
EBENEZER BAYLIS AND SON LIMITED
THE TRINITY PRESS, WORCESTER, AND LONDON
AND BOUND BY W. & J. MACKAY LTD, CHATHAM

74-12236

CONTENTS

Dichtung ist Verdichtung, eine Essenz. Literatur ist dagegen Auflösung, ein Genußmittel, das das unbewußte Leben erleichtert, ein Narkotikum. *(G, 74-5)*

Poetic creation is intensification, an essence. In contrast, literature is dissolution, a means of self-indulgent pleasure which alleviates the unconscious life, a narcotic drug. *(C, 47)*

Die Kunst ist so wie das Gebet eine ins Dunkle ausgestreckte Hand, die etwas von der Gnade erfassen will, um sich in eine schenkende Hand zu verwandeln. *(G, 75)*

Art, like prayer, is a hand stretched out into the darkness which seeks to grasp some element of grace so that it may become transformed into a hand which bestows. *(C, 48)*

Der Dichter hat die Aufgabe, das isolierte Sterbliche in das unendliche Leben, das Zufällige in das Gesetzmäßige hinüberzuführen. Er hat eine prophetische Aufgabe. *(G, 231)*

The creative writer has the task of bringing over what is isolated and mortal into the life of eternity, of bringing over what is accidental into a total pattern. His is a prophetic task. *(C, 172)*

Die Spannung zwischen der subjektiven Ich-Welt und der objektiven Außenwelt, zwischen Mensch und Zeit, das ist das Hauptproblem aller Kunst. *(G, 248)*

The tension between the subjective world of the ego and the objective world outside, between man and time, is the chief problem of all art. *(C, 186)*

ACKNOWLEDGEMENTS

We are grateful to the following for permission to quote extracts:

Martin Secker & Warburg Ltd.:
Franz Kafka DIARIES edited by Max Brod
Franz Kafka LETTERS TO MILENA, Willy Hass (ed.), Tania and
  James Stern, London, 1953

Andre Deutsch Ltd.; and New Directions Inc.:
Gustav Janouch CONVERSATIONS WITH KAFKA translated by
  Goronwy Rees

S. Fischer Verlag:
Gustav Janouch GESPRACHE MIT KAFKA, Frankfurt, 1968

Alfred A. Knopf, Inc.:
Franz Kafka THE CASTLE translated by Edwin and Willa Muir

Schocken Books Inc.:
GERMAN LANGUAGE
1. 3,756 words from DAS SCHLOSS
2.   88 words from BRIEFE AN MILENA
3. 216 words from BRIEFE AN FELICE
4. 333 words from BRIEFE 1902–1924
5. 199 words from TAGEBÜCHER
6. 475 words from HOCHZEITSVORBEREITUNGEN

CREDIT LINES FOR ABOVE:
1. Reprinted by permission of Schocken Books Inc. from DAS
   SCHLOSS by Franz Kafka. Copyright © 1946 by Schocken
   Books Inc.
2. Reprinted by permission of Schocken Books Inc. from BRIEFE
   AN MILENA by Franz Kafka. Copyright © 1952 by Schocken
   Books Inc.

ABBREVIATIONS

The figures which follow the German quotations from *Das Schloß* refer to pages in Franz Kafka, *Das Schloß*, Lizenzausgabe, Schocken Books, New York, 1962.

The figures which follow the English quotations from *The Castle* refer to pages in Franz Kafka, *The Castle*, Willa and Edwin Muir (trans.), Penguin Books, London, 1962.

Where English translations of German passages are not my own, they have been based on the standard English translations of Kafka's and Schopenhauer's works which are detailed on this page.

G = Gustav Janouch, *Gespräche mit Kafka*, Frankfurt, 1968.

C = Gustav Janouch, *Conversations with Kafka*, trans, Goronwy Rees, London, 1971.

H = Franz Kafka, *Hochzeitsvorbereitungen auf dem Lande und andere Prosa aus dem Nachlaß*, Max Brod (ed.), New York, 1953.

W = Franz Kafka, *Wedding Preparations in the Country and other posthumous prose writings*, Ernst Kaiser und Eithne Wilkins (trans.), London, 1954.

BF = Franz Kafka, *Briefe an Felice*, Erich Heller und Jürgen Born (eds.), New York, 1967.

BM = Franz Kafka, *Briefe an Milena*, Willy Haas (ed.), New York, 1952.

LM = Franz Kafka, *Letters to Milena*, Willy Haas (ed.), Tania and James Stern (trans.), London, 1953.

B = Franz Kafka, *Briefe 1902–1924*, Max Brod (ed.), New York, 1958.

T = Franz Kafka, *Tagebücher 1910–1923*, Max Brod (ed.), New York, 1954.

D1 = Franz Kafka, *Diaries 1910–1913*, Max Brod (ed.), Joseph Kresh (trans.), New York, 1948.

D2 = Franz Kafka, *Diaries 1914–1923*, Max Brod (ed.), Martin Greenberg and Hannah Arendt (trans.), New York, 1949.

WV = Arthur Schopenhauer, *Die Welt als Wille und Vorstellung, Sämtliche Werke*, Bd. 1, Wolfgang Freiherr von Löhneysen (ed.), Darmstadt, 1968.

WI = Arthur Schopenhauer, *The World as Will and Idea*, Vol. 1, R. B. Haldane and J. Kemp (trans.), 6th ed., London, 1907.

INTRODUCTION

At a crucial point in *Das Schloß*, the sceptical and intelligent Amalia comes over to the place where Olga is telling K. about her family's afflictions and wryly remarks:

»*Schloßgeschichten werden erzählt? Noch immer sitzt ihr beisammen? Und du hattest dich doch gleich verabschieden wollen, K., und nun geht es schon auf zehn. Bekümmern dich denn solche Geschichten überhaupt? Es gibt hier Leute, die sich von solchen Geschichten nähren, . . .«* (298)	'*Is it Castle stories you're telling? Still sitting with your heads together? And yet you had wanted to leave us the moment after you came, K., and now it's nearly ten. Are you really bothered with stories of that sort? There are people around here who feed on such stories, . . .*' (193)

These are ominous words, for the critic who decides to add yet more pages to the vast number which already surround Kafka's tantalising novel inevitably runs the risk of incurring the same sardonic comments. Is he simply projecting his own obsessions onto the notoriously complex narrative of *Das Schloß*? Is he simply retelling the same old 'Castle stories' without reaching any new conclusions? Is he presuming to have found the key to *Das Schloß* where his predecessors have failed and when at least one of them denies that such a key exists?[1] The Castle has the uncanny ability to tempt K. into revealing his worst traits of arrogance and presumption, and *Das Schloß* can do the same to the reader who ventures into its labyrinths with excessive confidence or inadequate awareness of the difficulties which he will encounter there. Consequently, if the critic of *Das Schloß* is to avoid making mistakes which parallel K.'s and to avoid fabricating yet more 'Castle stories', he has to proceed with the utmost care, using all the insights which previous

[1] Marthe Robert, *L'Ancien et le Nouveau*, Paris, 1963, p. 277.

2

explorers have left him and ensuring all the while that he has said
nothing that is simply a derivative of his subjective and therefore
relative point of view.

Although *Das Schloß* is very like a hall of mutually reflecting
distorting mirrors which throw back different patterns as one moves
between them, the business of orientating oneself within the novel
has become considerably easier thanks to several excellent critical
studies. Ronald Gray[2] has shown us how to read the novel as a work
of literature rather than as a non-literary allegory. Friedrich Beissner,[3] Martin Walser[4] and Klaus-Peter Philippi[5] have provided us
with descriptions of the narrative structure of the novel. Ronald
Gray, Walter Sokel[6] and Heinz Politzer[7] have offered penetrating
analyses of K.'s psychology. Marthe Robert[8] has situated the novel
within a number of overlapping literary traditions, and Herbert
Tauber[9] and Erich Heller,[10] among others, have broached the intricate problem of the meaning of the Castle itself. At the same time,
however, these studies by no means add up to one coherent or ex-
haustive account of the novel. The question of the relationship of the
narrator to K. has only been partially resolved. The problem of how
it is possible to say anything unequivocal about a fictional world in
which the narrator has refused to use his authoritative voice has
never been systematically investigated. The accounts of K.'s psychology, although convergent in several respects, diverge over the
question of whether K. undergoes a change of state during the
course of the novel, and there is considerable disagreement and
confusion over the status and meaning of the Castle itself. Thus, as
well as offering some new suggestions about certain aspects of *Das
Schloß*, I hope that this study will draw attention to, and perhaps

[2] Ronald D. Gray, *Kafka's Castle*, Cambridge, 1956.
[3] Friedrich Beissner, *Kafka der Dichter*, Stuttgart, 1958.
[4] Martin Walser, *Beschreibung einer Form: Versuch über Franz Kafka*, Munich, 1961.
[5] Klaus-Peter Philippi, *Reflexion und Wirklichkeit: Untersuchungen zu Kafkas Roman, 'Das Schloß'*, Tübingen, 1966.
[6] Walter H. Sokel, *Franz Kafka: Tragik und Ironie*, Munich and Vienna, 1964, pp. 391–500.
[7] Heinz Politzer, *Franz Kafka*, Ithaca, 1962, pp. 218–81.
[8] Robert, pp. 173–311.
[9] Herbert Tauber, *Franz Kafka*, London, 1948, pp. 131–85.
[10] Erich Heller, 'The World of Franz Kafka', *The Disinherited Mind*, Penguin Books, London, 1961, pp. 175–202.

resolve some of the problems raised by the secondary literature which surrounds the novel.

The first section of this book consists in a discussion of the narrative structure of the novel. The second section asks by what criteria it is possible to say anything with certainty about a fictional world on which its very creator refuses to pass explicit judgement. In the third section, the psychology of K. will be discussed at some length. The final section investigates the status of the Castle authorities—asking whether they are good or evil, gods or men—and concludes by attempting to define the relationship of K. to the Castle. If then, this study makes mistakes which resemble those made by K., it will not, I hope, be because its author has been unwilling to pay attention to the 'Castle stories' which others have told before him or has failed to study the available maps before setting foot inside a labyrinth which may lead nowhere.

CHAPTER ONE

The Narrative Problem

Die Form ist nicht der Ausdruck des Inhaltes, sondern nur sein Anreiz, das Tor und der Weg zum Inhalt. Wirkt er, dann öffnet sich auch der verborgene Hintergrund. (G, 213)

The form is not the expression of the content, but simply its initial impulse, the gateway and the path which lead to the content. If it functions as it should, then the hidden background opens up as well. (C, 158)

Der Virtuos steht durch seine Fertigkeit eines Gauklers über der Sache. Kann aber ein Dichter über der Sache stehen? Nein! Er wird von der Welt, die er erlebt und darstellt, so wie Gott von seiner Schöpfung gefangen gehalten. (G, 219)

Because of his charlatan's dexterity, the virtuoso stands above the matter in hand. But can a creative writer stand above the matter in hand? No! He is held captive by the world which he experiences and puts before us just as God is held captive by His creation. (C, 163)

Das Leben ist so unermeßlich groß und tief wie der Sternenabgrund über uns. Man kann nur durch das kleine Guckloch seiner persönlichen Existenz hineinblicken. Und da spürt man mehr als man sieht. Darum muß man das Guckloch vor allem rein halten. (G, 253-4)

Life is as immeasurably great and deep as the chasm of stars above our heads. One can only look into it through the little peep-hole of one's personal existence. And then one senses more than one actually sees. For that reason, one must, above all else, keep that peep-hole free from dirt. (C, 191)

It is now established as a matter of first principle among critics of *Das Schloß* that it is impossible to understand the novel without appreciating its peculiar narrative form. The two principal characteristics of this form are the absence of explicit comment by the narrator on the events of the novel and the fact that everything that happens in the novel is accessible to the reader only after it has been filtered through the mind of the main protagonist K. Kafka originally wrote *Das Schloß* in the first person and only later substituted 'K.' for 'Ich'.[1] Thus it is argued that although he makes use of the third-person narrative form, he foregoes the privilege of God-like omniscience and the right to intervene in the narrative which, traditionally, this form has entailed. Moreover, he restricts himself to narrating only those experiences which K. undergoes and interprets. Consequently, the following statements are to be found in secondary works on *Das Schloß*:

Es geschieht nichts ohne K., nichts ohne Beziehung auf ihn und nichts in seiner Abwesenheit. Alles geschieht, indem es ihm widerfährt. Und alles wird so erzählt, so klar und so undeutlich, so verzerrt und so genau, wie er es in seiner Enttäuschung, seinem Verdruß, seiner Müdigkeit wahrnimmt. Der „Schriftsteller" steht nicht erläuternd, dozierend, reflektierend neben ihm.[2]

Nothing happens without K., nothing happens which is not related to him and nothing happens in his absence. Everything happens inasmuch as it happens to him. And everything is narrated just as clearly and just as indistinctly, just as distortedly and just as exactly as he experiences it in his disappointment, his vexation, his tiredness. The 'author' does not stand next to him interpreting, teaching or reflecting.

Der Held sieht nicht mehr so viel, dafür deutet er jetzt. Der Leser ist völlig auf diese Deutung angewiesen, da ja kein Erzähler da ist, der uns mehr sagen könnte als der

The hero does not see all that much any more, so he interprets to make up for it. The reader is entirely dependent upon this interpretation as no narrator is

---

[1] See Dorrit Cohn, 'K. enters *The Castle*—On the change of person in Kafka's manuscript', *Euphorion*, 62, 1968, pp. 28–45.
[2] Beissner, pp. 24–5.

Held sieht, weil eben durch den Helden erzählt wird.[3]

there who could tell us more than the hero sees, simply because all narration proceeds via the hero.

Der Erzähler greift nicht ein einziges Mal ein, um dieses konjunktivisch—vermutende Abtasten zu unterbrechen oder gar dem Leser etwas zu verraten, was ihn in einen Abstand zu K. bringen könnte.[4]

The narrator does not intervene even once in order to interrupt this subjunctively suppositional groping or to give something away to the reader which would allow him to gain distance from K.

In fiction, ordinarily, the community of author and reader stands as objective reality outside and above the points of view of the characters and forms a 'true' frame of reference. The traditional story-teller or novelist maintains this division by one or both of these devices: he switches the point of view from one character to another, and thus enables us to enjoy a relative omniscience since we can look into all minds of the story, which none of the characters can; or he keeps his own perspective separate, looks into his characters, and comments upon their thoughts and actions. These conventions are absent in Kafka's fiction. His stories know only a single point of view, that of the protagonist. Even in his third-person narratives—and his major works are all third-person narratives—objects, scenes, and persons are seen by us only through the protagonist's eyes.[5]

Die phänomenologische Einheit des Erzählens bedeutet auch, daß der Erzähler, der als solcher nicht mehr auftritt, keinen eigenen Wirklichkeitsbereich innerhalb des fiktionalen Ganzen haben kann. Dadurch, daß er nur durch

The phenomenological unity of the mode of narration also means that the narrator, who no longer appears as such, can have no area of reality of his own within the fictional whole. By virtue of the fact that he can be inferred only

---

[3] Walser, p. 24.
[4] Walser, p. 30.
[5] Walter Sokel, *Franz Kafka*, New York and London, 1966, p. 9.

die Fiktionalität der erzählten Welt hindurch erschließbar ist, die K. als quasi faktische gegenübersteht, besitzt er keine Distanz gegenüber der Wirklichkeitsebene des Erzählten, ist er selbst kein eigenwertiges Faktum mehr—auch nicht aus der präteritalen Erzählform erschließbar.[6]

from the fictional nature of the narrated world which stands over against K. as though it were real, he possesses no distance from the plane of reality of the narrative. He himself is no longer a fact in his own right—nor can his presence be inferred from the past historic form of narration.

Although such statements are near enough to the truth to be immediately acceptable, they are just far enough away from the truth to lead their authors into greater or lesser difficulties. This is because all of them seem to imply, more or less clearly, that the absence of explicit comment by the narrator is the same as the total absence of the narrator from his fictional world. Consequently, some critics are led to conclude either that the author has allowed his consciousness to become identical with that of K., or that the author has deliberately excluded his consciousness from the narrative altogether. Martin Walser, for instance, concludes that no author exists within the world of *Das Schloß* who could mediate between K.'s reactions to his world and our reactions to K.'s reactions to his world:

Den Leser treffen diese Dnthüllungen im gleichen Augenblick und mit der gleichen Schwere wie die K.s.[7]

These disclosures strike the reader in the same instant and with the same force as those of K.

Der Erzähler fehlt, das Medium [K.] ist die »wichtigste« Person des Werkes, also geschieht alles ohne Brechung, in sich selbst, von sich selbst her, und alle Deutung bleibt uns überlassen.[8]

The narrator is missing, the medium [K.] is the 'most important' character in the novel. Consequently, everything happens without interruption, within its own terms, under its own impetus, and all interpretation is left to us.

[6] Philippi, pp. 19–20.
[7] Walser, p. 29.
[8] Walser, p. 39.

And Klaus-Peter Philippi writes:

„Einsinnigkeit" ist so eine Erleb-niseinheit, die durch die jeweilige Interpretation des Geschehens durch K. geschaffen wird. In ihr ist alles erkennbar auf K. be-zogen. Die konkurrenzlose Dar-stellung der innerseelischen Verar-beitung des Begegnenden, einer inneren Welt überhaupt, macht K. zum integrierenden Zentrum des Romans, womit er eine Funktion des auktorialen Erzählers über-nimmt und auf eine verstecktere Weise ausübt.[9]

'Monopolised perspective' is thus a unified mode of experiencing that is created by the way in which K. interprets any given event. In this mode, everything is perceptibly related to K. The un-challenged depiction of the process of assimilation of events, indeed, of a whole inner world, makes K. the integrating centre of the novel. Because of this, K. takes over and exercises in a more elusive way a function of the authorial narrator.

In both cases, the writers seem to suggest that the relationship of the narrator to the fictional world of *Das Schloß* is that of a *Deus Absconditus* to a world which he has set in motion but from which he has withdrawn. This kind of suggestion seems to receive a great deal of legitimation from Kafka himself, who, throughout his life, made several remarks to the effect that he himself was not present in his novels. Writing to Felice Bauer [10] in 1913 he said:

Und Maxens Lob! Er lobt ja nicht eigentlich mein Buch, dieses Buch liegt ja vor, das Urteil wäre nachzuprüfen, wenn einer Lust dazu haben sollte; aber er lobt vor allem mich, und das ist das Lächerlichste von allem. Wo bin

And Max's praise! He doesn't actually praise my book; after all, the book exists, and his judgement could be examined, should anyone feel so inclined; but it is me he praises, and this is the most ridi-culous of all. For where am I?

[9] Philippi, p. 25.
[10] Felice Bauer was Kafka's first fiancée. He met her in 1912, became formally engaged to her in 1914 and broke off the engagement later on in the same year. In 1917 he became engaged to her once more, only to break off the engagement finally at the end of that year.

ich denn? Wer kann mich nach-
prüfen? Ich wünschte mir eine
kräftige Hand nur zu dem Zweck,
um in diese unzusammenhängende
Konstruktion, die ich bin, ordent-
lich hineinzufahren. (BF, 306;
dated 18–19.ii.1913)

Who can examine me? I wish I
had a strong hand for the sole pur-
pose of thrusting it into this in-
coherent construction that I am.

and:

Mein einziges Glücksgefühl be-
steht darin, daß niemand weiß,
wo ich bin. Wüßte ich eine
Möglichkeit, das für immer fort-
zusetzen! (BF, 472; dated
6.xi.1913)

The fact that no one knows where
I am is my only happiness. If
only I could prolong this forever!

Five years later, he wrote to his friend Max Brod:[11]

Darum scheint mir jede Kritik,
die mit Begriffen von Echt,
Unecht umgeht, und Wille und
Gefühl des nicht vorhandenen
Autors im Werk sucht, ohne Sinn
und eben nur dadurch zu er-
klären, daß auch sie ihre Heimat
verloren hat . . . (B, 241; dated
early April, 1918)

For that reason, all criticism
which deals in concepts of real
and unreal and looks in the work
for the will and the feelings of the
absent author, seems to me to be
senseless and only explicable by
the fact that its practitioners
have lost their homeland as well . . .

And Gustav Janouch reports him as saying during the years when he was working on *Das Schloß*:

Es gibt nur einen festen Punkt.
Das ist die eigene Unzulänglich-
keit. Von der muß man aus-
gehen. (G, 211)

There is only one fixed point and
that is one's own insufficiency.
That is where one must start from.
(C, 156)

[11] Max Brod (1884–1968) was Kafka's closest confidant, literary executor and biographer.

Throughout his creative life, Kafka was acutely aware of the relativity of his own point of view and profoundly anxious lest, in a world of uncertainty, he might, by the mere act of putting pen to paper, either be implying that his relative point of view was in some way absolute, or be indulging his own ego in order to compensate for an inability to come to terms with that uncertain world. Consequently, in his fictional writings, Kafka normally strives to eliminate his own personality as far as this is possible, and in his letters, he not only draws attention to this design, but also seems at times to imply that he has realised it. Nevertheless, it is impossible for any writer to eliminate himself completely from his work. His presence is bound to be betrayed by his selection of material, by the way in which the narrator is presented and by the very manner in which the tale is told. Correspondingly, therefore, the remarks of those commentators who suggest that Kafka the narrator is absent from *Das Schloß* do not quite measure up to the reality of that novel.

At a very obvious level, the idea that K. absorbs the consciousness of the narrator is made dubious by the consideration that the reader's relationship to K. is not constant but variable. When K. talks in direct speech, the reader identifies with K.'s perspective much more closely than he does when he hears what K. says or thinks in reported speech. *Pace* Philippi, when it is a case of reported speech, the very existence of signposts such as 'K. said' or 'K. thought' inevitably invites the reader to remember that he is hearing K.'s responses to his situation through the agency of a third person. The reader is thereby prevented from assuming uncritically that those responses are necessarily authoritative or accurate.[12] Even when the reader hears K. talk in direct speech, it is still not true to say that he acquiesces completely in K.'s point of view as though K. had taken over the traditional function of the narrator and was acting as the 'integrating centre' of the novel. When the reader hears K. speak directly, his acquired knowledge that K.'s point of view is not necessarily the only one possible invites him to measure K.'s estimates and opinions against other possibilities of interpretation that are unobtrusively inherent in the

---

[12] Compare Winfried Kudszus, 'Erzählhaltung und Zeitverschiebung in Kafka's "Prozeß" und "Schloß" ', *DVjS*, 38, 1964, pp. 192–207, especially pp. 193–6.

total situation in which K. finds himself. *Das Schloß* may sound like a first-person novel, but its structure is so much that of a third-person novel that, as Dorrit Cohn pointed out, the original first-person form of the novel was a grammatical accident rather than a structural necessity. Even though the narrator who informs that third-person structure has foregone the right to speak directly, his presence or consciousness forms a 'hidden background' to the entire narrative, suggesting indirectly to the reader that the authority which K. assumes may be spurious, that K. may simply be looking at the world through a 'peep-hole' which he may not have troubled to keep particularly clean.

More conclusively perhaps, the narrator's presence in *Das Schloß* is indicated by a small number of episodes which are reported 'above K.'s head', episodes of which K. either cannot or probably does not have personal experience. The first of these is constituted by the opening paragraph of the novel:

Es war spät abends, als K. ankam. Das Dorf lag in tiefem Schnee. Vom Schloßberg war nichts zu sehen, Nebel und Finsternis umgaben ihn, auch nicht das schwächste Lichtschein deutete das große Schloß an. (5)	*It was late in the evening when K. arrived. The village lay deep in snow. Nothing could be seen of the Castle hill, fog and darkness shrouded it, and not even the weakest glimmer of light indicated the presence of the great Castle. (9)*

Because the Castle is invisible, the newcomer K. can know nothing of its existence, and this speculation is confirmed one page later when K. asks whether there really is a Castle in the village. In the first paragraph then, the invisible narrator is reporting something which K., at this point in the novel, cannot himself see or know about.

The second such incident occurs in the fourth chapter when the maids cover up K. and Frieda after they have made love for the second time, and then, apparently, fallen asleep:

Erst die Müdigkeit ließ sie still und einander dankbar werden.	*Only when they were weary did they become still and grateful to*

Die Mägde kamen dann auch herauf, »*Sieh, wie die hier liegen*«, *sagte eine und warf aus Mitleid ein Tuch über sie. (69)*	one another. Then the maids came up as well. 'Look how they're lying here,' said one of them and out of compassion cast a coverlet over them. (49)

Because K. appears to have fallen asleep, he probably does not hear what the maids say and probably does not see them as they cover him and Frieda. Here again the narrator is allowing the reader to hear of something 'above K.'s head'.

A third example of this kind of break in the narrative perspective occurs during the course of K.'s interview with Bürgel. During K.'s first bout of sleep, he remains conscious of Bürgel's words, more conscious, it is said, than he had been when he was awake. In contrast, K.'s second bout of sleep is free from dreams and interruptions. Consequently, it is impossible for K. to have heard very much of Bürgel's long speech which comprises most of the last part of the eighteenth chapter.

Besides these three passages where it is either definite or highly probable that the reader is hearing or seeing things which K. does not, there is one other long incident in *Das Schloß* which seems to be there independently of K.'s experience, and that is the account of the long-standing relationship between Gisa and Schwarzer which extends from page 238 to 240 of the definitive German text.[13] Although this entire account is prefaced by the explanation:

Wie man im Brückenhof K. erzählt hatte . . . (238)	As K. had been told in the Brückenhof . . .

this signpost, whose ostensible purpose is to integrate the subsequent episode with K.'s experience, actually has the effect of making the reader aware that the episode in question cannot really form part of K.'s experience. To begin with, the generalised 'man', literally 'one', stands in contrast with the exact way in which K.

[13] This passage is missing from the Penguin edition used here, but were it included, it would begin after the paragraph which ends: '. . . warmth and nearness.' (156), continue for two pages, and then be followed by the paragraph which begins: 'The only astonishing thing . . .' (156).

normally identifies the source of any information that he receives. Then again, it is difficult to see when K. could have heard such a detailed and extended account of the Gisa-Schwarzer relationship, seeing that we remain with him throughout his waking hours in the village. Similarly, it is difficult to believe that the K. who was so self-obsessed and unreceptive to the words of others at the beginning of his stay in the village could have taken in such an apparently gratuitous anecdote in sufficient detail to be able to reproduce it so extensively several days later. Given the structure of the novel and K.'s mentality, it becomes hard to resist the suggestion that the entire Gisa-Schwarzer episode is, in reality, being imparted to the reader 'above K.'s head', the prefatory signpost notwithstanding. The direct speech in which the interpolated episode is narrated also supports this suggestion. If this episode really did represent K. turning over something which he had heard in his mind, in order to align it with his other experience, then it would be reasonable to expect it to be narrated in the subjunctive mood of German indirect speech which K. normally employs for such a purpose.

When, at the very end of the interpolation, the direct account of the way in which Schwarzer conducts his life is suddenly corrected by the particularized:

. . . *wie es ja auch K. erlebt* . . . as indeed had been K.'s ex-
hatte. (240)   perience too.

attention is again drawn to the fact that information which precedes this remark has been provided in a manner which is untypical of *Das Schloß*. Because such information is normally given only to the extent that it relates immediately to K., this second signpost gives the impression that the narrator has done something uncharacteristic and then tried to compensate for this retrospectively. Finally, it is worth comparing the way in which the account of the Gisa-Schwarzer relationship is worked into the narrative with the skilful way in which we hear about the *Herrenhof* landlady's frustrated struggle with the authorities at the beginning of the seventeenth chapter. Whereas the former account tends, for the reasons given, to stand out awkwardly from the narrative, it is entirely natural

that K. should hear local gossip about a person of immediate interest to the clients while these are waiting to be interviewed in the
establishment which she runs.

Admittedly, the status of the Gisa-Schwarzer passage is, as has
been implied, somewhat doubtful. Had Kafka lived to complete the
novel, it is quite probable that he would have assimilated this
episode more flawlessly into its narrative structure. Nevertheless,
within the definitive text as it stands, the episode is of great interest
because there the reader can see the narrator working hard to include
information which he specifically wants to be heard while doing his
utmost to make his own presence as unobtrusive as possible. Even if
Kafka had succeeded in integrating this episode fully into the
novel, the fact that the reader can see this process of integration
going forward inevitably indicates that a narrator is secretly at work
within *Das Schloß*.

Thus, just because the narrator of *Das Schloß* does not intervene
directly 'interpreting, teaching, reflecting', it does not follow that
he is necessarily a *Deus Absconditus*. Like the God to whom Kafka
refers in the second of the quotations which preface this chapter, the
narrator of *Das Schloß* is a captive of the world which he has created.
At key points, he reveals himself as directly as he dare, but more
typically, he exists within that world as a unifying substance or
nameless, shaping presence who provides the reader with a subliminal sense that K., appearances to the contrary, is himself under
judgement. Martin Walser, despite the apparent absoluteness of his
quoted statements about the absence of the narrator, seems, at other
points in his book, to be aware that a narrator is somehow present in
Das Schloß. Consequently, he is led to modify his original position
when he introduces the concept of 'Kongruenz' to explain the relationship of K. to the narrator. Whereas Walser first seems to use
this concept in order to suggest an identity between K. and the
narrator:

Wir haben bisher die Kongruenz   As yet, we have not examined
des Autors mit seinen Helden   more closely the congruence of the
noch nicht näher geprüft. Wir   author with his heroes. We have
haben sie festgestellt und ihre   simply established this congruence

Wirkungen in einer ganz bestimm-	*and pointed out the effects which it*
ten Richtung aufgezeigt.[14]	*has in one very definite direction.*

he later goes on to repudiate the identity of K. and the narrator and uses 'Kongruenz' to mean simply 'closeness':

Will man nun mutmaßen, warum	*If one wants to speculate why*
Kafka später vom »Ich« zum	*Kafka later went over from the*
»Er« fortgeschritten ist, so darf	*'I' to the 'he', one might per-*
man vielleicht sagen, daß ihm	*haps say that the 'I' allowed*
das »Ich« zu wenig Distanz	*him too little distance. In this*
gewährte. Hier war die Kon-	*case, congruence was in danger of*
gruenz in Gefahr, in eine Ident-	*turning into identity.*
ität umzuschlagen.[15]	

Whether he means to or not, Walser discovers that he has to revise his initial idea that implicit narrative presence is the same thing as explicit narrative intervention.

Walter Sokel too finally moves away from the suggestion that the narrator is entirely absent from Kafka's fictional world and concludes:

> *We have just shown that the protagonist's solipsistic perspective, through which we experienced the narrative, does not allow us to speak of authorial truth in Kafka's work. Yet there is an objective and verifiable authorial truth in most of his writings. It is obliquely smuggled in against the consciousness of the protagonist. In the contradiction between the reader's perspective, as given him by the protagonist, and the hidden truth of the work lies the fundamental concern of Kafka's art, the basis of its structure, and the secret of its unsettling effect.*[16]

And Ronald Gray seems also to come to the conclusion that a narrator may be present in *Das Schloß* even though he does not reveal himself through any explicit comment:

[14] Walser, p. 26–7.
[15] Walser, p. 38.
[16] Sokel, *Franz Kafka,* pp. 11–12.

And so throughout, while there is almost a compulsion on the reader
to experience the events of the novel as K. experiences them, one is
aware of a suggested overall scheme into which these experiences
may fit, of an invitation to see the experiences from other points of
view than K.'s. There is a mingling of objective narrative—the
narrator telling the reader what went on, and subjective reaction—
the limitation of all interpretation to what went on in K.'s mind.[17]

Although it seems, in the light of the foregoing discussion, that it
is permissible to speak of a 'narrative presence' in *Das Schloß*, this
conclusion leaves one very important question unresolved. Given
that an 'authorial truth', an 'overall scheme', do not exist in *Das
Schloß* in the form of stated comment or easily discernible attitude,
to what criteria or frame of reference is it possible for the reader to
appeal if he is to evaluate the events and characters of the novel?
Even if the sense of the author's presence does impel the reader to
maintain a critical distance from the mind of K. which dominates the
foreground of the novel, what is his authority for saying anything
definite about K. and his world, seeing that the narrator provides
him with no obvious clues?

This is a very real methodological difficulty, and it has been
ignored by those writers who select a more or less arbitrary frame of
reference—Freudian, Existentialist, Marxist, Christian, anthro-
pological, autobiographical, etc.—and discuss *Das Schloß* within
the terms thereby provided. Although many useful insights may be
generated by such procedures, they all beg the question of authority
and approach. If the author himself deliberately decides not to
provide the reader with the explicit frame of reference that he has
come to expect from the third-person novel, then it simply will not
do to impose an extraneous frame of reference onto the novel as a
substitute. Somehow or other, we must, if we are to establish an
authoritative frame of reference within whose terms K. and his relationship to the Castle may legitimately be discussed, adduce such a
frame from within the novel itself, and if this cannot be done, then,
as Walser suggests at one point, anything goes and any one reading
is as good as any other.

[17] Gray, p. 25.

3

Marthe Robert, very interestingly suggests that one way of dealing with this problem is to look at *Das Schloß* in terms of literary antecedents which provide parallels to it:

C'est ainsi qu'après avoir été le héros d'un roman de mœurs, d'un roman feuilleton, d'un conte de fées et d'une geste médiévale, il [K.] devient pour finir le suivant d'Ulysse qui, pour gagner de restaurer l'ordre, dut être comme lui un nomade et un Juste souffrant.[18]

Thus, after being the hero of a novel of manners, of a serial novel, of a fairy story and of a medieval gestus, he [K.] finally becomes the successor of Ulysses, who, so that order might be restored, had, like him, to become a wanderer and a righteous man who undergoes suffering.

Although this approach enables Mme. Robert to make some very illuminating comparisons between K. and the Knight of the Grail and between K. and Ulysses, the fact remains that K. himself shows no sign of being at all aware of his complex literary ancestry. Nevertheless, Mme. Robert writes at times almost as though this were not the case. She speaks, for instance, of his imitation of Ulysses;[19] says that this latter-day champion is ready to do anything to procure the benefits of the Grail[20] and contends that K. is the 'land-surveyor of books' just as Don Quixote was their knight-errant.[21] In fact, however, one of K.'s main characteristics is his almost total lack of a sense of tradition. Unable therefore to look consciously for parallels and contrasts between his own experience and that of any literary predecessors, he has to pull himself out of the marsh by his own hair and discover, with almost no help from the past, patterns of meaning within the world of the village and Castle. Mme. Robert amply shows that *Das Schloß* is situated at a point where several literary streams converge. But her approach leads her, in the first part of her work, to move towards the novel from an extrinsic frame of reference rather than evolve such a frame of reference from the novel itself.

[18] Robert, p. 215.
[19] Robert, p. 215.
[20] Robert, p. 213.
[21] Robert, p. 199.

Klaus-Peter Philippi suggests at one point [22] that the only criteria which can be used to say anything about K. and the Castle must, in the absence of an authoritative narrator, derive from the experience of the reader. At another point, however, he seems to suggest the possibility of establishing a frame of reference which is immanent within and specific to the novel. He says that within *Das Schloß*, an objective system of reference is replaced by a 'definite pattern of behaviour in the given situation.'[23] To take up this very helpful suggestion, K., during this time in the village, finds himself in a variety of situations, and if these situations are examined closely, regular patterns begin to emerge. K. reacts in similar ways to different situations or in different ways to a recurrent situation. K.'s interpretation of his experiences does not always do justice to the facts and realities of those experiences. The people whom K. encounters react to and act upon him with a certain consistency. Certain situations appear to be archetypal for the entire novel or to carry more meaning for K. than he is capable of understanding. K. encounters people whose fate parodies or parallels his own. Certain words, symbols and emotions come to characterise K. or those with whom he is most concerned. In short, as K. and the world of the Castle interact, certain features of that interaction become either recurrent or salient—and therefore significant. An ordinary word, a commonplace event, a detail of the environment, an unexceptional response, a change of tone, an uncharacteristic insight, a blatant oversight seem at first reading to be present in the novel by accident, but when this accident is seen to recur or to form a contrast, it begins to appear as part of a 'total pattern', becomes akin to a fixed point of reference which says something about K., his relationship with the surrounding world and the nature of that world. It is perfectly true that we see nearly everything through K.'s eyes. Nevertheless, the narrator's consciousness makes certain features of the narrative stand out in relief and prompts the reader to decipher the patterns which they create even though K. himself may be unaware of the patterns or may put a different interpretation on the elements which form them. To extend the theological analogy which was

[22] Philippi, p. 28.
[23] Philippi, p. 30.

employed earlier, K. is surrounded by a complex of hidden signs which signify the objective point of view of the narrator/God who has created them and which communicate an 'objective and verifiable authorial truth' about K. and his world to anyone who can make sense of them.

As the patterns generated within *Das Schloß* have the effect of distancing the reader from K.'s assessment of any given situation, of drawing attention to other possibilities of interpretation and of arousing the suspicion that the world external to K. has a secret life of its own, the means by which these patterns are created will be referred to as 'alienation-devices'. Before we can look more closely at the significance of those patterns, it is necessary to spend considerable time in an examination of the devices which create them. In this context, it is perhaps worth pointing out in advance that this method of reading *Das Schloß* differs extensively from that used, for example, by Marthe Robert (who makes relatively little of the narrative structure[24] and says relatively little about the way in which the consciousness of the narrator casts an obliquely critical light on K.). Both Marthe Robert and the present writer agree in seeing K. as a man whose vision is flawed and who goes on a pilgrimage during which he learns to adjust his vision to reality. But Mme. Robert argues that the world external to K. is either meaningless, or neutral,[25] or hostile,[26] or filled with a meaning which is for ever inaccessible to K.[27] Consequently, she attributes this change of vision mainly to K.'s own intellectual persistence.[28] In contrast, the present writer will argue that the world which exists outside K. attempts continually and obliquely to meet K. half-way in order to communicate something of great importance to him. If K.'s pilgrimage issues in the discovery of some truth, then this, it is claimed here, is due as much to the (ultimately benign) influence of the forces behind the external world as it is to his own efforts.

---

[24] Compare Robert, p. 194, where a passing reference is made to Friedrich Beissner's *Der Erzähler Franz Kafka*, Stuttgart, 1952, but where no reference is made to Beissner's *Kafka der Dichter* or Gray's book on *Das Schloß*.

[25] Robert, p. 294.

[26] Robert, p. 273.

[27] Robert, p. 307.

[28] Robert, pp. 275–6.

CHAPTER TWO

Alienation-Devices

Man entgeht keinem Gespenst, das man in die Welt hinausläßt. Das Böse kehrt immer wieder zu seinem Ausgangspunkt zurück. *(G, 65)*

One cannot escape any spectre that one releases into the world. Evil returns again and again to its point of origin. *(C, 40)*

Die Kunst fliegt um die Wahrheit, aber mit der entschiedenen Absicht, sich nicht zu verbrennen. Ihre Fähigkeit besteht darin, in der dunklen Leere einen Ort zu finden, wo der Strahl des Lichts, ohne daß dies vorher zu erkennen gewesen wäre, kräftig aufgefangen werden kann. *(H, 104)*

Art flies around the truth, but with the decisive intention of not getting itself burned. Its ability consists in finding a place within the empty darkness where the beam of light can be firmly grasped hold of, even though its presence had previously not been perceived. *(W, 98)*

It goes without saying that the means by which Kafka gradually generates a critical perspective on K. and a sense that he is involved in a world which has a secret life of its own are unobtrusive, closely-worked and complex. In *Das Schloß*, we are dealing not with one device, consistently used, but with a variety of devices which interact with and reinforce one another, and which are fused into so tightly-knit a unity by the invisible substance of the narrator's mind, that it is somewhat artificial to distinguish between them. Nevertheless, with this proviso in mind, it is possible to distinguish between eight broad types of alienation-device: parallelisms, discrepancies, leitmotivs, changes of register, reflection, indirect narrational comment, direct comment on K. by others and breaks in narrative perspective.

35

A. Parallelisms

(i) *People in parallel situations*

As K. moves through the world of the village and Castle, he time and time again comes into contact with people whose situations or predicaments offer him parallels with his own. Of these, the various members of the Barnabas family are the most important. For example, just as K., through his continued struggles, becomes spiritually and psychologically lamed, so too, Barnabas' parents have been lamed almost to the point of death by their futile attempts at self-exculpation, and when K. meets them for the very first time, the scene presents itself to him in the following manner:

Und alles ringsum entsprach dem nicht nur, überbot es noch, der alte gichtische Vater, der mehr mit Hilfe der tastenden Hände als der sich langsam schiebenden, steifen Beine vorwärts kam, die Mutter mit auf der Brust gefalteten Händen, die wegen ihre Fülle auch nur die winzigsten Schritte machen konnte. Beide, Vater und Mutter, gingen schon, seitdem K. eingetreten war, aus ihrer Ecke auf ihn zu und hatten ihn noch lange nicht erreicht. (47)	*His surroundings not only corroborated all that but even emphasised it, the old gouty father who progressed more by the help of his groping hands than by the slow movements of his stiff legs, and the mother with her hands folded on her bosom, who was incapable of any but the smallest steps because of her stoutness. Both of them, father and mother, had been advancing from their corner towards K. ever since he had come in, and were still a long way from reaching him. (36)*

The laboured gait of these old people simultaneously points forwards to the lameness which threatens K. if he does not give up his struggles with the Castle, and backwards to the nightmare experience of running with the greatest exertion while getting nowhere which he has just undergone in the company of Barnabas. Although K. cannot yet know it, he is seeing, in the ineffectual struggles of the old people to walk across the room, an image of their own spiritual state and an image of the fate which awaits him if he does not give up his struggles.

Similarly, although K. does not yet realise it, the fate of the messenger to whom he has entrusted himself, and the fate of the sister (Amalia) whose far-away glance, it later transpires, has soured his first visit to the Barnabas household, provide parallels with his own fate. Although Barnabas has, in his naïve wilfulness, spent years getting inside the Castle to the almost complete neglect of his life in the village, he has, K. discovers, gained nothing of substance from his exertions. Similarly, although Amalia has succeeded in imposing her will on all those who surround her, the only result of this is that she now exists in a state of isolation from other humans which is even more absolute and more enduring than that which K. achieves by his defiance in the *Herrenhof* courtyard at the end of the eighth chapter. Although K. cannot yet understand it, all the members of the Barnabas family have a crucial relevance for him inasmuch as their predicaments parallel his own, and it is consequently a matter of the greatest irony that K. should 'scarcely glance at them' (35) when first he meets them and should even go so far as to say to himself:

. . . *er hatte geglaubt, hier im Dorfe habe jeder für ihn Bedeutung, und es war wohl auch so, nur gerade diese Leute hier bekümmerten ihn gar nicht. (48)*	. . . *he had believed that in this village, everybody meant something to him, and that was probably true as well, it was just these particular people who didn't concern him at all. (36)*

Shortly after the beginning of Chapter Fifteen, K. comes to realise just how much importance the Barnabas family has for him (258), but he never becomes aware that there are many other people in the village whose situations exactly parallel his own and from whom he could learn the pointlessness of engaging in a struggle with the Castle. When, for instance, K. enters Lasemann's house early on in the book, he ignores the scene of rude but vital family life which greets him there and concentrates his gaze on the woman who describes herself as 'a girl from the Castle', who appears not to be one of the peasant family and whose eyes are directed 'unbestimmt in die Höhe'—'into the indistinct heights'. Although this woman bears a superficial resemblance to a Madonna because of the aura of light in which she is bathed, she, like K., gazes away from the realities of family life into the unknown distances above and she, like the *Brückenhof* landlady, whose gaze, metaphorically speaking, has never left Klamm, has become ill as a result. Thus, when K. looks at her sick and wasted form, he is looking at another image of the wasting psychic sickness which has debilitated Barnabas' parents and which will debilitate him so long as his gaze is directed 'unbestimmt in die Höhe', Castlewards. A little later on in the novel, K. notes to himself that the sheen of Barnabas' suit reminds him somewhat of the aura of light which surrounded this sick woman. One might therefore expect K. to realise that this aura is as deceptive as Barnabas' pseudo-official suit which covers a shirt that is full of holes. But K. nowhere makes this connection consciously. Nowhere does he see that the woman's sickness is also Barnabas' sickness, and that the sickness of them both is his own sickness as well.

K. is also unaware of the affinity which exists between himself and Brunswick. Like K., Brunswick is a 'Streber', a man who enjoys struggle for its own sake, and also the biggest 'Schuster'[1] in the village. Like K., Brunswick has entered upon a struggle with the Castle in order to attain the impossible—the appointment of a land-surveyor—and, because he, like K., is interested more in the process of struggle than in its final outcome, he is actually angered when his project appears to be realised and an ostensible land-surveyor arrives in the village. Consequently, instead of welcoming K. he helps to eject him from Lasemann's house without showing any interest in him at all. Although K. hears about Brunswick's enterprises from the Village Superintendent in words which could equally well apply to himself, and although K. realises at one point that Brunswick ought to have been an ally of his, he never consciously registers the similarity between their two natures and so fails to see that Brunswick's 'stupidity' and 'inability to keep still' are equally his own.

Later on in the book still, while K. is waiting for his interview

---

[1] Translated literally, the German word 'Schuster' means 'cobbler', but in colloquial Austrian usage, 'Schuster' also means 'rogue'.

with Erlanger, he comes across yet another little parallel to himself
in the person of the landlady of the *Herrenhof*. She, it is recounted,
has entered the lists against the Castle authorities in order to get
measures passed which will prevent the villagers who have to wait
for an interview with the officials from standing around in the corridors of the *Herrenhof*. However, the very obstinacy and immoder-
ateness with which the landlady has pressed her case has had the
effect of multiplying the number of people who have to wait in the
corridors of her inn in order to see the officials in connection with
her case! Thus, the incident ends as follows:

... *freilich war es eine empfind-* *liche Strafe für die Witin—man* *lachte ein wenig darüber—, daß* *gerade die Angelegenheit des* *Wartegebäudes zahlreiche Be-* *sprechungen nötig machte und die* *Gänge des Hauses kaum leer* *wurden. (350)*	... *and that really was a nice* *punishment for the landlady—* *and people laughed a little over* *it—that the very affair of the* *waiting-room should necessitate* *innumerable interviews so that* *the corridors of the house were* *hardly ever empty. (226)*

There is no obvious need, at this point of the story, to give us any
information about the *Herrenhof* landlady. It is probable therefore
that Kafka has provided this information to shed more light upon
K., who, through fighting with the authorities, only causes himself
added discomfort and frustration.

Then again, although K. identifies sufficiently with young Hans
Brunswick at an unconscious level to be angered by Frieda's good-
humoured attempts to make Hans pipe down, he never realises
consciously that this boy is a smaller version of himself. Like K.,
Hans is imperious and conducts his conversation 'as though, in his
opinion, he were the only one allowed to do the questioning . . .'
(138). Like K., Hans conceals his essential childishness beneath the
appearance of an apparently 'energetic, clever and far-seeing man'.
Like K., Hans is more interested in overcoming hurdles than in
pursuing final aims. Like K., Hans misunderstands some of the
questions that are put to him, fails to answer others correctly and
even refuses to answer some at all. Even when Hans says that he

wants to be a man like K., K., in his complacency, fails to see that this desire is more an adverse judgement on his own childishness than a sign of Hans' maturity, fails to see that he, like Hans, is a 'mere schoolboy' who needs to learn much about himself and the world outside himself.

One can perhaps excuse K. for not recognising the parallels which are presented by the sick woman in blue, Brunswick and his son and the landlady of the *Herrenhof,* for these persons are peripheral figures. It is more difficult to excuse him for failing and even refusing to understand the parallel which exists between himself and Gardena, the landlady of the *Brückenhof.* Whereas K. comes across the above four parallels incidentally, in the sixth chapter, Gardena goes out of her way to reveal to K. the similarity between her past mode of life and the mode of life on which K. seems intent, precisely so that he may avoid making her mistakes. In this episode, Gardena summons K. to her bedside. Then, with an extraordinary politeness and restraint which contrast strikingly with her normal abruptness and impatience with K., she recounts at great length and with complete lack of reserve, the story of the failure of her marriage with Hans. K., however, proves to be completely incapable of consciously grasping the all-important fact that Gardena's marriage has failed because she, like the Barnabas family, the woman in blue and himself, has been obsessed with the Castle and its mysteries, has allowed them to become a quasi-daemonic influence upon her, and has, in consequence, neglected her marriage and family life. Throughout her marriage, Gardena has dwelt to such an extent upon her fleeting relationship with Klamm and the mementos which he left her that she has been unable to give herself to her husband as a person. So weighed down, so exhausted is she by 'the burden of her memory', that she has become 'herzkrank', 'sick in her heart', incapable of forming relationships with other people in the present. Gardena tells K. all this quite plainly and gratuitously, but K. is unwilling, at this stage of the novel, to accept that his own frenetic obsession with the Castle is leading him down the same road towards existential sickness and failure as a human being. Although it is recorded that:

K. fühlte sich unbehaglich gegen-	K. felt uneasy listening to these
über diesen Geschichten, sosehr sie	stories, much as they concerned
ihn auch betrafen. (117)	him. (80)

K. fails to ask himself how he could learn from Gardena's experiences. Although Gardena's photograph of Klamm's messenger is 'faded with age, cracked in several places, crumpled and dirty', it exercises sufficient power over her to ruin her marriage and prevent her from 'realising the blessing' which is within an inch of her grasp. Similarly, K. will be misguided enough to allow his 'peep-hole' memory of Klamm and his recollection of the ramshackle, crumbling Castle which he saw on the day after his arrival in the village to deprive him of Frieda, the one person who might reconcile him with the village and with himself.

A further parallel with K. is provided by Pepi, who, like K., suffers from ambition, assertiveness and a desire to be what she is not. K. looks down on her when he first meets her and criticises her faults mentally as though he had none of his own. But by the end of the novel, when the multiple parallels which K. has unconsciously assimilated begin to break into his conscious mind, forcing him to recognise himself in other people, he comes to see that Pepi's situation is also his own, that his criticisms of her could equally well apply to himself and that both he and she had gone badly wrong in the conduct of their dealings with others.

Lastly, it is worth pointing out that K. not only meets people who mirror himself, but that he also forces people, and especially the Castle authorities themselves, to act in ways which parallel his own actions. Just as K. takes Frieda from Klamm, so Frieda is taken from him. Just as K. struggles with the Castle, so the Castle struggles back. Just as K. rejects Brunswick's family for the woman in blue, so Brunswick's family rejects him and forcibly throws him out into the street. In *Das Schloß*, inner and outer are one, the village and the Castle are, to an extent, an externalisation of the inner processes of K.'s personality, and whatever he does to the external world, he does to himself as well. As the second quotation which prefaces this section suggests, evil always returns to its place of origin in order to exact its due.

(ii) *Paradigm Situations*

Throughout *Das Schloß*, K. finds himself in situations which at first sight appear to be particular, but which, on closer investigation, prove to symbolise and summarise the book as a whole. Perhaps the first example of such a situation is provided by K.'s visit to Lasemann's house during the very first chapter of the book, an episode which gives the reader a picture *in nuce* of K.'s entire life in and dealings with the village. When K. enters Lasemann's house, he is described as 'the outsider', 'der von draußen Kommende', and can at first see nothing of what is going on inside the house. This of course exactly parallels K.'s general position in the village. As an 'outsider', he can discern nothing clearly there because his vision is 'steamed up', not adapted to the new circumstances in which he finds himself. Because of this inability to see, K. soon becomes confused in Lasemann's house. Impressions flood in on him from every side and cause him to lose his bearings completely. Thus, when he is asked about his identity by a 'hectoring voice' whose source he does not know (but which belongs to him as much as to anyone else), he responds to the question in exactly the same way as he had done when his identity was challenged in the inn shortly after his arrival in the village. He claims out of desperation to be the Count's land-surveyor:

... »*Ich bin der gräfliche Landver-*   ... "*I am the Count's land-*
messer«, *sagte K.* .... (*19*)   *surveyor,*" *said K.* .... (*18*)

The narrative then goes on to suggest that this assertion is, in some unspecified way, false, for immediately after K. has made it, the narrator, moving a little way back from K., adds the remark:

... *und suchte sich vor den noch*   ... *trying to justify himself before*
immer Unsichtbaren zu verant-   *the still invisible personage* (*18*)
worten. (*19*)

This remark is of more than immediate relevance, for K.'s whole existence in the village is, as will be discussed later at greater length,[2]

---

[2] See pp. 55-8, 153-4 below.

based on a despairing attempt to justify himself before an invisible personage by clinging obstinately to an identity which he has arbitrarily invented for himself. At last, the steam in Lasemann's house clears and K. is faced with what amounts to a choice. He can focus his gaze either on the scene of familial vitality or on 'the girl from the Castle' in blue whose affinity with K. has already been discussed. This implicit choice is of course the choice with which K. is faced throughout his stay in the village, and he is presented with it explicitly a few pages later (after he has been pushed out into the road by Lasemann and Brunswick), and then again, in the following chapter, when he receives Klamm's first letter. In the first of these two incidents, one of the two men asks him:

»Wohin wollt Ihr gehen? Hier führt es zum Schloß, hier zum Dorf.« (22)	"Where do you want to go? This way leads to the Castle, that way to the village." (20)

And in the course of the second incident, K. realises that the letter faces him with the choice of becoming either a real village worker or an ostensible village worker whose real allegiance is with the Castle. In a sense though, it is unnecessary for K. to be confronted with one choice three times over. When he is confronted with it for the first time, he makes what amounts to a decision, the nature of which is evident from the structure of his experience in Lasemann's house, from the fact that he has eyes only for the woman in blue who is a mirror-image of himself. Consequently, it is not surprising that Lasemann and Brunswick eject K. from their house by force 'as though there were no other means of making him understand' (20). Because K. has rejected their home and their way of life for the sake of vague aspirations towards the Castle, they reject him in order to try and make him understand the implications of that decision for the Castle which all his behaviour indicates that he has unconsciously made.

Furthermore, although the scene in Lasemann's house seems, at first sight, to be 'an ordinary wash-day', Kafka seems to suggest that this wash-day is a kind of purgatorial experience. Children's screams come from one corner, smoke rolls out of one corner turning the half-light into deep darkness, the unknown voice seems to address itself to 'dem Alten', 'the old one', men are bathing (i.e. cleansing themselves) in a huge wooden tub, full of steaming water, which is connected explicitly with a bed (and beds are, as we shall see, associated in *Das Schloß* with the experience of death and re-birth). Before K. falls asleep on the bench, men are in the water: when he awakes, they have been replaced by children as though a process of rejuvenation has taken place. In short, the whole scene summarises the course of the novel. K. is invited to undergo a pur-gatorial experience and become a new man, to fall asleep and awaken renewed. And indeed, it begins to seem at one point in Lasemann's house as though K. is prepared to allow this to happen to him. K. awakes from his sleep 'somewhat refreshed' and 'with somewhat greater acuteness of hearing than previously' (19). In-stead of being angered by Lasemann and Brunswick, he is 'glad at their open words' and instead of being rude or aggressive to them, he uncharacteristically thanks them and everyone else in the house. But then, suddenly, the effect of the purgatorial scene and his short bout of sleep wears off, K.'s obsessions reassert themselves and his attention reverts without warning to the woman in blue:

Und unerwartet für jedermann kehrte sich K. förmlich in einem Sprunge um und stand vor der Frau. (22)	*And unexpectedly for everyone, K. turned right round in one jump and stood in front of the woman. (20)*

A second paradigm situation occurs in the second chapter of the novel when K. attempts, by attaching himself to Barnabas, to pene-trate the Castle at night by force—and fails. Despite the most vio-lent exertions, the duration of which cannot really be measured, for the nightmare journey takes Barnabas and K. outside space and time into a featureless nothingness, K. comes no nearer to the Castle. Finally, he arrives at Barnabas' house, a place which cannot be all that far from his point of departure. Thus, the entire incident symbolically shows K. where all wilful attempts to take the Castle by storm must lead. During the course of this journey, when the hold of K.'s rational mind is weakened by physical strain, several thoughts slip out which give the reader an insight not simply into this one particular incident, but into the psychology which underlies all K.'s dealings with the village and the Castle:

Doch hielt er solche Besorgnisse von sich fern, auch tröstete es ihn, daß Barnabas schwieg; wenn sie schweigend gingen, dann konnte doch auch für Barnabas nur das Weitergehen den Zweck ihres Beisammenseins bilden.
Sie gingen, aber K. wußte nicht wohin; nichts konnte er erkennen ... (44)

But he kept all such anxieties far from him, and he was comforted too by Barnabas' silence, for if they went on in silence then Barnabas too must feel that the business of moving forwards was the sole point of their being together.
They went on, but K. did not know where they were going; he could make nothing out at all, ... (33-4)

K., it is said, does not know where they are going—a strange remark in view of the fact that the whole point of attaching himself to Barnabas was ostensibly to get inside the Castle. It also seems, from the presence of the word 'too', that the real motive behind K.'s actions is not the wish to arrive anywhere so much as the will to engage in motion forwards for its own sake. Thus, this little paradigm incident suggests that K.'s apparently purposeful activity conceals a fundamental purposelessness, and that the manner of his actions must, inevitably, result in despair, disillusionment and frustration as the surrounding nothingness encroaches upon him and shows up the futility of his strivings.

By the beginning of the eighth chapter, K. has become more conscious of the futility of trying to make the Castle accede to his will—though he is not yet sufficiently conscious of this to undergo a change of heart. And at this juncture, the sight of the Castle buildings themselves provides yet another paradigm. When K. first goes out from the *Brückenhof* into the snow, he is glad to be away from other people and stares up at the Castle which towers above the village in the dusk. Despite the fact that K. can distinguish nothing more clearly by doing so, he persists in staring up at the

Castle just as he persists in striving towards it even when it has become patent that his strivings are getting him nowhere. By the end of the second paragraph of the eighth chapter, K. comes to the realisation that the longer he looks at the Castle, the less he can make out and the more deeply everything becomes lost in the twilight. Were K. sufficiently self-aware, he might generalise from this incident and give up his pointless struggle with the Castle authorities which reaches its climax with his pyrrhic victory in the snow at the end of the chapter in question. But K. is not yet self-aware, and so he both fails to reach this conclusion and overlooks the implications of the illuminating thought that his eyes 'wollten die Stille nicht dulden', 'would not stand the silence'. As has been suggested twice already, K.'s life in the village consists of motion forwards for its own sake, and it is therefore not surprising that his eyes are unable to deal with something that generates motionlessness and silence. Stillness is the very antithesis of striving, and if K. could sit still, he would have learnt the futility of his eternal 'Weitergehen'. In connection with this particular incident, it is worth making the general point that whenever K. looks at the physical Castle buildings, his thoughts and reactions nearly always provide a paradigm of his dealings with the Castle and the village. When for instance, K. gazes up at the Castle buildings on the very first day of his stay, it is recorded:

Die Augen auf das Schloß gerichtet, ging K. weiter, nichts sonst kümmerte ihn. (14)	*With his eyes fixed on the Castle, K. went onwards, nothing else concerned him. (15)*

This sentence can, of course, be read as a description of K.'s reactions to the Castle on one particular occasion, but in view of what has already been said about K.'s inability to sit still, it seems fair to read this sentence as a general statement about K.'s overall relationship with the Castle. Throughout *Das Schloß*, right up to his interview with Bürgel, K. 'goes onwards' without 'bothering about anything else'. Consequently, he fails to grasp the possibilities which exist for relating to the village and loses Frieda together with all that she stands for.

A further paradigm situation occurs about half-way through the book in the course of the thirteenth chapter. K. hears a knock at the school-room door and rushes to open it on the assumption that Barnabas is there:

Über den Namen mehr als über alles andere erschrocken, sah ihn Frieda an. Mit den unsicheren Händen konnte K. das alte Schloß nicht gleich öffnen. »Ich öffne schon«, wiederholte er immerfort, statt zu fragen, wer denn eigentlich klopfte. Und mußte dann zusehen, wie durch die weit aufgerissene Tür nicht Barnabas hereinkam, sondern der kleine Junge, der schon früher einmal hatte K. ansprechen wollen. K. hatte aber keine Lust, sich an ihn zu erinnern, (207)

Frieda stared at him, shocked and frightened more at the name than at anything else. With his uncertain hands, K. could not open the old lock immediately. 'I'll get it open in a minute,' he kept on repeating instead of asking who was actually knocking. And then he had to watch, as through the wide-open door there came, not Barnabas, but the little boy who had tried to speak to him once earlier on. But K. had no desire to remember him. (136-7)

Again, this single short extract contains within itself the essence of all that happens to K. in the novel. K. tries to wrench open 'das alte Schloß'[3] by force and is unsuccessful. But, because K. is more interested in the process of wrenching open than in achieving any aim beyond that, he neglects to ask who or what is on the other side of the door and simply assumes that the person who is there is the person who he wants to be there. Then, when he does manage to get the door open, he discovers that the person who comes in does not correspond to his preconceptions. Consequently, he loses interest in him, stupidly as it happens, for the little boy who stands there, out of all proportion to the wide-open door, is a mirror-image of himself and could teach him far more about his situation in the village than could Barnabas, around whom K. has woven superhuman fantasies. The parallel with K.'s situation in the village is

---

[3] The German word 'Schloß' means both 'castle' and 'lock'.

4

striking. K., because of his obsessive preconceptions, attempts re-peatedly to open 'das alte Schloß' by force. At first he fails, but when, impossibly, he almost succeeds during the interview with Bürgel, what he discovers is so unlike what he has expected to dis-cover that he does not appear to be capable of consciously under-standing what is within his grasp. Finally, this paradigm suggests something very fundamental about K. which will be discussed at greater length later.[4] Despite the apparent self-assurance with which K. does everything, he is said to attempt to open 'das alte Schloß' with *uncertain* hands, an indication perhaps that a profound anxiety lies concealed beneath the apparently self-possessed surface of his personality.

Thus, as K. moves through the world of the village, he repeatedly undergoes experiences whose particular structure corresponds in important respects to the structure of his experience in the village as a whole. Although these incidents must have an impact on K.'s unconscious mind, his conscious mind never even begins to think about their possible meaning. But the reader, who can re-live K.'s experience as often as he cares to, registering those significant words and thoughts which come to K. unnoticed, can learn to see how apparently incidental occurrences shed light intensively on K.'s entire way of life and combine to indicate the presence of an elusive 'total pattern'.

(iii) *Parodies*

A third form of parallelism is to be found in Kafka's use of parody, a device which above all explains the presence of the assistants in *Das Schloß*. Both Walter Sokel and Ronald Gray have provided detailed studies of the ways in which the assistants parody K. and it is not necessary to reproduce their analyses here in detail. It is only necessary to say that by their mocking mimicry they expose K.'s arrogance, greed for forbidden knowledge and pretentiousness. By their laughable and superficial consequentiality they parody K.'s purposelessness.[5] By their infuriating inability to accomplish

---

[4] See pp. 152-5 below.
[5] See pp. 140-6 below.

anything they parody the futility of K.'s apparently purposeful struggles. By their childishness they show K. how he must appear to the inhabitants of the Castle and village. By their perpetual spying on K. they indicate that his perspective on the world is a 'Guckloch-perspektive'[6] and that, perhaps, that 'Guckloch' has not been kept as free from dirt as it should have been.[7] The assistants do not simply parody K.'s behaviour, however, they also externalise those dimensions of K.'s personality about which he is unconcerned to know. By their lasciviousness, they parody the will to erotic power which underlies much of K.'s treatment of women in general and of Frieda in particular and which, because it is unadmitted, is instrumental in destroying that relationship. By their childlikeness (as opposed to their childishness), they point to a quality of pre-lapsarian innocence which, throughout much of the novel, seems to be missing from the personality of the calculating and ostensibly sophisticated K. The assistants embody the entire a-rational side of K.'s personality of which his conscious mind prefers to remain in ignorance. The 'tender' Artur and the 'passionate' Jeremias (362) embody K.'s destructive 'irrational' energies and his creative 'transrational' energies. And when, in the school-room, they force K. into rejecting them with violence, they reveal that his whole existence is characterised by a fear of and an inability to come to terms with a very large part of himself. As Jeremias finally says to K.:

... *du fürchtest mich doch als Gehilfen überhaupt, du fürchtest Gehilfen überhaupt, nur aus Furcht hast du den guten Artur geschlagen. (344)*	... *you are in general afraid of me as an assistant, you are afraid of assistants in general, it was only fear that made you strike good old Artur. (222)*

K. is afraid of those parts of his personality which should 'assist' him in finding an answer to the riddle of the Castle. Thus, Jeremias'

---

[6] 'Gucklochperspektive' means 'peep-hole perspective' and refers in the first place to the way in which K. gets his one and only glimpse of Klamm. More generally, it is suggested here that K.'s entire perspective on the Castle is a 'peep-hole perspective', and that as a result, his vision is extremely limited.

[7] See the third prefatory quotation on p. 19.

name suggests that he is a prophet whose task is to compel K. to discard his illusions, see some basic and unpleasant truths about his fear of himself and alter the behaviour which flows from it. And Artur's name suggests that he represents, after his *fashion* (German 'Art' = fashion, sort, kind) something which is basic and *primeval* (the German prefix 'Ur-' = primal, original, basic), something which a human being overlooks or neglects only at his peril. Between them then, the assistants fulfil a dual rôle in relation to K. On the one hand, they erode K.'s illusions by their parodies, and on the other hand, they embody certain unadmitted parts of K.'s personality which K. must learn to accept if ever he is to become what he most truly and completely is. The assistants aim to show K. both what he ought not to be and what he might become. As Walter Sokel put it:

Das Wichtigste aber ist nicht seine Berufung, sondern sein Wesen. Dieses unzustimmen, vom fanatischen Eugensinn zum Humor zu lenken, sind die Gehilfen da.[8]	*The most important thing, however, is not his appointment but his nature. And it is to transform this, to turn it from fanatical, egoistical wilfulness to humour, that the assistants are there.*

This should not be taken to mean, however, that if the self-conscious K. is to be diverted from his strivings, then he must return to the mindless 'grace' of a Kleistian marionette, or to the childish state of dependence which seems to characterise so many of the village-dwellers. To continue the Kleistian analogy, K. must 'make a journey around the world',[9] experience to the full the futility and desperation of his wilfully individualistic way of life, and reach that other point at which 'grace' can reconcile his mind and his will with the rest of his personality.

Although much comment has been devoted to the ways in which the assistants parody K., it has not been generally noticed that they also parody Frieda, and, surprising though it may seem, the Castle authorities as well. A striking example of the latter form of parody

[8] Sokel, *Franz Kafka: Tragik und Ironie*, p. 489.
[9] The reference here is to Kleist's essay *Über das Marionettentheater* (1810).

is provided during K.'s interview with the Village Superintendent. Just after K. has heard about the absurd bureaucratic zeal of Sordini and the disproportionate administrative activities which characterise the Castle, the assistants are seen to be busy stuffing a great mess of official papers, higgledy-piggledy, into an already overloaded filing cabinet. This activity in no way appears to parody K. at that point. So it would seem, in the context of the office of the sick Superintendent (who does not, oddly enough, appear to care very much about the papers) to parody the inability of the Castle bureaucracy to create any real order in the affairs of the village and to indicate that as an administrative body, the Castle bureaucracy is very much an end in itself, making little real difference to the lives of the inhabitants of the village. Similarly, several pages later, we hear of the assistants' 'zeal to perform their duty which was always inappropriate'. This too seems to be a parody of the ridiculously excessive measures and effort which are involved in the regulation of the affairs of one tiny village. If this suggestion is acceptable, then it is perhaps not too much to say that much of the assistants' parodistic activity points in two ways—towards the Castle *and* towards K. Thus, the assistants' greed during K.'s meal with Frieda in the school-room and their general lasciviousness parody both K's sexual rapacity and the sexual rapacity of the Castle officials. Their inability to achieve anything concrete parodies the ineffectiveness of both K. and the Castle administration. Their apparent purposiveness and consequentiality parody the show of flawless purposiveness which characterises both K. and the Castle administration. Their mock spying parodies K.'s attempt to spy on the officials and the officials' attempts to spy on everyone else. The closer one looks, the more apparent does it become that K. and the Castle authorities are, in many respects, mirror-images of each other, reflected in the antics of the assistants. Thus, the Castle, as an administration, only has as much repressive power over K. as he is prepared to allow it. It is probably too much to say, as Marthe Robert does, that:

...l'organisme administratif n'est	*...the administrative organisa-*
qu'un rêve où le rêveur tenterait	*tion is nothing but a dream in*
d'embrasser d'un seul coup d'œil	*which the dreamer tried, with one*
une réalité totale déjà representée,	*single glance, to take in a total*
classée et jugée par lui.[10]	*reality which he had already*
	imagined, classified and judged.

But the parodistic activity of the assistants does seem to indicate that the authority of the Castle administration derives to a considerable extent from its ability to foster the fantasies which the inhabitants of the village project onto it. If the assistants show K. on the one hand that his way of going about things will never achieve anything, they show him on the other hand that the Castle authorities are, as an administration, a splendid illusion whose repressive power is by no means as great as at first sight it appears to be.

The assistants also have something to say about Frieda. As will be argued later in much greater detail,[11] Frieda, for all her very positive qualities, is by no means a perfect or an idealised character, and of her flaws, perhaps the most important is her inability to deal in an adult fashion with the animal energies of K. and herself. The assistants provide a perpetual reminder of this inability which K. seems to perceive when he says to Jeremias:

Frieda hat nur um eines gebeten:	*Frieda only asked me to do one*
sie von den wildgewordenen, hünd-	*thing: to free her from those las-*
isch lüsternen Gehilfen zu be-	*civious swines of assistants who*
freien; ... (345)	*were running wild; ... (223)*

Both Frieda and K. are asked to learn to live with the assistants, the embodiments of their own shortcomings and weaknesses. Because they are unable to do so, they are unable to live with one another and thus forfeit the one possibility of a full relationship which the world of the village offers them.

Because there is ultimately no distinction between the inner world of K.'s mind and the outer world of the village and Castle, K.'s

[10] Robert, p. 307.
[11] See pp. 167-70 below.

person is reflected all around him if only he had the imagination to see this. But because K. is characterised for most of the novel by a competent intellect rather than a compassionate imagination, he overlooks or defends himself against the reflections which surround him. But the reader can observe this blindness and this defensiveness, can observe K. refusing to understand what is impressing itself upon his mind, and can also watch these impressions bringing about a change in his personality after the interview with Bürgel.

B. Discrepancies

(i) *Over-reactions to K.*

The logical question of how it is possible to recognise discrepancy cannot be satisfactorily answered. One cannot, in the abstract, say how it is possible to tell when something is out of proportion to something else. Nevertheless, within *Das Schloß*, it is possible to recognise discrepancies in practice and to distinguish between various kinds of discrepancy. First of all, it frequently happens that for no apparent reason, someone reacts to something that K. has said or done in a way which seems, at first sight, absurdly disproportionate. For instance, in the very first chapter, the teacher reacts to K.'s seemingly innocuous question about Count Westwest with a secretiveness which to the reader, seeing everything through the eyes of K., appears grotesque:

»*Wie sollte ich ihn kennen?*« *sagte der Lehrer leise und fügte laut auf französisch hinzu: »Nehmen Sie Rücksicht auf die Anwesenheit unschuldiger Kinder.*« *(17)*	'*How should I know him?*' *replied the teacher quietly, and added aloud in French: 'Please remember the presence of innocent children.' (16)*

Clearly, K. has touched upon a taboo, a matter in which his assumptions are fundamentally at variance with those of the village community, and the teacher's response would seem to suggest either that the Count is so holy a figure that his name cannot be mentioned, or that he does not exist at all. Of these two possibilities, the latter would seem the more probable in view of the fact that the teacher reproves K. for mentioning the Count in front of innocent children. Had the Count been a holy or a God-like figure, the very mention of him would have been enough to shock the teacher and the question of whether this mention had been made in front of the children would be irrelevant. Furthermore, the non-existence of the Count is suggested by the fact that the whole Castle administration resembles a hive from which the queen bee has been removed, and in which the surviving bees swarm about frenetically and pointlessly.[12] The whole Castle seems to be a shell from which meaning has all but disappeared; a vast, shambling edifice which is in perpetual danger of falling apart when it is threatened by someone as headstrong as K.; a system of forces which provides a surface illusion of order, but within which, seething administrative disorder is the rule. Nevertheless, the fiction must be upheld that the Count, the nerve-centre and divinity of the Castle, is still alive for the benefit of the 'children', the innocents who populate the village. Although K. fails to realise it, his simple question has called the entire Castle into question and must not be answered.

Another example of disproportionate response is provided by an incident at the very end of the novel. K. has allowed himself to make an apparently insignificant remark to the effect that the clothes of the *Herrenhof* landlady seem somehow out of keeping with her station in life and her surroundings. To K.'s obvious surprise, the landlady responds not simply by snubbing him for his innocent tactlessness, but by challenging his right to pass aesthetic judgements on clothes in general. To K., who by this time is no longer in a fighting mood, this challenge seems uncalled-for. As with the question to the teacher, K. again fails to realise that his comments imply far more than he is aware of. Most of the landlady's clothes are 'dark, grey, brown and black', colours which characterise the landscape of the village and Castle and the dress of the villagers and the officials. Thus, by questioning the landlady's taste in clothes, K. is unwittingly saying something about the entire Castle world, sug-

[12] The parallel between the Castle and a hive from which the queen has been removed was suggested by Chapter XI of Book XI of Tolstoy's *War and Peace*, where Moscow on the eve of the French invasion is described in similar terms.

gesting that Castle society, like the landlady, is 'over-dressed' in inappropriate garments, covered in a clothing of institutions which are outsize, and which, handed down from an age in which they may have meant something, have become mourning garments for the Count who is no more. If the 'children', the inhabitants of the village, ever discovered that the Count was dead and that their institutions, for all their impressiveness and apparent solidity, were merely a lifeless surface of flesh around a corpse in which a few circuits were still active even though the heart had stopped beating, their entire world would fall to pieces. Consequently, it is necessary for the landlady to see whether K. really does understand the explosive implications of his own remarks. Is he a fool, a child who asks his question in innocence, or a very wicked, dangerous person who asks his questions because he wants to destroy the apparently seamless robe covering the Castle and the village? In both cases then, the disproportionate reaction of a second person to K. provokes the reader into searching for the cause of the disproportion and hence, into suspecting that K., unwittingly, has come very near to tearing apart that world into which he wants to gain entrance.

(ii) *An Over-reaction by K.*

If a disproportionate reaction to K. acts as an 'alienation-device', then the converse, a disproportionate reaction by K., operates in a similar way. An excellent and highly revealing example of over-reaction is provided by the incident where the receipt of Klamm's apparently ordinary first letter causes K. to pore over its lines with all the exegetical skill of a Talmudic scholar. Why should K. over-react like this? The answer is suggested in the following passage:

Der Brief verschweig ja auch nicht, daß K., wenn es zu Kämpfen kommen sollte, die Verwegenheit gehabt hatte, zu beginnen; es war mit Feinheit gesagt, und nur ein unruhiges Gewissen—ein unruhiges, kein schlechtes—konnte	*Nor did the letter conceal the fact that if it should come to a struggle, K. had had the temerity to make the opening move; it was said with subtlety, and only an uneasy conscience—an uneasy, not a bad conscience—could sense it. It lay*

es merken, es waren die drei	*in the three words 'as you know'*
Worte »*wie Sie wissen*« *hin-*	*which referred to his engagement*
sichtlich seiner Aufnahme in den	*in the Count's service. (30)*
Dienst. (39)	

K.'s guilty conscience is not indicated simply by his neurotic response to the three harmless words 'as you know'. All his pedantic worrying at this seemingly innocuous letter betrays a deep sense of guilty anxiety. The source of this almost certainly lies in the facticity of his claim to be a land-surveyor and the knowledge that he has, on the basis of that false claim, absolutely no right to remain in the village. Copious evidence exists for making this apparently outrageous assertion. First of all, during his initial conversations in the *Brückenhof* on the night of his arrival in the village, K. asks: 'What village is this I've wandered into? Is there a Castle here then?', a question which suggests that he has no prior knowledge of the Castle and cannot therefore have been appointed as its land-surveyor. A page later, K. tells Schwarzer that he knew very well that he had to report to the Castle authorities and did not need Schwarzer to tell him to do so. In view of the question quoted above, this latter claim must be a lie, and if K. can lie about knowing what formalities must be gone through on taking up an appointment, then there is no reason to suppose that the rest of his story about the appointment is true. Similarly, after Schwarzer has reported over the telephone K.'s claim to be a land-surveyor and has given his opinion that K. is probably nothing but a 'common, lying tramp', it is said that K., in order to avoid the first onslaught by the peasants, 'crept completely under the blanket'. Now the German word for blanket ('Decke') also means 'cover' (German 'Deckname' = cover-name, pseudonym). In view of Kafka's predeliction for apposite word-plays, it may be that the narrator is dropping the oblique hint that K.'s identity of land-surveyor is a 'cover' under which K. is attempting to hide. Then again, in the same chapter, when K.'s appointment as a land-surveyor is confirmed over the telephone, K.'s reaction is not that of a man who genuinely is a land-surveyor, for he says to himself:

Und wenn man glaubte, durch diese geistig gewiß überlegene Anerkennung seiner Landvermesserschaft ihn dauernd in Schrecken halten zu können, so täuschte man sich; es überschauerte ihn leicht, das war aber alles. (10)

And if they thought that they could keep him in a permanent state of terror by this recognition of him as a land-surveyor (which was certainly a highly intelligent thing to do), then they were mistaken; a certain thrill went through him, but that was all. (12)

Why should a man of good conscience who was a genuine land-surveyor assume that the authorities had an ulterior motive in confirming his appointment? Surely, a man who assumes that the Castle authorities are simply trying to out-manœuvre him by recognising him as a land-surveyor cannot be a land-surveyor? Surely, the man who feels a certain thrill when the authorities apparently respond to his demands is more interested in struggle than in truth? The suspicion which is built up in the first chapter that K.'s claim may be false is reinforced strongly in the second chapter when the assistants arrive on the scene. K. is completely unconcerned by the non-arrival of the two assistants who, he had claimed, were following on in a carriage with his surveying instruments. Conversely, when Jeremias and Artur arrive without warning or explanation, K. seems to be equally unperturbed and his subsequent dealings with them are riddled with implausibilities. When, for instance, K. asks them: 'What . . . are you my old assistants whom I told to follow me and whom I am expecting?' and they reply in the affirmative, the unreality of K.'s claim to be a land-surveyor becomes plain. If Artur and Jeremias *are* his old assistants, then clearly, K. would not need to ask the above question, and if they are *not*, then K. must know this anyway—in which case he does not need to ask the question at all, and ought, logically, not to accept their affirmative answer. Then again, K. claims during the same conversation that he cannot tell Artur and Jeremias apart, and yet, if they are who they claim to be, then he must know who is who. And when it transpires that neither of the two assistants knows anything about land-surveying, K. does not seem to be at all concerned professionally. As a further indication that K. is not what he claims to be, one can point to an unguarded moment during some musings half-way through the novel. Here, K. lets slip the thought that he is no land-surveyor with a definite appointment but simply a 'Wanderbursche' (241), a 'journeyman' (157), who had happened to arrive in the village by accident, who had been provoked into claiming that he was a land-surveyor by Schwarzer's unexpected intervention in the inn, who would have found accommodation somewhere else as a hand, and who would have moved on after a couple of days unless the improbable had happened and he had found some temporary work in the village. All in all, it begins to look as though K. is not an existential hero who is deprived of his right to exist by a faceless authority or an oppressed individual whose right to an identity has been radically threatened. Rather, he is a man who has invented an identity with which to justify himself before the disembodied voice that he heard when he entered Lasemann's house, and which, by some mysterious chance, just happens to link up with some half-forgotten case that is buried in the official archives of the village. A final indication that this is so is provided in K.'s last conversation with the *Herrenhof* landlady. When she asks him who he is, he replies, very laconically this time, with the single word: 'Landvermesser'. On explaining the nature of this employment to the landlady, she yawns and accuses him of not telling the truth—whereupon K. replies:

»*Auch du sagst sie* [*die Wahrheit*]   'You're not telling the truth
nicht.« *(455)*   either.' *(297)*

The existence of the word 'either' implies that K. is now prepared to admit that he has not been telling the truth, that his assumed identity has been a fiction. Appearances to the contrary, K. knows this all along, knows that he has no right to be in the village as a private person let alone as a land-surveyor, knows that he is trying to foist his self-made identity onto the community out of a love of struggle. It is perhaps because of this secret knowledge that he reacts so disproportionately and so guiltily when he reads those three little words in Klamm's letter: 'as you know'.[13]

[13] Sufficient comment has already been devoted to the name-symbolism in *Das Schloß* and no part of this book will deal specifically with this topic. Nevertheless, it is

(iii) K.'s Under-reactions

K. over-reacts in some situations and under-reacts in others. For example, he frequently responds to an advance which someone else makes with a remark which indicates either that he has completely misunderstood the meaning of the advance, or that he has been insensitive to its tone. Early on in the thirteenth chapter for example, Frieda breaks out into an ardent protestation of her love for K.:

»*Klamm sollte mir fehlen?*« *sagte Frieda.* »*Von Klamm ist hier ja eine Überfülle, zu viel Klamm; um ihm zu entgehen, will ich fort. Nicht Klamm, sondern du fehlst mir, deinetwegen will ich fort; weil ich mich an dir nicht sättigen kann, hier, wo alle an mir reißen. Würde mir doch lieber mein Körper elend, daß ich in Frieden bei dir leben könnte.*« *(201)*

'You think that I miss Klamm?' said Frieda. 'There's a surfeit of Klamm around here, too much Klamm; it's to escape from him that I want to get away. It's not Klamm that I lack but you. It's for your sake that I want to get away because I can't sate myself with you here, where everyone grabs at me. I would gladly let my body become sick and ailing if only I could live with you in peace.' *(133)*

But from all of that outburst, it is said explicitly that K. hears only one thing:

»*Klamm ist noch immer in Verbindung mit dir?*« *fragte er gleich. (201)*

'Is Klamm still in contact with you?' he at once asked. *(133)*

Clearly, K. is so obsessed with his dream of Klamm and the Castle that he is incapable of appreciating the reality of Frieda's love,

---

worth making the point here that the German word 'Landvermesser', lexically 'land-surveyor', is closely linked with the German verb 'sich vermessen'—'to get above oneself', 'to presume', 'to make an error of reckoning'. Thus, the title of 'Landvermesser' is an apt one, for K. 'presumes' to maintain the fiction of an identity which he does not possess and makes several 'errors of reckoning' in his attempt to impose this fiction on the village community.

which the village offers him as a 'Gnadengeschenk', 'a gift of grace'.

Something similar happens when K. has his long interview with Gardena in the sixth chapter. As has been said, the landlady exposes her most personal secrets to K., tries to show him where she has gone wrong in order to prevent him from doing likewise. For a time it looks as though K. is managing to grasp what she is trying to tell him. He sees that Gardena has thrown herself into her work at the inn in order to forget Klamm. He sees too that her neurotic industriousness has caused her 'Herzkrankheit', her 'sickness of heart', her inability to relate to or appreciate the value of her husband Hans. Indeed, K. even goes so far as to say:

... und ich glaube auch den Fehler zu erkennen, den sie gemacht haben. Äußerlich scheint ja alles gelungen, Hans ist gut versorgt, hat eine stattliche Frau, steht in Ehren, die Wirtschaft ist schuldenfrei. Aber eigentlich ist doch nicht alles gelungen, er wäre mit einem einfachen Mädchen, dessen erste Liebe er gewesen wäre, gewiß viel glücklicher geworden; wenn er, wie Sie es ihm vorwerfen, manchmal in der Wirtsstube wie verloren dasteht, so deshalb, weil er sich wirklich wie verloren fühlt—ohne darüber unglücklich zu sein, gewiß, soweit kenne ich ihn schon—, aber ebenso gewiß ist es, daß dieser hübsche, verständige Junge mit einer anderen Frau glücklicher, womit ich gleichzeitig meine, selbständiger, fleißiger, männlicher geworden wäre. (125)

... and I think too that I can discern the mistake that they made. On the surface, everything seems to have gone well of course. Hans is well provided for, he has a handsome wife, he is looked up to and the inn is free from debt. But in reality, things have not succeeded so well: he would have certainly been much happier with a simple girl whose first love he was; and if he, as you complain, sometimes stands there in the tap-room as though he were lost, it's precisely because he really does feel as though he is lost—without being unhappy about it, of course, I know him that well already—, and it's just as certain that this good-looking, sensible lad would have been a lot happier with a different wife, and by happier, I mean more independent, more industrious, more manly. (85)

Although it reflects adversely on her, Gardena seems to accept K.'s estimate of her situation without demur, for, instead of becoming angry, she rolls over onto her back, and, lying there in a position of complete openness, puts the key question to K.:

»*Was hat man denn versäumt?*«   '*Then what was overlooked?*'
(125)   *(85)*

to which K. makes the completely inane reply:

»*Klamm zu fragen*«, . . . *(126)*   '*You forgot to ask Klamm*', . . .
                                       (85)

It is plain that this answer is inappropriate in this context, for, as the landlady has just told him, Klamm forgets his women completely once they have left him or he has tired of them. Nothing could therefore be gained by 'asking Klamm' for he would already have forgotten Gardena. Over and above that, however, it is worth asking what exactly K. thinks Gardena should have 'asked Klamm'. If K. means that Gardena should have asked Klamm's permission before getting married to Hans, then he would more probably have said that she had forgotten: 'Klamm zu *bitten*'. By using the verb '*fragen*', however, K. suggests that Gardena, Hans and their relatives ought to have asked Klamm a question (the exact nature of which K. fails to specify). This suggestion is quite irrelevant since there is nothing that Hans and Gardena could have needed to know that they did not know already. Thus, by his final response to the landlady's story, K. shows, as the landlady is quick to perceive, that he is reading his own vague aspirations into her case instead of listening carefully to her story and thinking about it on its own terms. At the very point when K. could discover something about himself by entering into the mind and experience of someone else, he projects his own preconceptions onto the matter in hand and answers: 'You forgot to ask Klamm' instead of: 'You failed to put Klamm completely out of your mind.' Annoyed at K.'s blindness, the landlady then challenges K. outright by asking him what it is that *he* wants to ask Klamm, and K., as will be shown in detail later,[14] provides only

[14] See pp. 143-5 below.

the vaguest and most implausible of answers to this challenge. Furthermore, the tone of K.'s reply to Gardena is deeply insulting. Although she has told him some highly personal secrets, K. is able to respond only in a tone of moralising condescension. This suggests that even though he is able to understand Gardena's revelations to a certain extent intellectually, he is unable to grasp their import emotionally. Instead of showing his gratitude to Gardena by trying to suspend his prejudices, he virtually tramples on her feelings and so, by his under-reaction, effectively deprives himself of an important key which could help him unlock the secret of the Castle.

(iv) *Discrepancies between K.'s Description and the Reality Described*

Besides betraying himself through discrepancies in the tone and content of his responses, K. also betrays himself through discrepancies between his interpretation of reality and the nature of that reality as he experiences it or as we come to know it. For example, when K. first comes to the village, he tends to attribute his own hostility and arrogance to the people who he meets there even though he has no reason for making these attributions. Similarly, at the beginning of the fifth chapter, K. ascribes the fact that he can go where he likes in the village to bad motives on the part of the authorities. But here again, he has no real grounds for doing this. The bad motives exist in his assertive personality as much as they exist in the Castle authorities, and the darkness and impenetrability which he experiences all around him are due as much to his own inability to see aright as they are to any inherent deficiency in village life. Thus, although K. says to the Village Superintendent that the only certainty is his ejection from the village, the Village Superintendent quite rightly replies that no one has attempted to do such a thing. However, he might more accurately have replied that if anyone has tried to throw K. out of the village, it is K. himself, and that he has done this by refusing the identity which the village has offered him.

Then again, when K. meets Frieda for the first time, he describes her rise to the position of barmaid in the following terms:

»*Nur eines noch, Fräulein Frieda*«, sagte er, »*es ist außerordentlich und eine auserlesene Kraft ist dazu nötig, sich von einer Stall-magd zum Ausschankmädchen vorzuarbeiten, ist damit aber für einen solchen Menschen das end-gültige Ziel erreicht? Unsinnige Frage. Aus Ihren Augen, lachen Sie mich nicht aus, Fräulein Frieda, spricht nicht sosehr der vergangene, als der zukünftige Kampf. Aber die Widerstände der Welt sind groß, sie werden größer mit den größeren Zielen, und es ist keine Schande, sich die Hilfe selbst eines kleinen, ein-flußlosen, aber ebenso kämpfend-en Mannes zu sichern.*« (58)

'Just one thing more, Fräulein Frieda,' he said. '*it is quite ex-traordinary to have worked one's way up from byre-maid to bar-maid, and an exceptional strength is necessary for such a feat. But when that has been accomplished, is that the end of the line for such a person? A stupid question. Your eyes—don't laugh at me, Fräulein Frieda—speak to me far more of struggles still to come than of struggles past. But the oppo-sition of the world is great, it gets greater as one's goals get greater, and it's no disgrace to accept the help of a man who's struggling too, even though he's small and without influence.'* (42)

Although we are not to know it at this stage of the book, the terms in which K. has described Frieda's 'career' are totally inapplicable to her. As we come to know Frieda better, it becomes patent that struggle, goal-directedness, force and ambition are entirely foreign to her nature. Unlike Pepi, who is her caricature, Frieda has not wilfully struggled to become barmaid, she has been called to that position, and her promotion is not the result of her own efforts but a 'gift of grace'. As the narrative unfolds, so we discover that there is a complete discrepancy between K.'s account of Frieda's rise and her real nature. In the light of this it becomes entirely understand-able in retrospect why Frieda should have replied by saying to him: 'I don't know what you're getting at.' Although Frieda does not consciously understand K.'s alien thought processes at this stage of the novel, she has sufficient insight to see that K. is talking about the way in which his personality works rather than about the way in which her personality works.

More important still, there seems to be a very wide discrepancy

5

between K.'s assumptions about the Castle and the reality of that institution as an official body. When K. ruminates over Klamm's first letter for example, the narrator tells us:

Den einer solchen Behörde gegen-über wahnwitzigen Gedanken, daß hier Unentschlossenheit mit-gewirkt habe, streifte K. kaum. (37)	*K. scarcely even considered the thought, an insane one in connec-tion with an authority of that kind, that indecision could have played a part here. (29)*

When this sentence is first read, the massiveness of the first German phrase and the tone of voice in which K. dismisses the thought as a whole impresses the reader. Thus he overlooks the possibility that there may, in fact, be some justification for that 'unthinkable thought', that the Castle authorities may, perhaps, not be so admin-istratively efficient as they appear to be. But when this sentence is considered at greater length, it becomes difficult to say why K. should think that the Castle authorities are administratively so im-pressive. At this early stage in the narrative, K. has met one minor official, had an inconclusive conversation on the telephone with an-other, received an ambiguous official letter which could have been sent to anybody, and persuaded the authorities to accept an identity which he knows is fictitious. In other words, his experience of the authorities in no way entitles him to assume that the Castle auth-orities are as infallible or as resolute as the above quotation suggests that he thinks they are. Similarly, at the beginning of the fifth chapter, K. speaks of the 'admirable uniformity of the official ser-vice'. But again, on the basis of what evidence does K. arrive at this unqualified admiration? Although he has by now met Barnabas and seen Klamm through a peep-hole, his fragmentary contacts with the world of the officials add up to surprisingly little. Then again, although the reader is told, two pages later, that K.'s conception of the officials was confirmed by his meeting with the Village Super-intendent, that man, far from being the efficient and majestic repre-sentative of infallible officialdom, is said to be sick and gouty and proves to be bogged down in excessive administration. Finally, at the end of the eighth chapter, although K. feels that the Castle has broken off all relations with him, we are explicitly told that a gleam of light still shines down into the courtyard, providing the wandering gaze with a certain point of reference. In other words, K. seems to overestimate both the efficiency and the malice of the Castle bureaucrats. In his imagination, they become an enormously repressive and massively efficient superego, and as a consequence of this, K. cannot see that they may intervene in his life in benevolent and unofficial ways. Throughout K.'s time in the village, there is a discrepancy, sometimes more and sometimes less blatant, between his experience of the Castle authorities and his interpretation of that experience. Once that is realised, then the possibility begins to emerge that the Castle authorities may be by no means as malignant as K. would have them be.

At first sight, the existence and significance of such discrepancies are not apparent. K.'s interpretation of the world seems entirely plausible because of the tone of assurance in which it is delivered, and the reaction of others seems, in comparison, merely absurd. Only when the reader has acquired considerable experience in the ways of the village and has accustomed himself to discerning those elements in K.'s experience which do not tally with K.'s interpretations, does it become possible to question K.'s estimation of the world and of his place within it.

(v) *Discrepancies between K.'s Intentions and K.'s Acts*

When K. has pondered the first letter that Klamm sends him, he comes to the following conclusion:

... es war ihm überlassen, was er aus den Anordnungen des Briefes machen wollte, ob er Dorfarbeiter mit einer immerhin auszeichnenden, aber nur scheinbaren Verbindung mit dem Schloß sein wolle oder aber scheinbarer Dorfarbeiter, der in Wirklichkeit sein ganzes Arbeitsverhältnis von den	...it was left to him to make what he wanted out of the directions contained in the letter, to decide whether he wanted to be a village worker with a distinctive but merely apparent connection with the Castle, or whether he wanted to be an ostensible village worker who in reality had his entire

Nachrichten des Barnabas be-
stimmen ließ. K. zögerte nicht zu
wählen, hätte auch ohne die Er-
fahrungen, die er schon gemacht
hatte, nicht gezögert. Nur als
Dorfarbeiter, möglichst weit den
Herren vom Schloß entrückt, war
er imstande, etwas im Schloß zu
erreichen, . . . (37/38)

area and terms of work deter-
mined by Barnabas' messages. K.
did not hesitate in his choice, and
would not have hesitated even
without the experiences which he
had already undergone. Only as a
worker in the village, removed as
far as possible from the gentlemen
of the Castle, was he in a position
to achieve something in the Castle,
. . . (29)

His subsequent actions, however, run completely counter to the
conclusions that he reaches here. Apart from his brief and abortive
attempt at working as the school janitor, K. never accepts his lot
as a village worker. Even though he realises in the passage quoted
above which choice is the right and reasonable one, he fails to carry
out his intention and constantly chases after 'connections with the
Castle' which promise much but lead nowhere. What happens,
after the eighth chapter, to his plan to meet Klamm face to face?
What happens to his desire to meet Hans Brunswick's mother?
Somehow or other, K.'s theoretical purposefulness never seems to
issue in the actual pursuit of his stated aims, and the force with
which he initially makes his decisions seems to coexist with an
undecidedness about final ends.[15] Ultimately, as has already been
suggested, all these factors indicate that K. is more concerned with
'movement forwards' for its own sake than with the realisation of
anything concrete.

From all of this discussion, I hope that it has become clear that
the reader of *Das Schloß* has to train himself perpetually to question
the appropriateness of K.'s thoughts, words and actions and to ask
himself whether and how these fit in with the rest of the evidence
provided by the novel. This is difficult to do because the structure
and perspective of the novel continually tempt the reader to
acquiesce in K.'s judgement, to believe in the appropriateness of
what K. says and to stare uncomprehendingly at anything which

[15] See pp. 140-6 below.

contradicts or goes against him as though it were inherently meaningless. Much has been written about the 'absurd', 'Kafkaesque'
quality of the world of Kafka's novels, but it needs to be remembered
that the distortion and absurdity lie to a very great extent in the
consciousness of the person through whom that world is viewed.
It is not so much that the world of the Castle and village is inherently incomprehensible, but that it is incomprehensible to K., who
insists on disregarding what it says to him obliquely and assumes
that his ideas about it are accurate and authoritative. If the reader
can accustom himself to standing back from K. and looking at him
within the total context of the narrative, then it gradually becomes
apparent that the events which K. experiences have a hidden logic
of their own which is obscured by the inapposite workings of K.'s
mind.

C. Leitmotivs

The concept of the leitmotiv is not usually associated with Kafka.
Nevertheless, this device occurs in *Das Schloß* in three forms: repeated patterns of action and response, recurrent images and recurrent words and phrases. It may seem at first sight that the first
of these is the paradigm situation under a different name, but
there is in fact a difference between the two categories. Whereas
the paradigm comprehends the entire action of the book in one
symbolic situation, the recurrent pattern of action or response
stresses and draws attention to one aspect of K.'s personality or
endeavours.

(i) *Recurrent Patterns of Action and Response*

Perhaps the three patterns of action and response which are most
frequently encountered in *Das Schloß* are: K.'s inability to make
out details at first sight; K.'s tendency to build up false expectations
about someone or something; and K's tendency to evaluate people
on the basis of their apparent usefulness to him. Thus, in the first
chapter, K. is so incapable of making out the details of the picture
hanging on the wall that he at first imagines that the picture has been
removed from its frame. A few pages later, K. is unable to see the

details of the Castle at first glance, and it appears to him, rather un-clearly and abstractly, as:

...eine ausgedehnte Anlage, die aus wenigen zweistöckigen, aber aus vielen eng aneinander stehend-en niedrigen Bauten bestand. (14)	*...an extensive complex of build-ings which consisted of a small number of two-storied units and a lot of squat units which were all closely packed in together. (15)*

Only later does he see more concretely that it is:

...ein recht elendes Städtchen, aus Dorfhäusern zusammengetra-gen, ... (14)	*...a really wretched little town, made up of village houses, ... (15)*

Shortly after that, when K. enters Lasemann's house, he is, as we have seen, unable at first to discern any details of the scene what-soever. Then again, although Frieda can tell the assistants apart, K. cannot and never makes any effort to learn to do so. Shortly before the end of the second chapter, K. remarks on the similarity of the houses in the village. At the beginning of the third chapter, when K. enters the *Herrenhof* for the first time, he remarks of the servants who are sitting there:

Es waren kleine, auf den ersten Blick sehr ähnliche Männer ... (54)	*They were little men who, at first sight, looked very much like one another ... (40)*

In the sixth chapter, when K. goes in to see Gardena, he records:

Erst wenn man eingetreten war und die Augen sich eingewöhnt hatten, unterschied man Einzel-heiten. (113)	*Only when one had gone in and one's eyes had become accustomed to the darkness, could one make out details. (77)*

Then, in the same episode, he is unable to make out any features

in the photograph which the landlady shows him. Further examples
of this trait could be provided, but the harm it can do becomes clear
in the thirteenth chapter when Frieda asks K. whether he has
noticed the advances which the assistants have been making to her,
to which K. responds by saying 'no' and then vainly trying to remember details. This particular trait is a symptom of K.'s more
general solipsism. He is unable to make out details because he is not
concerned at first with the world outside his own ego. He has to
learn, slowly and painfully, to suspend judgement, mistrust first
impressions and look for the significant detail which might allow
him to discover the immanent logic of events and a genuine identity
for himself.

The second recurrent pattern of response, K.'s tendency to build
up false expectations, complements the first. K. thinks initially that
Barnabas is a superhuman figure, a divine messenger sent to him by
the gods of the Castle, who will permit him to gain entry to the
Castle. When, however, K. becomes more acquainted with Barnabas, he discovers that he is simply a man like himself who has holes
in his shirt and no real influence in the Castle. Consequently, disillusion sets in:

Jetzt in der Nacht, unbeachtet, hätte er ins Schloß dringen wollen, von Barnabas geführt, aber von jenem Barnabas, wie er ihm bisher erschienen war, einem Mann, der ihm näher war als alle, die er bisher hier gesehen hatte, und von dem er gleichzeitig geglaubt hatte, daß er weit über seinen sichtbaren Rang hinaus eng mit dem Schloß verbunden war. Mit dem Sohn dieser Famil- ie aber, zu der er völlig gehörte und mit der er schon beim Tisch saß, mit einem Mann, der be- zeichnenderweise nicht einmal im	*K. would have been willing to force his way into the Castle now, by night, unnoticed on Barnabas' arm, but it would have had to have been on the arm of that Bar- nabas who had existed in his imagination up to that point—a man who was closer to him than anyone else he had seen here up to now, and of whom he had at the same time imagined that he had intimate connections with the Castle far in excess of those which his apparent rank suggested that he had. But to go in broad day- light, on the arm of the son of this*

Schloß schlafen durfte, an seinem
Arm am hellen Tag ins Schloß zu
gehen, war unmöglich, war ein
lächerlich hoffnungsloser Versuch.
(48)

family, to whom he completely
belonged and with whom he was
already sitting at table, on the
arm of a man who, significantly
enough, was not even allowed to
sleep in the Castle, was impossible. Such an attempt was laugh-
ably futile. (36)

The irony of this disillusion is patent. K. stands to learn a considerable amount from Barnabas once he stops thinking of him as a
superhuman figure. But at the very moment when he begins to see
Barnabas as a man like himself, he stops paying attention.

Similarly, in Chapter Eleven, K.'s fantasies about the effect that
his message will have on Klamm prevent him from truly appreciating the extent to which Frieda has made the school-room habitable.
He acknowledges her efforts, but this, as we are specifically told,
was not difficult for him 'because in his mind, he was still with
Barnabas, repeating his message word for word, not however, as he
had given it to Barnabas but as he thought it would sound in front
of Klamm' (121). Although K.'s conscious mind makes the right
response to Frieda's efforts, the realisation of what she is doing for
him fails to sink deeper into his psyche and destroy the fantasy
world in which he habitually lives. If only K. could focus his whole
attention on Frieda and sacrifice his fantasies to an appreciation
of reality, he would not need to undergo the painful experiences
to which he is increasingly exposed in the second half of the
novel.

K. weaves similar fantasies around the Castle buildings when he
sees them from a distance (which are shown to be false the nearer
he comes to the Castle); around Klamm's first letter (which the
Village Superintendent demolishes); around the Village Superintendent (which are destroyed when he discovers that the central
figure of the village administration is not the Village Superintendent himself but his unobtrusive and hence overlooked wife
Mizzi); and around Hans Brunswick and his mother (who, on the
basis of the most meagre scrap of impressionistic hearsay, K.

assumes to be a vital link between the village and the Castle). K. is attracted to the sick Madonna-figure in Lasemann's house because the light from outside gives her clothes the appearance of silk and he has to be ejected from that house if he is to understand the groundlessness of his fantasies. Similarly, K. sees a sweet-smelling cognac turn into a coarse 'liquor that a coachman might drink'. Time and time again, K. discovers that people and things do not correspond to his preconceptions about them. But, right up to his interview with Bürgel, K. does not really learn from his discoveries. Instead of despairing of his fantasy, attempting to identify his prejudices and trying to decipher what events mean in themselves, he represses the despair which could act on his ego as a corrosive, refuses to draw out the lesson which it implies, and turns his fantasy towards something else. Thus, after being ejected from Lasemann's house in the first chapter for reasons which have already been discussed, K. finds himself alone in the street and thinks to himself:

»Gelegenheit zu einer kleinen Verzweiflung«, fiel ihm ein, »wenn ich nur zufällig, nicht absichtlich hier stünde«. (23)

'An occasion for a little fit of despair', it occurred to him, 'if I were only standing here by accident and not by design'. (21)

K. does *not* stand in the street by his own design but because of his lack of perception. Because his fantasy allows him to obscure the significant details of what has happened to him by covering the events with a semblance of intentionality, he succeeds in forcing down his despair and the self-knowledge which he could have derived from succumbing to it. K. is always attracted by the grandiose illusion, the promise of the unknown, the seductiveness of the apparently extraordinary. Consequently, he overlooks the small and apparently banal details of a situation which could open up that situation to him. So concerned is he to chase after illusions that he frequently fails to be grateful for the unobtrusive riches by which he is surrounded.

Finally then, the third recurrent pattern of response complements the other two. K. nearly always responds to people when he first comes across them by considering how useful they will be to him. For instance, when he first meets the two assistants, his immediate reaction is to think:

... *ihre Bekanntschaft schien ihm zwar nicht sehr ergiebig, aber gute, aufmunternde Wegbegleiter waren sie offenbar. (23)*	... admittedly he didn't expect to gain very much from their acquaintance, but they were obviously good companions who would cheer him up. (21)

When K. first enters Barnabas' house, he sums up the situation in purely utilitarian terms. When he first meets Frieda, he regards her primarily as a means of reaching Klamm, and only later, completely unintentionally and unconsciously, does he begin to value her for what she is in herself. When K. meets Hans Brunswick, he is so concerned to make use of him and his mother that he fails to see that Hans is a smaller version of himself. Throughout *Das Schloß*, K. tends to subordinate people to his obsessive schemes, and when they do not fit in with these, he loses interest in them.

In summary then, all three patterns of action suggest that K. is a highly egocentric being, locked up in his own personality and generally unable to relate to the world as it stands. If the world of the village and the Castle appears to be distorted, it is largely because it is viewed in the first place through the eyes of a man, who, by straining for what is beyond the horizon, has only a blurred perspective on the middle distance and is almost completely unable to see what is going on in the foreground. K. looks without seeing and sees without comprehending what he sees. But the reader, who is able to watch K. doing the same thing in a variety of situations, who is able to interpret events differently from K., and who is able to focus on things that K. registers incidentally and uncomprehendingly, can gain a critical distance from K.'s characteristic behaviour and build up a coherent picture of K.'s personality.

(ii) Recurrent Images

Besides recurrent patterns of response, Kafka makes much use of recurrent images of which the most important are perhaps: table and table-cloth, eye, bed and cross.

When K. first enters Barnabas' house, he is twice invited to sit down at the family table and twice refuses to do so. From then onwards (and this suggestion is endorsed by K.'s thought, in one of the rare moments when he relaxes, that it was not at all unpleasant to be sitting at *table* drinking the good coffee that Frieda had fetched), the table becomes the symbol of familial togetherness and reconciliation with the ordinary. At the end of the sixth chapter, for instance, after K. has failed, or perhaps refused, to understand that the landlady's marriage has been a failure because of her secret obsession with her memory of Klamm, his attention is drawn to another family table:

Nur an einem kleinen Tisch in einem Winkel saß schon ein Ehepaar mit einigen Kindern; der Mann, ein freundlicher, blauäugiger Herr mit zerrauftem, grauem Haar und Bart, stand zu den Kindern hinabgebeugt und gab mit einem Messer den Takt zu ihrem Gesang, den er immerfort zu dämpfen bemüht war; vielleicht wollte er sie durch den Gesang den Hunger vergessen machen. (130)	*Only at one little table in a corner was a married couple already sitting with several children; the husband, a friendly, blue-eyed gentleman with tousled grey hair and beard, stood bent over the children, beating time to their singing with a knife and trying all the while to keep the noise down; perhaps he was trying to make them forget their hunger by their singing. (88)*

Although K. does not note any conscious response to this apparently gratuitous detail, it is one of the many features which impress themselves on his unconscious mind and suggest to him how he might be reconciled with the village and the Castle. The table imagery occurs again at the beginning of the seventh chapter when K. returns to his room in the *Brückenhof* to find that it has been cleaned, ordered and made habitable by the efforts of Frieda:

... der Tisch, der einem früher, wohin man sich auch wendete, mit seiner schmutzüberkrusteten Platte förmlich nachgestarrt hatte, war mit einer weißen, gestrickten Decke überzogen. (131)

... the table, whose top had been literally stiff with a crust of dirt and had earlier seemed to stare after one no matter where one turned, was covered with a white knitted cloth. (88)

In Chapter Eleven, the assistants greedily snatch food from K.'s and Frieda's table and thus symbolise that greed of K.'s which will contribute to the break-up of his marriage. In Chapter Twelve, Gisa, in anticipation of the same break-up, sweeps Frieda's food and coffee-pot from the table. During the narration of the Gisa-Schwarzer relationship, Schwarzer is said to find a certain happiness with Gisa sitting at a 'little table'. Finally, K. realises the import of the table image and the meaning of his actions in relation to it when, in the course of the long conversation with Pepi towards the end of the book, he says:

... nur wenn ich mich mit dir vergleiche, taucht mir etwas Derartiges auf, so, als ob wir uns beide zu sehr, zu lärmend, zu kindisch, zu unerfahren bemüht hätten, um etwas, das zum Beispiel mit Friedas Ruhe, mit Friedas Sachlichkeit leicht und unmerklich zu gewinnen ist, durch Weinen, durch Kratzen, durch Zerren zu bekommen—so, wie ein Kind am Tischtuch zerrt, aber nichts gewinnt, sondern nur die ganze Pracht hinunterwirft und sie sich für immer unerreichbar macht. (448)

... only when I compare myself with you, the following kind of notion begins to dawn on me. It is as if we had exerted ourselves too much, too noisily, too childishly and with too little experience, in order to get something by crying and scratching and tugging that could have been obtained easily and unobtrusively had we had, say, Frieda's calm and matter-of-factness. We've been like children who tug at a table-cloth, but gain nothing by doing so, and only bring all the splendid things down onto the floor where they are out of reach for ever. (293)

By the time of this conversation with Pepi, K. has come to see that in Frieda, he had been offered the opportunity of sitting down to eat at a family table, of finding reconciliation and meaning within the world of the Castle without becoming mesmerised into mindlessness by its authority. Instead of accepting the table, however, he has preferred to chase wilfully after illusions of his own devising, and in so doing, he has overturned the table and destroyed what stood upon it.

Kafka's own reverence for family life is well known, and a clear and typical statement of this attitude is to be found in the famous letter to his father:

Heiraten, eine Famile gründen, alle Kinder, welche kommen, hinnehmen, in dieser unsicheren Welt erhalten und gar noch ein wenig führen, ist meiner Überzeugung nach das Äußerste, das einem Mensch überhaupt gelingen kann. (H, 209–10)

To marry, to start a family, to accept all the children who arrive, to support them in this insecure world and even to guide them a little, is, I am convinced, the greatest thing at which a person can succeed. (W, 204)

It is less frequently noted, however, that Kafka was also afraid of marriage because of its ability to diminish, narrow and, in a sense, kill an individual's creativity with its routine, stability and solidity. Thus, in one of his letters to Felice Bauer, he recalled the time when they had gone to buy furniture in Berlin:

Schwere Möbel, die einmal aufgestellt, kaum mehr wegzubringen schienen. Gerade ihre Solidität schätztest Du am meisten. Die Kredenz bedrückte mir die Brust, ein vollkommenes Grabdenkmal oder ein Denkmal Prager Beamtenlebens. Wenn bei der Besichtigung irgendwo in der Ferne des

Heavy furniture which looked as if, once in position, it could never be removed. Its very solidity is what you appreciated most. The sideboard in particular—a perfect tombstone, or a memorial to the life of a Prague official—oppressed me profoundly. If during our visit to the furniture store

Möbellagers ein Sterbeglöckchen geläutet hätte, es wäre nicht unpassend gewesen. Mit Dir, Felice, mit Dir natürlich, aber frei sein, meine Kräfte arbeiten lassen, die Du nicht achten konntest, wenigstens in meiner Vorstellung nicht, wenn Du sie mit diesen Möbeln überbautest. (BF, 650; probably March, 1916)

a funeral bell had begun tolling in the distance, it wouldn't have been inappropriate. I wanted to be with you, Felice, of course with you, but free to express my powers which you, in my opinion at least, cannot really have respected if you could consider stifling them with all that furniture.

Kafka's ambiguous attitude towards marriage seems also to be detectable in *Das Schloß* where Frieda is both a possible answer to K.'s dilemma and a potential threat to him. Frieda is not simply a symbol of life and reconciliation as is often argued, she also possesses a quality of deathliness which will be discussed more fully later.[16] Two of the major symbols by which this deathliness is made manifest in *Das Schloß* are the 'weiße Decke' ('white [table-]cloth') which we have already met, and the 'Tuch' ('cloth') which is quite frequently associated with her. The deathly connotations of the cloth motif are established very early on in the novel when, after Frieda and K. have made love for the second time, a 'cloth' is thrown over them by the maids just as if they had died. Thereafter, both the German words for 'cloth' are used with deathly overtones. One of Gardena's souvenirs of Klamm, the symbols of her sick attachment to her fantasy, is an 'Umhängetuch', ('wrap' or 'shawl') of which Frieda also possesses an example. Frieda's most prized possession is a beautiful 'white cloth' of the sort that might be used to make a wedding-dress and therefore a shroud as well. Just before Olga tells Amalia's story, K. says that Barnabas cannot see what is being offered him by the Castle because of the 'cloth' which is bound round his eyes. Amalia's father tries to present his petition to the Castle officials standing outside Bertuch's nursery (German 'Bahrtuch' = 'pall') and wastes away for his pains. While he is waiting there, Bertuch, who, like the Devil, has a crippled foot, throws

[16] See pp. 167–9 below.

him a 'Decke'. After Frieda has left K. for Jeremias (who, by the end of the novel, is said explicitly to look like a corpse), she wraps him in damp 'cloths' just as though she were trying to mummify him or to prepare his corpse for burial in that dark, subterranean chamber of hers. The ghost-like officials in the *Herrenhof* who cannot bear the sight of K. peer at him over the tops of the doors with their faces almost entirely swathed in 'cloths' as though they too were corpses. Thus, if the table is a symbol of life and recon-ciliation, the cloth is a symbol of deathliness and blindness. While the 'cloth is on the table', the life and death forces in K.'s and Frieda's relationship are balanced out. But when the cloth is 'pulled off the table', as literally happens in the school-room, this crucial balance is destroyed. Consequently, K. and Frieda are given over to their worst impulses and so forego the chance of living with each other in peace.

The eye motif plays an equally important rôle in *Das Schloß*. In the first chapter, it is said of the dark picture of the official which hangs on the wall of the *Brückenhof* that one could scarcely see anything of the eyes, an indication, perhaps, that only a few faint glimmerings of life are still to be found in the depths of the Castle bureaucracy. Later on in the same chapter, the Madonna figure in Lasemann's house is said to have 'tired blue eyes'—a symptom of her existential sickness. When K. first meets Barnabas, he notices that his eyes are 'more than normally large', wide open with the naïve innocence of a child. But it is only when K. first meets Frieda that he really begins to understand the possible meaning of the eyes which surround him:

Das Bier wurde von einem jungen Mädchen ausgeschenkt, das Frieda hieß. Ein unscheinbares, kleines, blondes Mädchen mit traurigen Augen und mageren Wangen, das aber durch ihren Blick über-raschte, einen Blick von besond-erer Überlegenheit. Als dieser Blick auf K. fiel, schien es ihm,

The beer was served by a young girl called Frieda. A small, unob-trusive girl with fair hair, sad eyes and hollow cheeks, but who surprised one by her glance, for it was a glance of special superior-ity. When this glance fell upon K., it seemed to him that this glance had already achieved things

daß dieser Blick schon K. be-
treffende Dinge erledigt hatte,
von deren Vorhandensein er selbst
noch gar nicht wußte, von deren
Vorhandensein aber der Blick ihn
überzeugte. (54-5)

which concerned him, of whose
presence he was as yet completely
ignorant, but of whose presence
this glance convinced him. (40)

From that moment onwards, K. possesses a standard of comparison by which to assess people, even if he becomes aware of the existence of that standard only gradually and dimly. Hence, when he meets Pepi, although he is attracted by the thought that she may be just as well-connected with the Castle as Frieda, he realises, by thinking back to Frieda's eyes, that she possesses qualities which Pepi does not:

Und doch, trotz ihrem kindlichen
Unverstand hatte auch sie wahr-
scheinlich Beziehungen zum
Schloß; sie war ja, wenn sie
nicht log, Zimmermädchen ge-
wesen; ohne doch von ihrem
Besitz zu wissen, verschlief sie
hier die Tage, aber eine Umarm-
ung dieses kleinen, dicken, ein
wenig rundrückigen Körpers
konnte ihr zwar den Besitz nicht
entreißen, konnte aber an ihn
rühren und aufmuntern für den
schweren Weg. Dann war es
vielleicht nicht anders als bei
Frieda? O doch, es war anders.
Man mußte nur an Friedas Blick
denken, um das zu verstehen.
(148)

And yet, despite her childish lack
of comprehension, she too probably
had connections with the Castle.
Unless she was lying, she had been
a chambermaid; without knowing
anything of what she possessed,
she slept away her days here, and
although he could not wrest what
she possessed from her by taking
this little fat body with its some-
what rounded shoulders into his
arms, yet if he did that, the em-
brace might stir him and buoy
him up on his difficult way. Then
was her case much the same as
Frieda's perhaps? Oh no, it was
different. One only had to think
of Frieda's glance to understand
that. (99)

Then again, Pepi's eyes are said to be:

... mühsam geöffneten, schlaf-trunkenen Augen ... (146)	*... eyes which had been opened with effort and which were stupid with sleep ... (98)*

If these adjectives are understood metaphorically rather than literally and if it is remembered that Pepi forms a parallel to K., then it becomes clear that K. is looking at his own eyes in Pepi's eyes. His eyes are 'drunk with sleep' until he awakens transformed after his interview with Bürgel and are 'opened only with difficulty' as a result of his experiences in the village.

Similarly, after K. has spent some time in the proximity of Amalia, he is able, because of his earlier experience of Frieda's and Pepi's eyes, to make extensive and penetrating comments about Amalia's glance:

Ihr Blick war kalt, klar un-beweglich wie immer; er war nicht geradezu auf das gerichtet, was sie beobachtete, sondern ging —das war störend—ein wenig, kaum merklich, aber zweifellos daran vorbei, es schien nicht Schwäche zu sein, nicht Verlegen-heit, nicht Unehrlichkeit, die das verursachte, sondern ein fort-währendes, jedem anderen Gefühl überlegenes Verlangen nach Ein-samkeit, das vielleicht ihr selbst nur auf diese Weise zu Bewußt-sein kam. (244–5)	*Her glance was cold, clear and immovable as ever; it wasn't exactly directed at the thing she was looking at, but—and that was the disturbing thing—went slightly, almost imperceptibly, but quite definitely past it. This didn't seem to be due to weakness, embarrassment or dishonesty, but to a persistent longing for isola-tion which dominated every other feeling and which perhaps got into her conscious mind only in this fashion. (159)*

Within *Das Schloß*, the eye is a way into the soul, a means of seeing how it stands with a person in the depths of their personality, a means of discerning whether that person is dominated by the will or the spirit. In the above passage then, Amalia's glance be-trays the fact that her entire life, like K.'s, is one persistent attempt to look past the people in the foreground of her life for the sake of

6

the unattainable far distance, and to cut herself off from the rest of humanity as completely as possible.

A further important symbol which recurs throughout *Das Schloß* is that of the bed. K. is first challenged about his identity when he is lying on a rough bed. On three occasions in the novel, important truths are revealed to K. by people who are lying in bed. The sick Village Superintendent first explains to K. the insignificance and questionableness of his case as he lies in his bed. When Gardena wants to communicate something of vital importance to K., she takes to her bed and it is from his bed that Bürgel invites K. to put that question which could tear apart the entire fabric of the Castle administration. In other words, the bed is frequently a place of revelation and truth, a place where the hold of the striving will is relaxed and a sanctuary where hostility (such as that which exists between K. and Gardena or that which exists between K. and the Castle) can be suspended for the sake of something higher. It is in bed that K. and Frieda discover that their relationship is doomed to failure if their love-making is nothing more than the copulation of beasts who do not relate to one another, and that their relationship can succeed if they can learn to become 'still and thankful'.

Furthermore, as has been pointed out, the bed is connected with the rejuvenating 'wash-tub' in Lasemann's house (which is said to be as big as two beds), and when Gardena receives K. in Chapter Six, her situation in bed is also connected with the composite theme of death and rebirth. First, it is said that being in bed makes Gardena look younger *and* that her face is in a state of decay. And second, the 'little night-cap woven from delicate lace' which is too small for her is reminiscent of the kind of cap which might be worn *either* by a corpse *or* by a child. Later on still, K. stretches out to sleep on a kind of bed in Klamm's womb-like sledge and has to be 'reborn', forcibly ejected from that 'womb'. Thus, if the bed is one of the main places of revelation within *Das Schloß*, then one of the main truths imparted to K. there is that he must learn to 'go to sleep'; that he must be willing to die metaphorically if ever he is to be freed from his prison of wilfulness and egocentricity. Correspondingly, everything in the village conspires to make K. go to sleep once and for all, and the more he resists the pressure which is put upon him, the tireder he becomes. Very early on in the novel, K. remarks that 'every new acquaintance increased his feeling of tiredness' (17) and notes that his conversation with the teacher causes him to feel 'real tiredness' for the first time. But in reality, K.'s tiredness is due as much to his disinclination to accept and assimilate his new experiences as it is to the experiences themselves. Then again, when K. has read Klamm's second letter, which, as will be argued,[17] makes perfect sense if read carefully, a tremendous sense of tiredness overcomes him. Although K.'s conscious mind refuses to work out what the letter might mean, his unconscious mind seems to have grasped the hidden import of Klamm's letter, and the result of this tension is a sense of utter weariness.

K. is not the only person who suffers from this profound kind of fatigue. Amalia, whose whole life constitutes a defiant refusal to see the damage that her egocentric pride is causing herself and her family, is, when K. visits the Barnabas house for the second time, exhausted for a reason which is not explained. It is probable, however, that Amalia's exhaustion comes from the strain which is generated by her attempt to maintain herself in isolation while imposing her egocentric fictions upon all those who surround her.

K. fears his tiredness, for he knows that once it overcomes him completely and he is compelled to relax the hold of his will, he will have to give up his fictitious identity, cease to claim that he is a land-surveyor and become someone different. Thus, throughout the novel he fights sleep, and only succumbs to it completely during his interview with Bürgel. After this, he wakes up a new person, freed from the control of obsessive fictions and deriving his identity from sources of his personality which lie below the threshold of his will. Although this final bout of sleep will be fully discussed in the next chapter, it is worth pointing out at this juncture that this final 'death' and 'resurrection' is prefigured by six minor bouts of sleep. In Lasemann's house, K. falls asleep for a brief while and wakes up 'somewhat refreshed', with his sense of hearing 'made somewhat more acute'. After this awakening, he is, as we have seen, more inclined to appreciate openness in and to show gratitude to those people who surround him. Between Chapters Three and

[17] See pp. 122-123 below.

Four, K. falls asleep, wakes up 'much refreshed' and even begins to become reconciled with the possibility of life in the village as Frieda's husband. When, shortly after the beginning of the fourth chapter, K. and Frieda make love, it is only when they have ceased to struggle and their wills have died that they become 'still and grateful' to one another. The maids then throw a blanket over them to signify what has happened, and after a while, K. awakes, throws off the death-symbol of the blanket and stands up, whereupon the two assistants, the symbols of the life-force, salute him. K. offers no explanation for their action, but in the light of what has just happened, it is not implausible to suggest that they are paying K. a form of tribute for metaphorically dying to the wilful side of his nature and awakening in a new state of mind. K., however, remains unaware of the meaning of this incident, and when, towards the end of the eleventh chapter, he next goes to sleep, he is violently annoyed at being woken and deals a vicious blow to the assistant who has disturbed him. Throughout most of the novel, K.'s actions amount to a refusal to go to sleep properly and be re-awakened to a new way of life. Thus, the violence of his action in the eleventh chapter may well suggest that he unconsciously understands the wider implications of this particular action. Although K. becomes increasingly tired after the eleventh chapter, he remains awake right up to his interview with Bürgel, at which juncture the connection between sleep and death becomes explicit. K. is summoned to the *Herrenhof* by Erlanger, a name which, in German, means 'the one who attains'. This official limps (like Bertuch and the Devil), is famous for his memory and knowledge of men, leaves the *Herrenhof* at dawn (the time of awakening) and draws his brows together (like a pair of horns). If this death-symbolism were not conclusive enough, the first person K. meets outside the *Herrenhof* on this occasion is Gerstäcker, the 'inexorable driver', death, of the first chapter. To enter the *Herrenhof,* K. has to go down below the level of the ground, and as he does so, he hears the sound of hammer-blows (the noise of hammers on a cross or a coffin-lid?). The Frieda who meets him there is corpse-like, being twice described as 'starr' ('stiff' or 'rigid'), and is almost unable to remember him. Clearly then, K. is going down into the *Herrenhof* in order to 'die'. And this time, he really does undergo a form of death for he falls into a deep, dreamless sleep. Then, after his interview with Bürgel he is 'suddenly awakened' exactly as he was by Schwarzer in the first chapter and by Artur at the end of Chapter Eleven, but now he neither attempts to justify himself nor resists by lashing out blindly with his fists. Instead, he gets up in a state of semi-trance, goes into the tap-room and falls asleep for twelve hours, after which he rises devoid of the egocentric wilfulness which had characterised him earlier. In the Fourth Octavo Notebook, Kafka remarked:

Von einer gewissen Stufe der Erkenntnis an muß Müdigkeit, Ungenügsamkeit, Beengung, Selbstverachtung verschwinden, nämlich dort, wo ich das, was mich früher als ein Fremdes erfrischte, befriedigte, erhob, als mein eigenes Wesen zu erkennen die Kraft habe. (H, 110)	*When a certain stage of knowledge is reached, weariness, inadequacy, constriction and self-contempt have to vanish, and that stage is reached when I have the strength to recognise my own essential nature in that which formerly seemed alien to me, even though it did refresh, satisfy and uplift me. (W, 104)*

It may be said that after his interview with Bürgel, K. has passed through that 'certain stage of knowledge', so that his 'tiredness' and 'inadequacy' disappear, and he is enabled to see the world, which once he thought was 'alien' to him, as his 'own being'.

An imagery of crosses and crucifixion also runs through *Das Schloß*, complementing the sleep/death complex. This motif first occurs in the second chapter when K. recalls how he had scaled the churchyard wall in his youth, and how, on reaching the top of the wall, he had seen the crosses below him disappearing into the earth. When this incident is examined in more detail,[18] it will be seen to indicate that one of K.'s major unconscious urges is a desire to escape death, to evade crucifixion, to 'bury' the crosses. Up to his interview with Bürgel, K. seeks to deal with death not by accepting it and allowing an element of deathliness to have its rightful place

---

[18] See pp. 154–5 below.

within his life, but by running away from it and denying the fact of his own mortality. Correspondingly, whenever the cross motif appears in *Das Schloß*, one can be sure that K. is about to be invited in some way to undergo a 'crucial' experience, to die metaphorically and be reborn. Shortly before K. illicitly spends the night in the *Herrenhof* where he will meet Frieda for the first time, he sees the landlord of that inn standing against a wall with his legs crossed. When K. makes love to Frieda for the first time and is seduced into wandering into a country which is unknown to him, Frieda lies on her back with her arms outstretched in an attitude which suggests both open-hearted love and crucifixion. But the voice of Klamm recalls K. from the enchanted air of that unknown country and instead of permitting himself to be taken over by Frieda's love, his old fantastic ambitions assert themselves again. Gardena lies on her bed in a similar attitude when she reveals her secrets to K. in the sixth chapter and asks him to criticise his own way of life by saying what had gone wrong with her marriage. When K., is offered the job of janitor by the teacher and has to swallow some of his pride, he stands there, while he is making up his mind, 'with his arms crossed above his chest'. When K. goes into the *Herrenhof* just before his long wait in the snow, he notices how two corridors cross each other inside the inn, and when he leans back in the furs of Klamm's sledge, he does so 'with his arms outstretched and his head resting on the upholstery'. When K. drives the assistants from the school-room, they hang outside 'am Gitter', on the criss-cross trellis-work of the fence, with their arms stretched out towards the school. Similarly, Amalia's father undergoes his crucifixion 'am Gitter' outside Bertuch's nursery. Just before Sortini makes that 'Sprung über die Deichsel'[19] which, in effect, challenges Amalia to die from her proud isolation, he sits with his arms crossed upon his chest. Jeremias brings together the leitmotivs of 'Gitter', 'Kreuz' and 'Faust' (the significance of which will be discussed immediately below) shortly before K.'s crucial interview with Bürgel:

[19] Translated literally, this phrase refers to the 'jump over the shafts' of the fire-pump which Sortini makes in order to get near Amalia, but idiomatically, the phrase has the connotation of 'kicking over the traces'.

Diese Rücksichtslosigkeit, mit der	*That recklessness of yours which*
du uns am Gitter *frieren ließest,*	*made us freeze on the* railings;
oder wie du Artur, einen Mensch-	*or the way in which you nearly*
en, den ein böses Wort tagelang	*killed Artur, a man whom an*
schmerzt, mit der Faust *auf der*	*angry word causes pain for days,*
Matratze fast erschlagen hast	*with a blow of your* fist *on the*
oder wie du mich am Nachmittag	*straw-sack; or the way in which*
kreuz *und quer durch den Schnee*	*you chased me* all over the place[20]
jagtest, daß ich dann eine Stunde	*through the snow this afternoon so*
brauchte, um mich von der Hetze	*that it took me a whole hour to get*
zu erholen. (340) (my emphasis)	*over the upset. (219)* (my em-
	phasis)

Finally, during K.'s interview with Bürgel, Bürgel stretches out his arms in bed before K. and K. stretches out his arms before Bürgel. This time, however, K. does not refuse the crucifixion. He consents to die and his arms slip downwards like those of a dead man, whereupon Bürgel says:

So korrigiert sich selbst die Welt	*That is how the world corrects*
in ihrem Lauf und behält das	*itself in its course and maintains*
Gleichgewicht. (392)	*its balance. (254)*

Similar studies could be made of the *imagery* of clothing, light and children, but as these will be dealt with when the status of the Castle itself is considered, we shall now pass on to the final type of leit-motiv, the recurrent word or phrase.

(iii) *Recurrent Words and Expressions*

The consciousness of Kafka's artistry becomes very apparent from an analysis of the way in which he uses words. A word or phrase or object will be introduced unobtrusively into *Das Schloß* and then used two or three times again, sometimes within a matter of pages. Thus, at the beginning of the novel, K. stands on a 'Holzbrücke' (a 'wooden bridge'); he then finds accommodation at the *Brückenhof*

---

[20] Lexically, the German idion 'kreuz und quer' means 'all over the place', 'over hill and dale'. Literally, the idiom means 'across and athwart'.

(the 'Bridge Inn') and within twenty pages he walks across another bridge in the shape of the 'Brett' ('plank') which the occupants of Lasemann's house hold out to him. During his nightmare journey through the snow, he remembers how the 'Tuch' ('cloth') of the 'Fahne' ('flag') which he had planted on the wall in his youth had fluttered in the wind. Five pages later, when he enters the *Herrenhof* for the first time and sees the officials' flags fluttering over the door, the same two words ('Tuch', 'Fahne') occur again, indicating that his attempt to take the officials by storm forms a parallel to his attempt to climb the wall, and will probably end in the same manner. At the beginning of Chapter Eight, K. describes the Castle as 'free from care' ('unbekümmert') and five pages later, the same German adjective is used to describe the sledge-driver, an indication perhaps that the Castle is somehow behind the subsequent experience which K. undergoes in the courtyard. The unusual noun 'Gewecktwerden' ('awakening', 'process of being awakened') occurs three times in the novel. Schwarzer uses it in Chapter One and K. uses it at the end of Chapters Eleven and Eighteen. Thus, the reader is automatically invited to compare K.'s reactions to all the three incidents. The image of the cat is introduced half-way through Chapter Eight when K.'s approach to Klamm's sledge is compared to an approach by that animal. Soon after that, Gisa's cat helps to disrupt K.'s relationship with Frieda and is used by Gisa herself to scratch K.'s hand badly. Later on still, Jeremias compares Amalia to a wildcat. Thus, the reader is encouraged to make links between these three situations.

Perhaps, however, the three most important words to recur in *Das Schloß* are 'Faust', 'sich verhalten' and 'wollen' (together with their related concepts). Both Max Brod and Walter Sokel have pointed out the similarity between Goethe's Faust and Kafka's K.:

Mit diesem (allerdings sehr entfernten und ironisch gleichsam auf ein Minimum reduzierten) Anklang an Goethes »Wer immer strebend sich bemüht, den dürfen [sic] wir erlösen« sollte also das Werk

The novel, which one is entitled to describe as Franz Kafka's version of Faust, was thus supposed to end with this (admittedly very unobtrusive, and, as it were, ironically minimal) suggestion of Goethe's:

enden, das man wohl als Franz Kafkas Faust-Dichtung bezeichnen kann.[21]	*'The soul that still has strength to strive, We have the power to save.'*

Ein Teil seines Wesens ist Ehrgeiz, mystisch-faustisches Streben nach der Höhe und der Auszeichnung.[22]	*One part of his being is ambition, mystical-Faustian striving for the summit and distinction.*

Neither, however, to the best of my knowledge, has validated this comparison by calling attention to the frequent usage of the word 'Faust'[23] in *Das Schloß*. The phrase 'auf eigene Faust'[24] is used at least three times in the course of the novel: first by the *Brückenhof* landlady (128), second by the teacher (134) and third by K. himself (233). Furthermore, at least four references are made to K.'s readiness to use his 'fists' ('Fäuste') and to deal out 'blows' ('Faustschläge') when infuriated by his assistants. Like Faust, K., up to the time of his interview with Bürgel, is a man who strives wilfully and egocentrically for his own ends, and the suggestion that Faustian wilfulness, violence and solipsism were all closely connected in Kafka's mind receives endorsement from an isolated entry in the Third Octavo Notebook:

Aus eignem Willen, wie eine Faust drehte er sich und vermied die Welt. (H, 99; dated 16.i.1918)	*Of his own will, he turned round like a fist and avoided the world. (W, 94; erroneously dated 19.i.1918)*

Thus, it is completely apt that K., shortly before the interview with Bürgel which issues in his change of heart, should say to Frieda:

Laß also die Fäuste ruhen. (365)	*Put down your fists. (235)*

[21] Max Brod, *Nachwort zur ersten Ausgabe des Schloß-Romans, Das Schloß*, p. 527.
[22] Sokel, *Franz Kafka: Tragik und Ironie*, p. 407.
[23] The German word 'Faust' literally means 'fist'.
[24] Translated literally, this phrase means 'on one's own fist'. It therefore has to be rendered in English by such expressions as 'on one's own initiative' or 'off one's own bat' which completely miss the 'Faustian' overtones of the German original.

By extension, this injunction could equally well be addressed to himself and paraphrased as: 'may the Fausts rest in peace'.

Closely bound up with K.'s Faustianism is his frequent use of the verb 'sich verhalten'.[25] For instance, when he has just met Frieda he says of himself:

>». . . *und Sie werden über sie nicht mit jemandem reden, den Sie eine halbe Stunde lang kennen und der noch keine Gelegenheit hatte,* Ihnen zu erzählen, wie es sich eigentlich mit ihm verhält.« (57)

Talking to Gardena he says:

>». . . *es beweist aber, glaube ich,* daß sich auch sonst nicht alles genauso verhält, *wie Sie glauben.*« (75)

When he is with the Village Superintendent he asks:

>». . . *und* wie verhält es sich mit *meiner Berufung?*« (92)

and later remarks:

>». . . *angenommen,* daß sich alles so verhält, *dann hätte ich eine Menge guter Freunde im Schloß;*« *(109)*

And during his long interview with Gardena he says:

>». . . *dann will ich von ihm wissen,* wie er sich zu unserer Heirat verhält.« *(127)* (my emphasis in all cases)

[25] The German expression 'sich verhalten' is a reflexive verb which, translated absolutely literally, means 'to relate oneself'. 'Sich verhalten' is, however, frequently used as a synonym for the verb 'sein', 'to be'. As this verb is also used in a variety of highly idiomatic expressions, it is virtually impossible to provide one consistent translation for it and completely impossible to find an equivalent English expression which preserves the sense of 'to relate oneself'. Thus, in the first passage quoted, the phrase emphasised has to be translated by: '. . . to tell you how matters stand with him.' In the second passage, the phrase emphasised has to be translated by: '. . . that moreover, things aren't exactly as you think they are.' The third phrase emphasised has to be translated by: '. . . and how do matters stand with my appointment?' The fourth phrase emphasised has to be translated by: '. . . that things are as you say they are, . . .' And in the final example, the phrase emphasised has to be translated by: '. . . what his attitude is to our marriage.'

He uses the phrase once during his reflections in Chapter Fourteen; once during Olga's account of Amalia's secret; three times in the course of his long final conversation with Frieda and once more after his interview with Bürgel. At first sight, there is nothing exceptionable about this ordinary, if somewhat bureaucratic idiom. But if one forgets the translations which have been suggested in the footnote and considers the idiom's literal meaning of 'to relate oneself', then a certain amount of light is thrown on K.'s psychology. K., the land-surveyor, is so concerned to establish how things and people *relate* to other things and other people, that he completely neglects to discover what those things and people mean *in themselves*. For most of the novel, K.'s glance, like Amalia's, is unable to focus on anyone or anything and continually looks past them in order to see how they relate to what is beyond themselves. Hence, Frieda is important to him at first because she has a relationship with Klamm; Klamm and Barnabas are important to him because they have a relationship with the Castle; Hans Brunswick is important to him because he has a relationship with his mother, and so on. As will be argued later,[26] K. is completely unable to say with any definiteness or clarity what he really wants simply because all apparent ends are, in his mind, nothing more than means to attaining something which forever lies beyond them. Consequently, when K. is confronted by Bürgel, Bürgel gently mocks K.'s tendency to chase after 'relationships' by using the phrase 'sich verhalten' no less than three times. When Bürgel uses this idiom for the second time:

Wie verhält es sich denn mit der Landvermesserei? (376)   *How's the land-surveying business getting along then? (243)*

the derogatory overtones of the German suffix '-ei' gives a clear indication that Bürgel is being deliberately satirical.

The recurrent use of the verb 'wollen' and the various nouns which derive from or include it is closely connected with K.'s concern with relationships. Although it often appears that words like 'wollen' and 'Wille' are just used incidentally, the following passages

[26] See pp. 140–6 below.

indicate that Kafka is using such words with emphasis and deliberateness.

. . . *es gab Stellen* [*of Klamm's first letter*], *wo mit ihm wie mit einem Freien gesprochen wurde, dessen* eigenen Willen *man anerkannt,* . . . *(37)*

»*Wie* wollen Sie *das tun?*« *fragte der Vorsteher. (103)*

. . . *vielleicht war es gar nicht möglich, aus dieser Ferne etwas zu erkennen, und doch verlangten es die Augen und* wollten *die Stille nicht dulden. (145)*

Mögen Sie tun, was sie wollen. *(166)*

Von mir befreit, könntest du vielleicht alles erreichen, was du willst. *(200)*

Niemals werden sie mit meinem Willen *hereinkommen. (206)*

. . . *aber noch immer hatte er für die Alten und für die ganze Ecke des Familientisches dort kein Mitleid, nur* Widerwillen. *(275)* (my emphasis in all cases)

In all of these examples, the noun 'Wille' or the verb 'wollen' seem either to stand out in some kind of relief or to have been used in a rather unusual way. In the first example, 'eigenen Willen' ('own will') has clear overtones of 'Eigenwille' ('self-will' or 'wilfulness'). In the second example, 'wollen' is used where the simple 'werden' (the futuritive 'will' in German) or 'beabsichtigen' ('to intend') would have been more natural. In the third example, 'wollten . . . dulden' instead of the simple 'duldeten' gives the idea that K.'s eyes refused wilfully to tolerate the stillness. In the fourth and fifth examples, the placing of the verbs 'wollen' and 'willst' at the end of a sentence accentuates these verbs and stresses the fact that K. *wills* something beyond what is legitimately desirable. In the sixth example, K. draws attention to his own wilfulness by using the highly emphatic 'mit meinem Willen' instead of a less intransigent turn of phrase. And in the final example, the German 'Widerwillen' brings out the fact that K.'s will works *against* (German 'wider' = against) his acceptance of the family table. These seven examples were selected at random. Other emphatic uses of 'wollen' and 'Wille' are to be found on nearly every page, a frequency which underlines the fact that wilfulness and the values associated with it are fundamental to K.'s personality.

It is almost impossible to convey the full meaning of the words emphasised above to a reader who knows no German. In the first example, the overtones of 'self-will' are lost when 'eigenen Willen' is translated by 'independence' (29) or 'own will'.[27] In the second example, the force of 'wollen' is dissipated when the German verb is rendered by 'intend'.[28] In the third example, 'wollten' has to be translated by the less emphatic 'refused'.[29] In the fifth example 'willst' has to be translated by the weaker 'want'.[30] In the sixth example, the translator has either to alter the idiom and say something like: 'it is only against my will that they will ever come back in here' or translate 'mit meinem Willen' by the much weaker idiom 'with my consent'. And in the final example, it is necessary to use the less evocative 'aversion' or 'repugnance'.[31] Only the fourth example preserves in English something of the force of the original, for here one is able to say: 'You may do as you will.' More importantly, the various English translations of 'wollen' and its derivatives to which a translator necessarily has to resort, means that that steady accumulation of force around the word 'will' which takes place in the German text cannot come about in an English translation. It is that much more difficult for an English reader to see into K.'s mind. The English text is that much more opaque than the German text—and that, I would suggest, is in large measure the result of the very careful way in which Kafka uses unobtrusive

[27] '. . . there were passages where he was spoken to as though he were a free man whose own will is acknowledged.' (29)

[28] 'How do you intend to do that?' asked the Superintendent. (71)

[29] '. . . perhaps it wasn't at all possible to make out anything from this distance, and yet one's eyes demanded it and refused to endure the stillness.' (87)

[30] 'Freed from me, you could perhaps achieve everything that you want to.' (132)

[31] '. . . but he [K.] could still not feel any sympathy for the old people and for that whole corner where the family table stood—only repugnance.' (178)

verbal leitmotivs to illuminate the structure of K.'s mind and behaviour, and his relationship with the world around him.

D. Changes of register

Marthe Robert writes:

On l'a souvent noté, tous les
personnages de Kafka parlent un
langage uniforme où rien ne perce
de leur situation sociale, de leurs
habitudes ou de leur tempéra-
ment; aucun d'eux n'est avare,
timide, passionné, cultivé, grossier,
tous sont nivelés de telle sorte que
l'amoureux parle comme l'indif-
férent; . . .[32]

It has often been remarked that all
Kafka's characters speak a uniform language which bears no
trace of their social situations,
their idiosyncrasies or their temperaments. None of them is
miserly, timid, passionate, culti-
vated or boorish. All of them have
been reduced to the same level to
such an extent that the person who
is in love speaks like the person
who is unconcerned; . . .

Indeed, we have become so used to the featureless, tentative, almost
legal style of Kafka's narratives that mention is very rarely made
of variations in their register. Nevertheless, such variations do exist,
and it is precisely because they are so rare that they merit special
attention. In this section then, it will be shown how, by variations
in the apparently uniform register of Das Schloß, Kafka persuades
the reader to stand back from K. and consider him in their light.

(i) Moments of Uncertainty

At several points in the novel, K.'s normal tone of argumentative
self-assertion modulates into one of puzzled tentativeness, as though
he were encountering something which was of great importance to
him but which he himself was unable to grasp. When, for example, K. is sitting in the Brückenhof in the second chapter, he
senses that the peasants there want something from him whose
nature he cannot define. A page later, he senses that Barnabas'
manner is communicating some message to him of which Barnabas

[32] Robert, p. 237.

himself is probably ignorant. When K. first meets Frieda, he refers to some element in her glance of which he knows nothing, but of whose presence he is certain. Throughout K.'s long conversation with Olga, he senses that she and all her family have overlooked some factor which is of vital importance, but whose nature he cannot quite comprehend either:

Denn sieh, immer wieder hindert dich etwas—ich weiß nicht, was es ist—, voll zu erkennen, was Barnabas nicht etwa erreicht hat, aber was ihm geschenkt worden ist. (267)	*See here, something or other—I don't know what it is—prevents you time and time again from recognising clearly not what Barnabas may have achieved, but what has been given to him as a gift. (173)*

In all four cases, and they are by no means the only occasions when K. becomes aware of the inadequacy of his point of view, the reader is invited to stop and ask himself about the nature of the uncomprehended dimension. Because K. himself is, for most of the novel, ignorant of the answer to that question, it is doubly difficult for the reader to provide a definite answer. Nevertheless, it is perhaps worth suggesting that in the first case, the peasants are looking to K. for a change of heart. On the morning after he has made love to Frieda on the *Herrenhof* floor and begun to lose himself in an 'unknown country', they stream towards him as though in celebration of his discoveries. And after he has failed to tell the landlady 'what was overlooked' in the sixth chapter, they rush away from him when he appears, as though in disappointment at his failure. The peasants seem to function in *Das Schloß* as a kind of chorus. When K. conforms with their expectations, they react to him positively, and when he fails to do so, they react negatively. Thus, it may be that when K. first meets them, it is those unspoken expectations that he is intuitively recognising. It is possible to decipher Barnabas' secret message to K. with much more certainty. Barnabas, it ensues, is an unreliable messenger and must know this at the time of his first meeting with K. Thus, it is probable that K. already senses this in the *Brückenhof.*

As K. comes to know Frieda better, he begins to realise that the undefined quality in her glance of which he initially knows nothing, is, as her name suggests, peace. This peace is the antithesis of everything that the Faustian K. stands for at the outset of the novel and the source of all Frieda's other virtues—her ability to give, to love and to make habitable. As the novel unfolds, K. begins to learn something of this peace, largely, as he himself comes to see, because of his close contact with Frieda. Finally, that 'something or other' which prevents Olga and the Barnabas family from overcoming their situation is the same 'something or other' which prevents K., for three-quarters of *Das Schloß*, from making contact with the outside world on its own terms and from breaking out of the prison which his will and his fantasy have constructed for him. If we are to obtain some clearer idea of the nature of that undefined quality, then it is necessary to look at other moments in the novel when the register of the narrative changes in a rather different way.

(ii) *Moments of Lyricism*

At four points in *Das Schloß*, the tone of the narrative suddenly becomes lyrical and the mind of K., whether he knows it or not, is pervaded by a new quality. Three of these moments occur when K. is in the company of Frieda and the other occurs when K. is with Olga. Of these four moments, the first comes in the third chapter when K. spends the night in the *Herrenhof* with Frieda 'in the little puddles of beer and the other rubbish which covered the floor'. Walter Sokel sees this particular incident in a negative light:

Dies ist es, was die Liebesszene in den Bierlachen vor Klamms Tür beschreibt, eine der tragischsten Szenen in Kafkas Werk. Wenn so Wesentliches in der Liebe von Mann und Frau als Schmutz (Umherwälzen in Bierlachen und Unrat) und Niedrigkeit (Koitus auf dem Fuß-

And it is this that describes the love scene in the beer-puddles outside of Klamm's door, one of the most tragic scenes in Kafka's work. When such an important part of the love of a man and a woman is seen as dirt (rolling around in puddles of beer and detritus) and baseness (coitus on

boden) gesehen wird, wird eine
reife Liebesbeziehung kaum Geleg-
enheit haben, sich zu entfalten.[33]

the floor), a mature love relation-
ship will scarcely have the oppor-
tunity of developing.

But surely, the point of this scene is *not* to prefigure the eventual break-up of K.'s and Frieda's relationship in the degradation of their first sexual union, but to give K. an insight into Frieda's essential ability to make even the most squalid environment tolerable and habitable? It is not reprehensible but remarkable that both K. and Frieda are able to spend hours among the filth and detritus without being troubled by these in the least. Furthermore, it has to be noticed that the narrative here continues:

Dort vergingen Stunden, Stunden
gemeinsamen Atens, gemeinsam-
en Herzschlags, . . . (63)

Hours went past there, hours in
which they breathed as one, in
which their hearts beat as one, . . .
(45)

'Gemeinsam' ('mutual', 'communal') is a strange word to use in connection with the individualistic K. And in this context, it is extremely significant, for it means that we are seeing K.'s Faustian egoism being tempered by a power of love which introduces him to an entirely new scale of values. This experience of love is such a novel one for K. that he is completely confused and disoriented by it. Consequently, the passage continues:

. . . Stunden, in denen K. immer-
fort das Gefühl hatte, er verirre sich
oder er sei so weit in der Fremde,
wie vor ihm noch kein Mensch,
einer Fremde, in der selbst die
Luft keinen Bestandteil der Heim-
atluft habe, in der man vor
Fremdheit ersticken müsse und in
deren unsinnigen Verlockungen
man doch nichts tun könne als

. . . hours in which K. constantly
had the feeling that he was going
astray or had gone further into a
strange country than any man
before him, a country so strange
that not even the air had any-
thing in common with the air of
his native land, where one must
stifle because of this strangeness and
yet, in whose insane enticements,

---

[33] Sokel, *Franz Kafka: Tragik und Ironie*, p. 433.

7

weiter gehen, weiter sich verirren. *(63)*	*one could do nothing else but go further and lose oneself more and more. (45-6)*

K.'s sense that he is wandering into a strange country is so great that he experiences Klamm's voice which recalls him to his Faustian struggles as 'ein tröstliches Aufdämmern', 'a comforting re-awakening'. In this passage then, K. is faced with another version of the choice with which he has been confronted three times already. *Either* Frieda and the new, but to him strange existence which she represents, *or* the quest for Klamm and the Castle. *Either* a new 'Heimat' ('homeland') of love, *or* the old 'Heimat' which, as is clear from K.'s memory of its church spire, is synonymous with aggressive striving for impossibly transcendent goals. Walter Sokel goes on to make the following comment on this incident:

Daher fühlt K. den Sexualakt als ein »Sich-Verirren« und Verlorengehen. Er ist Untreue an der inneren Heimat und dem eigenen Wesen.[34]	*For this reason, K. experiences the sexual act as a 'going astray' and a getting lost. It involves infidelity to his inner homeland and to his own most essential nature.*

But it is worth asking whether the 'Gemeinsamkeit'[35] which flows from this sexual act does not represent an infidelity to K.'s *false* 'inner homeland' of Faustian struggle rather than an infidelity to his *true* 'inner homeland' of love? Far from estranging K. from his true being, this sexual act helps him to realise unconsciously that he can only truly discover himself in the peace and timelessness of a relationship with someone like Frieda. If this embryonic realisation seems, at this juncture, like self-betrayal to K., it is perhaps because he is not used to the idea rather than because the idea is inherently misguided.

The antics of the assistants on the morning after this night in the *Herrenhof* bear out the idea that K.'s experience with Frieda has

[34] Sokel, *Franz Kafka: Tragik und Ironie*, p. 433.
[35] 'Sense of community', 'togetherness'. The reference is to the passage from *Das Schloß* quoted immediately above.

been essentially positive. The narrator tells us that on that morning, the assistants were happy, and that their happiness was the kind that is produced by the conscientious fulfilment of duty. This is the only time in the whole novel that the assistants give the impression of having accomplished something, and when K. then shouts at them 'as though they were guilty of everything', he is doing no more than implicitly recognising the truth of the situation. The assistants, the personifications of the spontaneous parts of K.'s personality, are indeed responsible for him making love to Frieda and discovering a new country, and to this extent, they have begun to fulfil the task to which they were appointed.

By Chapter Thirteen, K. has become more conscious of what Frieda really means to him, and when, in this chapter, he again wanders into a 'strange country' with her, he does not notice the strangeness this time. Thus, when a conversation of intense tenderness takes place between K. and Frieda, K. passes no comment on it whatsoever:

»Nein«, sagte K. und legte tröstend den Arm um sie. »Alles das sind Kleinigkeiten, die mir nicht weh tun, und zu Klamm will ich ja nicht nur deinetwegen. Und was hast du alles für mich getan! Ehe ich dich kannte, ging ich ja hier ganz in die Irre. Niemand nahm mich auf, und wem ich mich aufdrängte, der verabschiedete mich schnell. Und wenn ich bei jemandem Ruhe hätte finden können, so waren es Leute, vor denen ich mich fluchtete, etwa die Leute des Barnabas.« (200)	'No', said K. and put his arm consolingly around her. 'All those things are trifles which don't hurt me, and it's not simply for your sake that I want to get to Klamm. And just think of all that you've done for me! Before I knew you, I was wandering around here quite lost. Nobody took me in, and if I imposed myself on anyone, I was soon sent packing. And if I did manage to find peace with anyone, it was always with people from whom I ran away, like the Barnabas family.' (132)

Human contact is rare in *Das Schloß* and it is impossible to overlook the gentleness with which K. puts his arm around Frieda and the genuineness of his appreciation of what she has done for him. In this passage, there is nothing of the self-justifying arrogance, cruel argumentativeness or subjunctive speculation which are more typical of K.'s tone of voice throughout the novel. Even if K. is incapable of sustaining this note of tenderness for very long, even if he soon leaves Frieda again, for this moment at least, he means what he says. He is, whether he knows it or not, in 'another country', and he seems to confess that his deepest desire is for peace there and not for struggle.

A comparable passage occurs when K. is sitting with Olga at the beginning of the fifteenth chapter:

K. *blieb mit etwas erstauntem Gesicht zurück, Olga lachte über ihn, zog ihn zur Ofenbank, sie schien wirklich glücklich zu sein darüber, daß sie jetzt mit ihn allein hier sitzen konnte, aber es war ein friedliches Glück, von Eifersucht war es gewiß nicht getrübt. Und gerade dieses Fernsein von Eifersucht und daher auch jeglicher Strenge tat K. wohl; gern sah er in diese blauen, nicht lockenden, nicht herrischen, sondern schüchtern ruhenden, schüchtern standhaltenden Augen. Es war, als hätten ihn für alles dieses hier die Warnungen Friedas und der Wirtin nicht empfänglicher, aber aufmerksamer und findiger gemacht.* (250)

Looking somewhat surprised, K. stayed where he was; Olga laughed at him and drew him to the settle. She seemed to be really happy that she could now sit here alone with him, but it was a peaceful happiness and certainly not clouded by jealousy. And precisely this absence of jealousy and thus of any feeling of constraint did K. good; he was glad to look into these blue eyes which were not seductive or imperious, but shyly tranquil, shyly steadfast. It was as though the warnings of Frieda and the landlady had made him not more susceptible to all this, but more observant and more discerning. (162)

Because of his experiences with Frieda, K. has become alive to the values which she represents and is able to recognise them in other people, even in Olga, to whose merits Frieda is persistently blind. In the above incident, K. completely forgets his Faustian aspirations and struggles and gives himself over with frank gratitude to the impressions of peacefulness and modesty which Olga makes upon him. Although K. never manages to reach the tenderness with Olga that he does with Frieda, the above passage is characterised by a very real sense of intuitive understanding for Olga's shy self-possession, sad good humour and freedom from jealous assertiveness.

Finally, attention must be drawn to K.'s last meeting with Frieda which takes place in the eighteenth chapter. Although Frieda is at first cold and dead towards K., he manages, without casuistry or impertinence, to break through her reserve because of the openness, perspicacity and resignation which he is beginning to learn. At this point, K. takes hold of Frieda's hand for the last time, and, with a calm simplicity and complete lack of vindictiveness, proceeds to give a sober and entirely accurate account of what has gone wrong between them:

Das Ganze ist nur eine bösartige, allerdings sehr kluge Ausnützung der Mängel unseres Verhältnisses. Jedes Verhältnis hat seine Mängel, gar unseres, wir kamen ja jeder aus einer ganz anderen Welt zusammen, und seit wir einander kennen, nahm das Leben eines jeden von uns einen ganz neuen Weg, wir fühlen uns noch unsicher, es ist doch allzu neu. Ich rede nicht von mir, das ist nicht so wichtig, ich bin ja im Grunde immerfort beschenkt worden, seit du deine Augen zum erstenmal mir zuwandtest; und an das Beschenktwerden sich gewöhnen, ist nicht schwer. (366)	*The whole thing is simply a malicious but very clever exploitation of the weaknesses of our relationship. Every relationship has its weaknesses, even ours. We came together from two very different worlds, and since we have known each other, our lives have taken quite new directions—we still feel insecure, for it's all too new. I'm not speaking of myself, I don't matter all that much, for in reality I've been continually presented with gifts from the very first moment that you turned your eyes towards me—and it isn't hard to get used to being given gifts. (236)*

The change which K.'s tone has undergone is remarkable. Instead of bitterness at being deprived of Frieda, there is a resigned humour. Instead of self-obsession, there is consideration for Frieda. Instead of insistence on what he has achieved, there is gratitude for what he has been given. Instead of the assumption that he and his relationships are central, there is an ability to look at himself and his relationships from a distance. Instead of a tendency to see everything in black and white, there is a readiness to admit the existence of various shades of grey. Indeed, K.'s whole speech is permeated with such a real sense of love and tenderness towards Frieda, that she responds with an outburst of lyrical emotion that is almost unique in *Das Schloß*:

Frieda hatte ihren Kopf an K.'s Schulter gelehnt, die Arme umeinander geschlungen, gingen sie schweigend auf und ab. »Wären wir doch«, sagte Frieda langsam, ruhig, fast behaglich, so, als wisse sie, daß ihr nur eine ganz kleine Frist der Ruhe an K.'s Schulter gewährt sei, diese aber wolle sie bis zum Letzten genießen, »wären wir doch gleich noch in jener Nacht ausgewandert, wir könnten irgendwo in Sicherheit sein, immer beisammen, deine Hand immer nahe genug, sie zu fassen; wie brauche ich deine Nähe; wie bin ich, seit ich dich kenne, ohne deine Nähe verlassen; deine Nähe ist, glaube mir, der einzige Traum, den ich träume, keinen anderen.« (367–8)

Frieda had let her head fall on K.'s shoulder, and with their arms entwined around each other, they walked up and down in silence. 'If only,' said Frieda slowly, quietly, almost serenely, as though she knew that only a short respite of calm on K.'s shoulder had been granted her, but which she wanted to enjoy to the full, 'if only we had gone away at once that night, we could be somewhere in safety, always together, your hand always near enough for mine to grasp; how much I need you near me, how lost I have been without you near me ever since I have known you; believe me, the only dream that I ever dream, no other, is that you are near me.' (237)

At this point in the narrative there is no reason to think that K. misunderstands Frieda or that Frieda is being insincere. The balanced tenderness of this entire passage suggests that a momentarily perfect relationship between K. and Frieda has been attained, in comparison with which Frieda's subsequent relationship with

Jeremias appears as the relationship of a smothering and over-indulgent mother to a sick child.

Moments of peace and stasis are rare within *Das Schloß*, but they are real, and their existence gives the lie to those critics who paint K. in unrelievedly dark colours. Heinz Politzer, for example, maintains that:

> *Frieda is right when she charges that he uses whatever knowledge he has for his own sake and in his own interest. The bitterness he spreads is the taste he leaves on the lips of his patients . . . Now we can see that this bitterness is not only a matter of taste but an integral quality of K. himself. K. not only embitters others by his deeds and words; bitterness is engrained in his life; it is his very substance.*[36]

And Walter Sokel goes so far as to say:

Ebenso plump-lüstern und gemein-sinnlich ist K.s Verhältnis zu seiner Frieda wie es die Wirtin sieht. Sie kam ihm zufällig in den Weg und mißfiel ihm nicht gerade. Von Liebe keine Spur![37]

K.'s relationship to his Frieda is just as clumsily lascivious and vulgarly sensual as the landlady sees it. He came across her by chance and she by no means displeased him. But of love there is not a trace!

and:

K. ordnet alles Menschliche dem Ziel unter.[38]

K. subordinates everything human to his goal.

In the light of what has just been said, however, all three of these statements seem somewhat exaggerated. K. *is* wilful, aggressive and egocentric, of that there is no doubt, but he is also capable of love. There *are* moments in the novel when deeper and more human resources of his personality emerge, and his relationship with

---

[36] Politzer, pp. 278–9.
[37] Sokel, *Franz Kafka: Tragik und Ironie*, p. 414.
[38] Sokel, *Franz Kafka: Tragik und Ironie*, p. 421.

Frieda *can* go beyond coarse-grained sensuality and hard-bitten exploitation. Kafka once wrote:

Der Mensch kann nicht leben ohne ein dauerndes Vertrauen zu etwas Unzerstörbarem in sich, wobei sowohl das Unzerstörbare als auch das Vertrauen ihm dauernd verborgen bleiben können. (H, 44)	*Human beings cannot live without a persistent faith in something indestructible within themselves. But, at the same time, it is perfectly possible for this indestructible element and this faith to remain permanently concealed from them. (W, 43)*

If we apply the terms of this statement to the central figure of *Das Schloß*, it is possible to say that throughout the novel, an indestructible power underlies K.'s conscious mind and will. This power is normally hidden from K.'s conscious mind because the two sides of K.'s personality are in secret conflict with each other, but it breaks through spontaneously to the surface of K.'s personality at certain times in the novel as a result of his relationships with Frieda and Olga. When K. feels that something is missing from his experience of the world outside himself, it is this dimension that he is missing. When K. fails to make contact with other people, he fails because of the absence of this dimension. As the novel progresses, however, this 'indestructible element' breaks down K.'s will more and more until, at last, after the interview with Bürgel, it corrodes his will altogether, suffuses the surface of his personality and allows us to see that the name of this 'something' is imaginative sympathy, love.

The lyrical moments of timelessness and love which K. occasionally experiences when he is with another person appear even more valuable if they are compared with his experience at the end of the eighth chapter when he breaks off contact with all other human beings. Whereas the four lyrical moments provide an insight into K.'s best self, the eighth chapter gives the reader a clear picture of the implications of K.'s Faustianism when this is taken to its ultimate conclusions. When K. opens the bottle of cognac which he finds in a pocket of Klamm's sledge, the narrative reads:

*Er holte eine [Flasche] hervor,
schraubte den Verschluß auf und
roch dazu, unwillkürlich mußte
er lächeln, der Geruch war so süß,
so schmeichelnd, so wie von je-
mand, den man sehr lieb hat, Lob
und gute Worte hört, und gar
nicht weiß, worum es sich handelt,
und es gar nicht wissen will und
nur glücklich ist in dem Bewußtsein, daß er es ist, der so spricht.
»Sollte das Kognak sein?« fragte
sich K. zweifelnd und kostete aus
Neugier. Doch, es war Kognak,
merkwürdigerweise, und brannte
und wärmte. Wie es sich beim
Trinken verwandelte, aus etwas,
das fast nur Träger süßen Duftes
war, in ein kutschermäßiges Ge-
tränk! (152–3)*

*He pulled one [a bottle] out, undid
the cap and smelt it. Although he
did not want to, he had to smile,
the scent was so sweet, so caress-
ing, like praise and good words
from someone who one holds very
dear, even though one does not
know what they are all about, and
is not concerned to know, and is
simply happy in the knowledge
that it is he who is saying them.
'Can that be brandy?' K. asked
himself doubtfully and took a sip
out of curiosity. Yes, strangely
enough it was brandy, and it
burned and warmed him. How it
changed as one drank it from
something that was almost nothing
other than the bearer of a sweet
perfume into a rough liquor that a
coachman might drink! (102)*

Perhaps one of the significant facts here is that in the fourth, sixth
and seventh lines, the German relative pronouns 'den' and 'der' and
the German personal pronoun 'er' are masculine, and not, as one
might reasonably expect, seeing that a man is speaking, feminine.
In other words, the feelings that the cognac arouses in K. are the
narcissistic and self-indulgent feelings of a man looking at his reflection in a mirror and deriving a sexual satisfaction from doing so.
Just as in such a situation it is not the presence of another, nor the
occasion of the praise, nor the terms of the praise that matter, but
the subjective feelings of gratification, so too, in K.'s situation, it is
not the objective reality of the cognac which is appreciated, but
simply the deceptive scent which it gives off and the self-indulgent
fantasies and feelings that K. obtains from it. Whereas, in the privileged moments with Frieda and Olga, K. gives himself unself-
consciously to the other person and derives an unself-conscious

pleasure from experiencing what these women are in themselves, in the *Herrenhof* courtyard, he fixes his fantasy on an object and wallows in the sickly emotions thus aroused. Consequently, when he is interrupted, his fantasies are shattered—the bottle drops onto the furs and as its sticky contents are spilt, K.'s fantasies are revealed as a form of masturbation.

If K.'s solipsism is shown to be infantile at the point just discussed (when, incidentally, he literally returns to the womb of Klamm's sledge and has to be ejected into the cold once more), then the end to which such infantilism must lead is revealed at the end of the same chapter:

. . . da schien es K., als habe man nun alle Verbindung mit ihm abgebrochen und als sei er nun freilich freier als jemals und könne hier auf dem ihm sonst verbotenen Ort warten, solange er wolle, und habe sich diese Freiheit erkämpft, wie kaum ein anderer es könnte, und niemand dürfe ihn anrühren oder vertreiben, ja kaum ansprechen; aber—diese Überzeugung war zumindest ebenso stark —als gäbe es gleichzeitig nichts Sinnloseres, nichts Verzweifelteres als diese Freiheit, dieses Warten, diese Unverletzlichkeit. (157)

. . . then it seemed to K. as though all relations with him had been broken off and as though he were indeed freer than he had ever been and could wait in this place, otherwise forbidden to him, as long as he wanted, and had won this freedom for himself in a way that scarcely anyone else could do, and as though no one might lay a finger on him or drive him away or scarcely speak to him; but— and this conviction was at least equally as strong—as though, at the same time, there was nothing more senseless, nothing more hopeless than this freedom, this waiting, this inviolability. (105)

Here at last K. has succeeded totally in imposing his fantasy world onto the real world, in forcing the real world to recede before him. Whereas after his first night with Frieda on the floor of the *Herrenhof*, the peasants and Olga stream in towards him as though in celebration, now the lights go out one by one and K. finds himself as alone as Amalia must be. K.'s victory, as he himself senses, is pyrrhic for it results in a profound tension in his personality. Whereas the freedom that K. experiences with Olga and Frieda is a freedom which takes account of and coexists with the realities of the external world, the freedom which K. attains at the end of the eighth chapter is a freedom which denies all rights to that world. Thus, just as K. was knocked off the wall when he was a child and hurt for his impertinent desire for power, so now the world will react convulsively against K. for having arrogantly assumed that he could wilfully impose his fictions upon it. Whereas the victories that K. wins with Olga and Frieda are real because K. is unself-conscious about them, the victory that he wins at the end of Chapter Eight is unreal precisely because he is so conscious of having won it.

(iii) *Mythical Events*

Although the world of the village and the Castle are characterised at first sight by an overwhelming banality and bleakness, behind that world lies a secret mythical dimension which is rarely per-ceived by K. even though it is of the greatest importance for him. The scene in Lasemann's house is, as has been shown, suggestive of purgatory. The fire-brigade festival has all the characteristics of a festival of procreation and renewal.[39] It takes place by a stream, the source of life, and it is presided over by the god of fate and fire (*Sort*ini) and the god of water (Seemann—Seaman—the head of the fire-brigade). Several of the people whom K. meets or hears about in the village are death-figures (Gerstäcker, the 'inexorable driver' whose name inevitably calls to mind the German word for grave-yard 'Gottesacker'; Bertuch and Erlanger). The name *Herrenhof* can be translated as 'The Gentlemen's Inn', but in German, it also suggests 'the court of the Lord' ('Herr' = 'Lord'; 'Hof' = 'Court') with all the overtones of justice and rejoicing which that idea carries. When K. listens to the telephone in the first chapter, he puts his ear to the 'Hörmuschel'. Now, although this word translates lexi-cally as 'ear-piece' or 'receiver', it literally means 'hearing-shell', suggesting therefore that the sound which K. hears through it is something primal like the noise of the sea. Klamm's sledge is like a

---

[39] See pp. 155–6 below.

womb into which K. is invited to return by the sledge-driver (who, because of his association with that other sledge-driver, Gerstäcker, is also a death-figure) and out of which he has to be ejected if ever he is to be reborn.

If at one level the Castle authorities and their village representatives operate in K.'s mind as an anomalous, disproportionate and repressive bureaucracy, at another level they seem to perform a more basic rôle in the life of the village by initiating and presiding over rituals and festivals of death and rebirth. Although K. can make no contact with the Castle inhabitants in their capacity as administrators, in their capacity as demi-gods, these beings continually and surreptitiously intervene in K.'s life. They confront him with situations in which he is invited to undergo an archetypal experience, ensure that he is provided with appropriate legends, and indicate what rites he must take part in if ever he is to die and be reborn, if ever he is to find a place within village society without being brutalised or mesmerised by its institutions. K. has little or no sense of the hidden realities of village life. But the reader can, by paying close attention to the implications of the precise words which Kafka uses and by divorcing the scenes which present themselves to K. from K.'s unimaginative response to those scenes, discern in the world of the village a secret play of forces which continually call into question K.'s ego, valuations and assumed authority.

(iv) *Metaphors and Similes*

A fourth technique by which Kafka significantly varies the register of *Das Schloß* and invites the reader to step back from the mind of K. is the sparing use of simile and metaphor. At the end of the ninth chapter, for example, a point in the narrative when K. has completed the obstinate wilfulness of the eighth chapter by refusing to answer Momus' questions, the *Herrenhof* landlord, to ease K.'s mind, says that it will not rain fire and brimstone just because K. has refused to submit to Momus' examination. To this, K. replies with an irony whose grimness only later becomes apparent:

»Nein... danach sieht das Wetter nicht aus.« (172)

'No ... the weather doesn't look as though it'll do that.' (114)

Although it does not actually rain fire and brimstone at the beginning of the next chapter, an extremely ugly storm does blow up which K. realises is somehow connected with his recent behaviour:

Ein böses, böses Wetter. Irgendwie im Zusammenhang damit fiel ihm ein, wie sich die Wirtin bemüht hatte, ihn dem Protokoll gefügig zu machen, wie er aber standgehalten hatte. (173)

An angry, angry storm. Somehow it occurred to him in connection with it how the landlady had exerted herself to make him accept the necessity of Momus' report, but how he had refused to do so. (115)

Thus, it is suggested here that the storm is both a metaphor of the convulsive reaction with which the external world is about to retaliate to K.'s self-assertion and an image of the tension which has accumulated in K.'s personality between his egoistical will and his capacity for appropriate imaginative response. Perhaps at no other point in Das Schloß is it so evident that inner and outer are one, that the spectres which have been released into the world always return to haunt their place of origin. Similarly, K.'s overheated temper in Chapter Eleven finds its metaphorical counterpart in the overheated school-room.

As far as the use of simile is concerned, K. is compared to a cat and to an animal at pasture, Amalia to a wild-cat, the assistants to beasts of prey, Bürgel to a Greek god and Klamm to an eagle. At the end of the novel, when K. is talking to Pepi, he compares himself and her to children who have tugged the table-cloth from a table, smashing everything on the ground as they do so. Although there is a measure of overlap between the ways in which symbolic objects and similes work in Das Schloß, the symbolic object is normally embedded in the narrative and therefore unobtrusive, whereas Kafka's use of simile draws the reader's attention to one thing specifically and invites him, because of the force of the comparison, to regard it as specially significant.

E. Reflection

In his discussion of narrative breaks in Kafka's *Der Prozeß*, K. Leopold remarks:

> *Only very rarely is [Josef] K. allowed to sit and brood and dream, and then his thoughts do not wander back to his childhood and adolescence or out into the world; instead they are concerned exclusively with the immediate problem of his lawsuit or with problems arising from it, . . .*[40]

Whereas Josef K. is almost totally unreflective about himself, K. subjects himself throughout *Das Schloß* to a process of indirect and unconscious self-evaluation which finally issues in the conscious self-analysis that takes place during his final conversation with Pepi. The notion of 'unconscious self-evaluation' may sound like a contradiction in terms. But by using it, I am trying to suggest that K.'s unconscious mind is at work throughout the novel, assimilating experience, digesting it, dreaming about it and comparing it with his previous experience and that of other people—though he does not focus on himself with consciousness and lucidity until the very end of the novel. Throughout *Das Schloß*, K.'s ego is subjected to a bombardment from outside, and whether he likes it or not, that bombardment causes him to engage in a process of oblique reflection and culminates in the change that comes about in his personality after his interview with Bürgel. Well may K. think to himself:

. . . aber die Gewalt der entmutigenden Umgebung, der Gewöhnung an Enttäuschungen, die Gewalt der unmerklichen Einflüsse jedes Augenblicks, die fürchtete er allerdings, aber mit dieser Gefahr mußte er den Kampf wagen. (38)

. . . but the force of the dispiriting environment and of the process of becoming accustomed to disillusionments, the force of the imperceptible influences of every moment —of these things he was indeed afraid; but it was in the face of this danger that he had to chance his struggle. (30)

[40] K. Leopold, 'Breaks in Perspective in Franz Kafka's *Der Prozeß*', *The German Quarterly*, 36, 1963, p. 31.

For all the power which K.'s conscious mind seems to exert over his personality, ultimately, it is unable to impede the osmotic growth and change which goes on below its threshold.

(i) *Memory*

During the course of *Das Schloß* K. three times casts his mind back to his previous life in order, by implication, to compare it with his present life in the village. The first of these passages occurs very early on in the first chapter:

Und er verglich in Gedanken den Kirchturm der Heimat mit dem Turm dort oben. Jener Turm, bestimmt, ohne Zögern geradewegs nach oben sich verjüngend, breit-dächig, abschließend mit roten Ziegeln, ein irdisches Gebäude— was können wir anderes bauen?— aber mit höherem Ziel als die niedrige Häusermenge und mit klarerem Ausdruck, als ihn der trübe Werktag hat. (15)	And in his mind he compared the church tower at home with the tower up there. The former tower, firm in line, soaring unfalteringly upwards to its tapering point, with a broad roof and topped with red tiles, an earthly building—what else can we build?—but with a loftier goal than the low throng of houses and with a more clearly expressed meaning than the dismal workaday world possesses. (15)

This is the first time that K. has seen the Castle itself, and it is natural that he should throw his mind back into the past in order to seek a landmark in relation to which he can orient himself in his new situation. Unfortunately, the one image on which his memory lights, the church tower of his native village, offers him a set of standards and a pattern for action which are completely inappropriate to his situation in the village. K., like the tower of church he remembers, tries to move 'ohne Zögern geradewegs nach oben', 'unfalteringly upwards'. K. neglects the world of the 'Werktag' and the 'Häuser-menge' and sets himself a 'high aim' which proves to be unattain-able. K. talks in 'klaren Ausdrücken', absolute judgements, which are incapable of comprehending the complexities of the greyish world of the Castle and village. Perhaps the Castle, the shambling state bureaucracy, is the anomalous and decadent descendant of a

great society whose human symbol was K.'s church tower—we are
never given any indication about this. But whether this is the case
or not, K. makes his fundamental error in assuming that the society
from which he has come and the society into which he has come are
continuous with one another, that a pattern of behaviour which may
have been appropriate in the one will be equally appropriate in the
other. As the novel develops, K. discovers the falsity of this assumption and begins to see that what may possibly have been legitimate
behaviour in the former society is hubritic in the latter. That
obsessive purposefulness which may have been permissible within
the firm structures of the former 'earthly building' becomes vicious
self-assertiveness within the 'low throng of houses' of the latter
'earthly building'.

The second reference to K.'s previous life comes at the beginning
of the second chapter. K. arrives back at the *Brückenhof* and is met
by the two assistants who had earlier passed him on the road:

. . . es waren die Männer, die er schon getroffen hatte und die Artur und Jeremias angerufen worden waren. Sie salutierten jetzt. In Erinnerung an seine Militärzeit, an diese glücklichen Zeiten, lachte er. (28)	*. . . it was the men he had already met and who had been addressed as Artur and Jeremias. Now they saluted him. That reminded him of his time in the army, a happy time for him, and he laughed. (23)*

The exact significance of this second recollection is not so easy to
determine, for the reference to the past is not sustained and developed as it was in the first case. Nevertheless, two features are
clear enough. First, given that the prime purpose of the assistants
is to parody K. and that at this early stage of the narrative K. is
still looking to the surrounding world for a confirmation of his preconceptions, we can, I think, assume that K.'s laughter is the re-
lieved laughter of someone who has found a familiar landmark
rather than the bemused laughter of someone who has learnt to
see the funny side of his own pretensions. Second, the fact that K.
looks back on his army days as a 'happy time' both links up with the
values of striving and achievement which were inherent in his

memory of the church tower and explains his rude, authoritarian treatment of people during the first half of the novel. K. is someone who seems to need a hierarchy, for he is very concerned that Barnabas should not confuse him with the peasants and intensely aware of the distinctions that exist between master and servant; land-surveyor, inn-keeper and castellan's son; janitor and part-time teacher. But the hierarchy that K. seems to need is not the hierarchy of calling, legitimised by the service of a vision or an ideal, but the hierarchy of a 'career structure' whose ranks are matters for individualist competition and within which everyone is the enemy of everyone else. In K.'s mind, promotion and advancement tend to mean the acquisition of personal prestige and power over others, not the administration of responsibility within a pre-ordained system.

The final and most important recollection occurs later on in the second chapter when, in the course of the nightmare journey with Barnabas through the snow, the hold of K.'s conscious and intentional mind is loosened, and memories of his childhood, when he had climbed an impossibly difficult wall and been frightened off by the teacher, well up inside him. This entire incident will be considered more extensively later,[41] and for now, it is sufficient to say that although the wall-climbing episode could be construed either as a defeat or as a victory, K. chooses to remember it as a victory and is encouraged by it when it might perhaps have been more useful for him to be discouraged:

Das Gefühl dieses Sieges schien ihm damals für ein langes Leben einen Halt zu geben, was nicht ganz töricht gewesen war, denn jetzt, nach vielen Jahren in der Schneenacht am Arm des Barnabas, kam es ihm zu Hilfe. (45)	*The feeling of this victory seemed at that time to give him a support which would sustain him throughout a long life, and that consideration had not been altogether foolish, for now, after many years in the snowy night on Barnabas' arm, it came to his aid. (34)*

[41] See pp. 136–7 and 154–5 below.

8

Consequently, instead of relaxing his hold on Barnabas' arm and
ceasing to struggle, ceasing, that is, to climb the village equivalent
of the impossible wall, K.'s memory stimulates him into hanging on
all the more tightly to Barnabas' arm. In summary, Kafka's re-
strained use of K.'s memories enables the reader to see that K.
has imported a definite set of readily identifiable values into his
new situation. Hence we gain a critical distance from K. by seeing
the effect that those values have on his actions and relationships
there.

(ii) *Dream*

Although the status of dream in *Das Schloß* is very close to that of
recollection, the dream-sequence which occurs during the interview
with Bürgel carries even more authority than the memories because the incident of which it forms a part constitutes the crux of
the whole novel. Beforehand, K. is one person: afterwards, he is
another, and the dream-sequence helps to make plain the nature of
the transformation which takes place.

As in the *Herrenhof* courtyard, K. experiences a feeling of liberation in his state of semi-slumber before Bürgel. But the feeling of
sweetness which he had known in the *Herrenhof* courtyard, resembles the sensation which comes from the experience of being
praised and shows the extent to which K. is dependent on the
Castle authorities. In contrast, the feeling of liberation which K.
experiences before Bürgel shows the extent to which K. has achieved
independence from Bürgel and the Castle authorities whom that
official represents.[42]

In his dream, K. throws a party in order to show the guests that
the Castle officials are of the same status as, and therefore as unreal
as Greek gods. At first, K.'s demonstration seems to be nothing
more than a game with the Greek god of the dream, a playful celebration of the fact that he has come near to being freed from his
Faustian will and obsessive fantasies and no longer feels that the
Castle authorities are worth bothering about. At first, K.'s dream
seems to indicate that he has realised that the Castle is, in many

[42] The name Bürgel suggests in German the noun 'Bürglein' ('little castle') and the
verb 'bürgen für', ('to stand surety, vouch for').

respects, a necessary fiction, an 'earthly building' without ultimate authority. But then, quite suddenly, K. falls back into his old ways. The playful show of strength becomes obsessive struggle once more, and as K. presses forward, driving the official on and on when there is no need to do so, the guests disappear and K. finds himself alone again:

Und schließlich war er [der griechische Gott] fort, K. war allein in einem grossen Raum, kampfbereit drehte er sich um und suchte den Gegner; es war aber niemand mehr da, auch die Gesellschaft hatte sich verlaufen, nur das Champagnerglas lag zerbrochen auf der Erde. K. zertrat es völlig. Die Scherben aber stachen, ... (383)	*And in the end, he [the Greek god] was gone, K. was alone in a great spacious room; ready for battle he turned round and looked for his opponent; but there was no longer anyone there, the guests had run away as well, and only the champagne glass lay shattered on the ground. K. trampled it to smithereens. But the splinters stabbed into him, ... (248)*

An incident which had begun as the demonstration of K.'s exorcism from daemonic obsession and integration into a community[43] ends in the same way as the incident in the *Herrenhof* courtyard: K. finds himself alone, looking for a fight. An incident which had begun as a party to mark the cessation of K.'s attempts at self-justification ends in the same way as his ascent of the churchyard wall: K. hurts himself. The beginning of the dream indicates that K. could resolve his dilemma by living within the village community in the knowledge that the gods of that community are necessary fictions and therefore have only as much power over him as he permits them. But the end of the dream shows how far K. is, even then, from realising that solution. Thus, because K. shows that he is still unable, of his own accord, to suspend the movement of his will, he must be broken completely and fall into that second bout of (dreamless) sleep which is a form of death.

---

[43] The German word 'Gesellschaft' means party, the guests at a party and a society (in all senses of that word).

(iii) *Projection*

As the narrative of *Das Schloß* unfolds, K. comes to know himself by thinking about the various people he meets in the village whose situations parallel his own. At first, K. fails to recognise the various parallels which are presented to him. But in the second half of the novel, when K. makes explicit remarks about Barnabas' futile struggles, Amalia's pride and indifference towards others, Olga's indulgence towards her family and Jeremias' motives for carrying off Frieda, he is also beginning to identify and come to terms with his own failings. When K. projects himself illegitimately onto the world outside himself, he imprisons himself more securely in his own prejudices and fantasies. But when he accurately diagnoses what is going on outside his own mind, he simultaneously liberates himself from the prison of his preconceptions and comes to know himself through knowing other people. It can, of course, be asked how it is possible to know when K.'s diagnosis is correct, seeing that the reader receives all his information through K.'s mind. This is not an easy question to answer. It is, however, possible to say that the reader can, with reasonable certainty, say that K.'s diagnosis of a situation is accurate when his interpretation accords with the full facts of that situation; when nothing that anyone says or does elsewhere in the novel provides an explanation that is more plausible or authoritative than his diagnosis; and when he does not visibly introduce illicit assumptions into a situation. In the abstract, it is not possible to say how one knows that K.'s account of a situation is accurate. But when faced with a concrete situation, it is usually possible, by careful application of the above three yardsticks, to say whether K.'s account is justified and thus to see whether K. is opening himself to or hardening himself against the outside world.

(iv) *Indirect Self-reflection*

It is a comparative rarity for the arrogant K. to stand back and reflect upon his situation consciously and at length. Nevertheless, while K. is actually involved in a situation, he occasionally carries on an oblique, inconclusive reflection about himself. Such indirect introspection can be found, for example, in the very first chapter, just after he has seen the Castle for the first time:

Wieder stand K. still, als hätte er im Stillstehen mehr Kraft des Urteils. (16)	*K. stood still again, as though he had more power of judgement by doing so. (16)*

and again in the scene where he and Frieda make love on the tap-room floor:

... Stunden, in denen K. immer-fort das Gefühl hatte, er verirre sich oder er sei so weit in der Fremde, wie vor ihm noch kein Mensch, einer Fremde, in der selbst die Luft keinen Bestandteil der Heimatluft habe, in der man vor Fremdheit ersticken müsse und in deren unsinnigen Verlockungen man doch nichts tun könne als weiter gehen, weiter sich verirren. (63)	*... hours in which K. constantly had the feeling that he was going astray or had gone further into a strange country than any man before him, a country so strange that not even the air had any-thing in common with the air of his native land, where one must stifle because of this strangeness and yet, in whose insane entice-ments, one could do nothing else but go further and lose oneself more and more. (45–6)*

or at the end of the eighth chapter:

· .. da schien es K., als habe man nun alle Verbindung mit ihm abgebrochen und als sei er nun freilich freier als jemals und könne hier auf dem ihm sonst verbotenen Ort warten, solange er wolle, und habe sich diese Freiheit erkämpft, wie kaum ein anderer es könnte, und niemand dürfe ihn anrühren oder vertreiben, ja kaum ansprechen; aber—diese Über-	*... then it seemed to K. as though all relations with him had been broken off and as though he were indeed freer than he had ever been and could wait here in this place, otherwise forbidden to him, as long as he wanted, and had won this freedom for himself in a way that scarcely anyone else could do, and as though no one might lay a finger on him or drive him away*

zeugung war zumindest ebenso stark—als gäbe es gleichzeitig nichts Sinnloseres, nichts Verzweifelteres als diese Freiheit, dieses Warten, diese Unverletzlichkeit. (157)

or scarcely speak to him; but— and this conviction was at least equally as strong—as though, at the same time, there was nothing more senseless, nothing more hopeless than this freedom, this waiting, this inviolability. (105)

The technique is similar in all three cases. A tentative but complex proposition, introduced, for example, by 'K. hatte das Gefühl . . .' ('K. had the feeling . . .') or 'es schien K. . . .' ('it seemed to K. . . .'), is made up of clauses in the subjunctive mood. By this means, the narrator can attribute incisive thoughts to K. without having to make him commit himself actively or definitively to those thoughts or work out their implications in full. Furthermore, this process of oblique self-reflection has the advantage that the narrator can either distance himself from or endorse K.'s interpretation of an incident without having to intervene directly. Thus, by allowing K. to make use of this form of oblique self-analysis, Kafka has discovered a highly flexible form which, while appearing to be used consistently, in fact permits the narrator to advance towards or retreat from K.'s judgement in accordance with the demands of the narrative situation. So powerful is the illusion of consistency created by this form of self-reflection that it is easy to overlook the fact that Kafka may change his relationship of distance to the mind of K. even within a single passage. The end of Chapter Eight, for instance, comprises a sentence which extends over nineteen lines. During its course, Kafka approaches closer and closer to K. For the first nine lines, the narrator describes how the courtyard empties, and then, when only one ray of light shines down into the courtyard as a point of orientation, K. begins to feel the vanity of his actions in a sequence of subordinate clauses. These, predominantly verbal at first, resolve themselves and culminate after a period of stress and tension, in the finality of the three nouns 'diese Freiheit, dieses Warten, diese Unverletzlichkeit'. During these nineteen lines, one can feel Kafka moving closer and closer to K.'s thoughts until he reaches such a measure of agreement with his estimate of the situation that, by the time the concluding clause is reached, the subjunctive mood is a formality only. In reality, the subjunctive mood has been transcended to such an extent that it is impossible not to feel Kafka's very close alignment with K.'s thoughts about himself and his relations with the outside world.

As the novel progresses and the force of K.'s experiences begins to affect his conscious mind, K.'s self-reflection becomes less oblique. Thus, by the time Frieda deserts him, he is capable of standing back from himself and of reflecting on himself not obliquely, but with the full force of his not inconsiderable intellect.

Although K. only comes to a critical self-awareness during the last fifth of the novel, it would not be true to say that he remains unaffected by the stimuli to which he is exposed all along. Somewhere in the depths of his consciousness, all the oblique reflection in which he engages contributes to a process of self-comprehension. Throughout the first four-fifths of the novel, this unconscious process is largely invisible to the reader precisely because it is through K.'s conscious mind that he sees the world of the village. Nevertheless, the effects of this process occasionally become manifest in a moment of insight, illumination or self-doubt, or in the occasional pertinent remark which seems out of character with the compulsive K. who normally monopolises the centre of the novel.

F. Indirect Narrational Comment

Because the peculiar narrative form of *Das Schloß* allows the narrator to vary the extent of his endorsement and withdrawal, the narrator is able to make indirect comments on K. without actually seeming to do so:

K. aber, undankbar, *machte sich von Olga los und nahm den Wirt beiseite. (50)*	*K., however,* ungrateful, *let go of Olga's arm and drew the landlord to one side. (36)*
»*Wie?*« *fragte K., aus einer gewissen Zerstreutheit aufwachend,* aufgeregt mehr von der Neugierde als von Ärger. *(73)*	'*What?*' asked K., *waking up from a kind of absent-minded distraction,* excited more by curiosity than by annoyance. *(51)*

Darauf, was ihm angeboten wurde, achtete K. zunächst kaum, *aber die Tatsache, daß ihm etwas angeboten wurde, schien ihm nicht bedeutungslos.* (*134–5*)	At first, K. paid scarcely any attention to what was offered him, *but the fact that something was being offered to him did not seem to him to be without significance.* (*90*)
»*Ihr habt wohl euere Sachen noch niemals gewaschen*«, sagte K., es war nicht böse, sondern mit einer gewissen Zuneigung gesagt. (*143*)	'*You've probably never ever washed your things,*' said K., and this was said not maliciously but with a certain sympathy. (*96*)
Da sah K., *wie er* ziellos *umherblickte, weit in der Ferne an einer Wendung des Ganges* Frieda . . . (*355*)	Then, as he was looking around aimlessly, K. saw Frieda in the far distance at a bend of the corridor . . . (*229*)

(My emphasis in all cases.)

It is perfectly true, as Friedrich Beissner puts it, that Kafka does not stand behind K. in the above extracts 'interpreting, teaching or reflecting'.[44] Nevertheless, the manner in which the narrator describes K.'s actions and reflections, taken in the context of all the other alienation-devices which operate in *Das Schloß*, involves a continuous evaluation of K. If one scrutinises the above five extracts, it becomes apparent that Kafka manages this indirect evaluative comment by three principal means. These can be termed: particularisation, the avoidance of adjectives and description that is also evaluation.

(i) *Particularisation*

First of all, it needs to be noticed that the indirect narrative comment in *Das Schloß* proceeds so immediately from the realities of the situation in which K. finds himself, that any commentative words are, in the first place, validated by and understood in relation

[44] Beissner, p. 25.

to that situation alone. Only later, when a particular pattern of action or response has been repeated a number of times, does any particular commentative word acquire a more general significance. Thus, in the first example given above, 'undankbar', 'ungrateful', at first seems to be an unobtrusive and self-evident epithet which applies solely to K.'s initial neglect of Olga in a particular situation. Only when K. has repeated his ingratitude several times does the reader begin to see that ingratitude is a salient feature of his personality right up to his interview with Bürgel.

(ii) *The Avoidance of Adjectives*

Intimately connected with Kafka's technique of particularisation is his persistent refusal to attach generalised evaluative adjectives to the person of K. Thus, in the first example quoted above, 'undankbar' is more of an adverb than a predicative adjective. In the second example, even the adverb 'neugierig' is avoided and K.'s curiosity is communicated by the use of an adverbial phrase which itself is part of a carefully constructed comparison. In the third example, K.'s ingratitude is implied and not made at all explicit. In the fourth example, 'böse', 'maliciously', is an adverb and 'mit einer gewissen Zuneigung', 'with a certain sympathy', an adverbial phrase. And in the final example, 'ziellos', 'aimlessly', is firmly attached to the verb 'umherblickte'. Thus, although we are dealing with a scale of evaluative comments of which the first passage provides the most direct and the fourth passage provides the least direct example, none of the passages includes an unequivocal comment upon K. as a person. By refusing to provide generalised evaluative comment and by attaching commentative words to particular actions alone, Kafka avoids passing irrevocable judgements on K. He thereby implies that K.'s character is an incidental and changeable phenomenon rather than a fixed complex of unalterable qualities. Consequently, he leaves the possibility open that K.'s attitudes and behaviour will undergo radical change.

(iii) *Description that is also Evaluation*

The third feature of Kafka's narrative technique is an ability to use apparently neutral and value-free words in order to communicate implicit value judgements. Kafka creates a fictional world in which conventional value judgements lose much of their normal force and in which new value judgements are evolved from the close and surreptitious analysis of a situation. Thus, in the third passage quoted above, the simple description of K.'s failure to take what is offered him contains a latent evaluative charge, the full force of which only becomes apparent when it is seen that this failure is one of K.'s most persistent weaknesses. Likewise, the final passage given above provides an example of a descriptive adjective which contains a hidden value judgement. On the surface, the adverb 'ziellos' seems an unexceptional, not to say redundant word. But, seen in the context of K.'s life in the village, 'aimlessness' represents a complete suspension of all the values that have apparently shaped his life up to that point. For a moment, K. has stopped striving, and while he is in this state of suspension, perhaps the most moving scene of *Das Schloß*, K.'s final parting from Frieda, takes place. If read with unattuned eyes, 'ziellos' is the most insignificant of words. Read with eyes which have become adjusted to the values by which *Das Schloß* is governed, the word 'ziellos' indicates that a fundamental change is coming about in K.'s personality, that K. is moving away from his obsessive Faustianism to that stillness which he has persistently tried to avoid.

G. Direct Comment on K. by others

If, through the indirect and unobtrusive means detailed above, Kafka gives us a series of insights into K., then, throughout *Das Schloß*, we continually meet other characters who, with less charity and restraint than the narrator, let K. know exactly what they think of him. Although many individual comments are passed on K., the most sustained passage during which K. is presented to the reader through the eyes of a third person occurs in the thirteenth chapter, shortly after K.'s interview with young Hans Brunswick. During this section of the narrative, the reader sees K. simultaneously through the eyes of the *Brückenhof* landlady and through the eyes of Frieda who has been influenced by, and even taken over Gardena's

estimate of K. Correspondingly, therefore, this passage involves
two shifts in perspective. At first, Frieda reports Gardena's words
in indirect speech. She then talks to K. in direct speech, using the
landlady's words as though they were her own. Finally, she reverts
to indirect speech again. The two transitions can be seen in the
following two passages:

> *Da dir an mir nichts, am Preise alles liegt,* seist *du hinsichtlich*
> *meiner zu jedem Entgegenkommen bereit, hinsichtlich des Preises*
> *hartnäckig. Deshalb* ist *es dir gleichgültig, daß ich die Stelle im*
> *Herrenhof verliere, . . . (227)*[45]

> *. . . und hilft nichts anderes, dann* wirst *du im Namen des*
> *Ehepaares K. einfach betteln. Wenn du aber dann,* so schloß die
> Wirtin, *sehen wirst, daß du dich in allem getäuscht hast, . . .*
> *(228)*[46]

(My emphasis in all cases.)

The accusatory and absolute style of Frieda's speech stands in complete contrast to Kafka's own tentative and provisional evaluations
of K. Thus, it is to K.'s credit and credibility that when the ground
begins to give way under his feet as his worse motives are exposed,[47]
he has developed enough self-awareness not to become either dis-
mayed or hysterical. Instead, he is able, after listening to a further
outburst from Frieda herself, to stand back from the accusations
and reply:

[45] In this passage, the first verb emphasised is in the subjunctive because Frieda is
reporting the landlady's words, and the second verb emphasised is in the indicative
because Frieda is now expressing her own thoughts. Not surprisingly, the lack of an
English subjunctive mood makes it almost impossible to render this shift in perspective
so unobtrusively in a translation.

[46] In this passage, the first verb underlined (which is in the indicative) indicates that
Frieda is expressing her own opinion, but then, in her final remarks, she adds the
'sign-post' (emphasised): '. . . the landlady concluded, . . .', as though the previously
expressed opinions had not in fact been her own.

[47] The narrator informs us that the pile of logs on which K. is sitting begins to roll
away from under him.

| »... alles, was du sagst, ist in gewissem Sinne richtig; unwahr ist es nicht, nur feindselig ist es.« (231) | '... there is a certain amount of truth in everything that you say; it's not untrue, it's simply said from a hostile point of view.' (151) |

K. has acquired enough insight into himself to see the justice of Frieda's charges, and sufficient self-possession to realise that there is more to him than they imply. To use a *Betrachtung* of Kafka's that has already been cited,[48] K. is beginning to arrive at a faith in 'something indestructible' and hidden in his personality that is the very opposite of assertive egocentricity. Forced to compare himself as he knows he really is with the distorted image of himself that exists in the mind of someone else, K. is unable, at that particular point, to say exactly what distinguishes him from that distorted image. But the sobriety, charity, lucidity and tenderness with which he answers Frieda gives us a certain insight into the nature of those hidden, but real qualities of which he is becoming aware, and entirely justify the narrator's refusal to pass any absolute judgements upon him.

A second form of indirect comment upon K. and his life in the village is provided by Klamm's second letter. If this is taken literally, it is either a nonsense, or, as Heinz Politzer puts it, 'one of the malicious specimens of Klamm's peculiar sense of humour.'[49] But if it is read metaphorically, it begins to make perfect sense. The 'surveying-work' which K. has so far carried out (his attempts to discover where he stands in the village) are 'pleasing' to Klamm because they have taught K. much about himself and the futility of his Faustianism. The assistants 'deserve praise' because they have been to a great extent instrumental in teaching K. these lessons. Klamm hopes that this work will issue in the 'happy conclusion' of K.'s transformation, assures K. that his interest in him will persist and concludes by promising that K. will receive his 'just due', 'Entlohnung'. Although K. is proceeding in a misguided way, Klamm implies that it is necessary for him to do this so that he

[48] See p. 102 above.
[49] Politzer, p. 263.

may discover the hidden resources within himself, learn to trust in the disposition of the world and become what he truly is.

H. Breaks in the Narrative Perspective

In the first chapter of this book, attention was drawn to the fact that at four points in the definitive text of *Das Schloß*, the typical narrative perspective is broken in such a way that the reader hears the narrator's voice telling him something 'above K.'s head'.

What then do these four untypical passages communicate? The first passage seems to indicate two things. First, it is interesting to notice that in German, the 'ihn', grammatically masculine, can refer either to 'der Schloßberg' ('the Castle hill') or to K. Thus, it is suggested that both K. and the Castle hill are shrouded in snow and darkness in one sense or another. Second, the passage seems to suggest that the status of the Castle within the novel is ambiguous. Whereas in one sense the Castle exists, in another sense it does not exist and this ambiguity relates directly to the last-mentioned of the four passages in question. On the one hand, Schwarzer accepts the Castle's reality to the extent that he delivers his father's messages there. But on the other hand, the Castle barely exists for him at all, since, from what the narrator tells us, it appears to be peripheral to his major concern—his relationship with Gisa.

Schwarzer dagegen brachte ihr das ständige Opfer, daß er im Dorfe blieb; Boten des Vaters, die ihn öfters abzuholen kamen, fertigte er so empört ab, als sei schon die kurze, von ihnen verursachte Erinnerung an das Schloß und an seine Sohnespflicht eine empfindliche, nicht zu ersetzende Störung seines Glückes. (239)

Schwarzer, on the other hand, made a ceaseless sacrifice for her sake by staying in the village; messengers who his father frequently sent to fetch him were sent angrily about their business by him, as though the memory of the Castle and his filial duty which they aroused, were a drastic and irremediable disruption of his happiness.

Unlike Gardena, K., Olga and Barnabas, Schwarzer has direct and

legitimate access to and real connections with the Castle. But, unlike those four people, he sets no store by his privilege. Indeed, he
finds a much greater sense of fulfilment and happiness sitting at a
'little table' watching Gisa correct exercise books or listening bliss-
fully at her door to the 'most total, incomprehensible silence' behind it. Although there is a faint and not ill-humoured note of the
ridiculous in Kafka's presentation of the Gisa-Schwarzer relationship, that relationship seems real and valuable enough to the two
parties involved. Whereas K. might conceivably have fallen in love
with Gisa because her unresponsive passivity presented him with
an impossible challenge, Schwarzer, the reader is three times in-
formed, loves Gisa because of the peace and stillness which he finds
with her. Thus, the interpolation of this incident seems to imply
two things. First, it seems to imply that if Schwarzer can neglect
the Castle for Gisa's 'ponderous nature', then the Castle cannot be
all that fascinating once it has been entered. Second, it seems to
imply that if Schwarzer can be contented with a human relationship
where scarcely a word is spoken and where physical contact is non-
existent, then K. ought much more to be thankful for and contented with the infinitely richer gifts that Frieda perpetually offers
him.

The second passage during which the reader is privileged, is,
because of its brevity, less easy to explicate. Perhaps its main point
is to draw the reader's attention to the special importance of the
incident in which it appears. But the third passage is clearly crucial.
At that very point in time when K. is all but convinced of his own
insignificance and the futility of his strivings, and when it is beginning to dawn upon him that it is possible to live in the village without reference to the Castle bureaucracy, Bürgel reveals to him that
if he were only willing to persist a little longer, he could tear apart
the whole fabric of that bureaucracy by asking the one question
which the officials have to answer. K., however, proves to be incapable of realising the power that he has and Bürgel's revelations
pass him by.

The preceding discussion has, I hope, shown the way in which a critical perspective and a coherent, if paradoxical 'authorial truth' is, almost imperceptibly, built up within *Das Schloß*. Just as no one beam of light tells the scientific observer where the point of parallax lies behind a lens, so too, no one piece or even category of evidence can give the reader of *Das Schloß* an authoritative insight into the mind of K. and the nature of the Castle authorities. Just as it is necessary to observe several beams of light before the location of the point of parallax emerges, so too, the reader needs to examine several types of alienation-device in considerable detail before reliable patterns begin to form. As K. himself says of the stories about the Castle:

Noch viel verständiger allerdings wäre es, wenn Barnabas sich, wenn er oben ist, gleich bei mehreren Leuten erkundigte wie sich die Dinge wirklich verhalten; es stehen doch seiner Angabe nach genug Leute in dem Zimmer herum. Und wären auch ihre Angaben nicht viel verläßlicher als die Angabe jenes, der ungefragt ihm Klamm gezeigt hat, es mußten sich doch zumindest aus ihrer Mannigfaltigkeit irgendwelche Anhaltspunkte, Vergleichspunkte ergeben. (266)

It would, of course be even more understandable if Barnabas, when he gets up there, were to enquire straight away from more than one person just how matters really stood; according to him, there are enough people standing around in the room. And even if their information wasn't much more reliable than the information of the man who pointed out Klamm to him without being asked to do so, some leads or points of comparison at least would surely have to emerge from the various things that were said. *(172)*

As the reader moves deeper into *Das Schloß*, certain convictions begin to form subliminally in his mind because of the variety of stimuli which are received and the variety of ways in which he is persuaded to stand back from K. Thus, by the time he comes to Pepi's long final speech, he knows instinctively that what she says is wrong even if he is unable, at first reading, to say why this should be so. Pepi's account of what has gone before provides the tangible proof that even when it is a question of a fictional world in which the narrator has refused to exercise omniscience and authority, there is no need to despair and assume that it is impossible to say anything conclusive about that world. But, when that has been said, the proviso needs to be made that interpretation of *Das Schloß* is always a matter of probability, dependent on a close and consistent reading of the text. Where the narrator refuses to intervene directly but simply exists in his work as a shaping presence, there it is necessary to work with great tact and scrupulosity. K.'s initial errors are to be unaware of the care that is needed to decipher his world and to assume that his point of view is absolute. But the reader, who can look through K.'s eyes with the narrator nudging him from behind, is able to discover consistent patterns—'leads' and 'points of comparison'—of which K. never really becomes aware but which have worked on his unconscious mind in order to attune him to the world in which he finds himself.

The centre of *Das Schloß* is occupied not by K. but by the luminous mind of the narrator, and, as one of the epigraphs to this chapter suggests, that centre is the place within the empty darkness where the ray of light can be grasped even though its presence had not previously been perceived. It is towards this centre that K. slowly and painfully makes his way. Finally, he goes through the interview with Bürgel and emerges permeated with something of the light that is both at the centre of the novel and in the blueness of the sky behind the shambling Castle buildings. As the novel progresses, so K.'s personality becomes more translucent until he ceases to be, as it were, a piece of smoked glass which stands between the mind of the narrator and the blue of the sky and becomes something akin to a clear lens which transmits the light that emanates from each. K. learns to 'clean the dirt from his peep-hole', and in the next chapter, this process of enlightenment will be examined on the basis of the authority which has been provided by an analysis of the alienation-devices that operate within the text.

CHAPTER THREE

A Twentieth-Century Faust

Das Gewöhnliche selbst ist ja schon ein Wunder! Ich zeichne es nur auf. Möglich, daß ich die Dinge auch ein wenig beleuchte, wie der Beleuchter auf einer halbverdunkelten Bühne. Das ist aber nicht richtig! In Wirklichkeit ist die Bühne gar nicht verdunkelt. Sie ist voller Tageslicht. Darum schließen die Menschen die Augen und sehen so wenig. (G, 108)

The commonplace itself is already miraculous! I merely register it. Possibly I illuminate things a little like the lightning-assistant illuminates a half-darkened stage. But that isn't right! In reality, the stage isn't darkened at all. It is full of daylight. And it is for that reason that people shut their eyes and see so little. (C, 74)

Im Kriminalroman handelt es sich immer um die Aufdeckung von Geheimnissen, die hinter außerordentlichen Ereignissen verborgen sind. Im Leben ist es aber gerade umgekehrt. Das Geheimnis sitzt nicht verkrochen im Hintergrund. Es steht—im Gegenteil!—ganz nackt vor unserer Nase. Es ist das Selbstverständliche. Darum sehen wir es nicht. (G, 181–2)

The detective story always deals with the discovery of secrets which are concealed behind extraordinary events. But in real life, exactly the opposite is the case. The secret doesn't sit huddled away in the background. On the contrary, it stands completely naked in front of our noses. It is that which is taken for granted. And for that reason, we fail to see it. (C, 133)

Man muß geduldig alles in sich aufnehmen und wachsen. Die Grenzen des ängstlichen Ich lassen sich nur durch die Liebe sprengen.

One must take everything patiently into oneself and grow. The limits of the Angst-ridden ego can only be burst by love. One must

9

Man muß hinter dem abgestorb-
enen Laub, das uns umraschelt,
schon das junge, frische Früh-
lingsgrün sehen, sich gedulden und
warten. Die Geduld ist das ein-
zige wahre Fundament der Ver-
wirklichung aller Träume. (G,
252)

see the young, fresh spring green-
ness behind the dead foliage
which rustles all around us, be
patient and wait. Patience is the
only true basis on which all one's
dreams can come true. (C, 189)

From the discussion which has preceded this chapter, it should have become apparent that the present writer wishes to suggest that the inner history of K. is a twofold struggle—between his ego and the external world[1] and between his Faustian will and other, deeper powers of his personality. Furthermore, it is suggested that the Faustian will to power by which K. is initially dominated has, by the end of *Das Schloß*, been overcome by another power whose nature K. comes to understand only dimly, but which enables him to relate more adequately to the world outside himself. K., be-cause of his egocentricity, begins by assuming that 'the stage is darkened' and that 'the secret lies cowering in the background'. But, because of his experiences in the village, he comes to see that 'in reality, the stage is full of light', that the 'secret' lies in 'what is taken for granted' and that he has failed to realise this because of the limitations of his '*Angst*-ridden ego'. As K. discovers resources within his personality which enable him to be himself without assertiveness, so too, he discovers that that same power is latent in the external world, and that to become reconciled with himself is to become reconciled with the world outside himself.

It is perhaps worth remarking at this point that this dualism distinguishes the view of K. which is taken here from the view of K. which is taken by Walter Sokel in his major work on Kafka. On the whole, Walter Sokel seems to regard the wilful, Faustian K. as the entire K., and if he occasionally hints at the existence of another side of K.'s personality, then he does so incidentally rather than deliberately. Consequently, Walter Sokel paints K. in darker colours than is done here, saying for instance:

[1] Compare the fourth prefatory quotation on p. 9 above.

Rücksichtsloser Kampf um die Verwirklichung phantastischer Ambition stellt das Wesen des Landvermessers dar.[2]	*The essential nature of the land-surveyor consists in ruthless struggle for the realisation of fantastic ambition.*
In ihm schwelt kein unbewußter Konflikt.[3]	*No unconscious conflict seethes within him.*
Trotz aller seiner Beteuerungen ist es klar, daß für K. wesentlicher als die Gegenwart Friedas der Traum von Klamm und dem Schloß ist.[4]	*Despite all his reassurances, it is clear that the dream of Klamm and the Castle is more important to K. than the presence of Frieda.*

These statements, I would suggest, are somewhat harsh. First of all, the 'essential nature' of the 'land-surveyor' is indeed struggle. But K. seems to forget about the fiction of being a land-surveyor approximately half-way through the book, after which point it becomes increasingly clear, from the changes which are observable in his personality, that the 'essential nature' of K. the man is different. Then again, as will be discussed in this chapter in detail, K.'s personality *is* torn by a conflict—between his fantasy and his ability to love; between his will and his spirit; between his desire to be what he wills to be and his instinct to be what he really is. Because, however, we know K. in the first place through his conscious mind, and because this mind wills to remain in ignorance of the conflict which goes on below its threshold, it is easy to overlook those signs, fear and guilt above all, which betray its subliminal presence.

Finally, although Walter Sokel's third statement holds good of K. to a great extent up to his interview with Bürgel, K., as will be shown,[5] comes to realise after that interview that the Castle is relatively unimportant, and that in Frieda he has lost someone who is far more essential to him than all his fantasies about the Castle,

[2] Sokel, *Franz Kafka: Tragik und Ironie*, p. 404.
[3] Sokel, *Franz Kafka: Tragik und Ironie*, p. 438.
[4] Sokel, *Franz Kafka: Tragik und Ironie*, p. 439.
[5] See pp. 185-6 below.

corresponding as she does to the deepest regions of his personality. Perhaps then, it is not unfair to say that a major weakness of Professor Sokel's monumental study of *Das Schloß* is his disregard of K.'s 'trans-Faustian' nature, which, admittedly, K. does his best to conceal for most of the novel's length.[6]

Kafka knew and respected the writings of Schopenhauer,[7] and there is a striking and unmistakable similarity between Schopenhauer's account of the psychology of Faustian man, man under the domination of the Will, and K.'s initial manner of life. In this chapter, the characteristics of K.'s Faustianism, the transformation which comes about in his personality and what Kafka's acquaintance, Martin Buber, would have called the 'metapsychological' basis of this transformation will be considered with reference to the guide-lines established in the previous chapter and to some of the major insights contained in Schopenhauer's *Die Welt als Wille und Vorstellung*.

A. The Psychology of Faustian Man—the Characteristics

Das Streben der Materie kann daher stets nur gehemmt, nie und nimmer erfüllt oder befriedigt werden. So aber gerade verhält es sich mit allem Streben aller Erscheinungen des Willens. Jedes erreichtes Ziel ist wieder Anfang einer neuen Laufbahn, und so ins unendliche. (WV, 240)

The tendency to strive which is inherent in matter, can therefore only be inhibited but never fulfilled or satisfied. And that is exactly the case with the tendency to strive which is inherent in all the phenomena of the Will. Every goal which is attained is also the beginning of a new career and thus it goes on ad infinitum. (WI, 214)

---

[6] For criticisms of other passages from Walter Sokel's book which seem to involve an excessively harsh estimate of K., see pp. 101–2 above and 147–8 below.

[7] Compare T. J. Reed, 'Kafka und Schopenhauer: Philosophisches Denken und dichterisches Bild', *Euphorion*, 59, 1965, pp. 160–72. In this essay, Mr. Reed shows how Kafka's interest in Schopenhauer developed at the time when he was writing the Octavo Notebooks and links this growing interest with the emergence of the Castle image in Kafka's writings. Mr. Reed does not, however, make use of Schopenhauer's ideas to elucidate K.'s temperament and actions.

Alles Wollen *entspringt aus Be-dürfnis, also aus Mangel, also aus Leiden. Diesem macht die Erfüll-ung ein Ende; jedoch gegen einen Wunsch, der erfüllt wird, bleiben wenigstens zehn versagt; ferner, das Begehren dauert lange, die Forderungen gehn ins unend-liche; die Erfüllung ist kurz und kärglich bemessen. Sogar aber ist die endliche Befriedigung selbst nur scheinbar: der erfüllte Wunsch macht gleich einem neuen Platz; jener ist ein erkannter, dieser ein noch unerkannter Irrtum. Dau-ernde, nicht mehr weichende Be-friedigung kann kein erlangtes Objekt des Wollens geben: son-dern es gleicht immer nur dem Almosen, das, dem Bettler zuge-worfen, sein Leben heute fristet, um seine Qual auf Morgen zu verlängern.—Darum nun, solange unser Bewußtsein von unserm Willen erfüllt ist, solange wir dem Drange der Wünsche mit seinem steten Hoffen und Fürchten hin-gegeben sind, solange wir Subjekt des Wollens sind, wird uns nim-mermehr dauerndes Glück noch Ruhe. Ob wir jagen oder fliehn, Unheil fürchten oder nach Genuß streben, ist im wesentlichen einer-lei: die Sorge für den stets ford-ernden Willen, gleichviel in wel-cher Gestalt, erfüllt und bewegt fortdauernd das Bewußtsein;*

All willing *arises from want, therefore from deficiency, there-fore from suffering. Fulfilment puts an end to willing—and yet, for one desire that is fulfilled, there remain at least ten which are denied. Furthermore, desire lasts long, the demands are in-finite; the satisfaction is brief and its portion is miserly. But even the final satisfaction itself is only apparent: the wish which is ful-filled at once makes room for a new one; the earlier desire is recognised as an error and the latter desire has not yet been recognised as an error. No object of the Will, once it is attained, can provide sustained and lasting satisfaction. It is always like alms thrown to the beggar which keep him alive today so that his torments may be prolonged into the morrow.—Therefore, as long as our consciousness is filled with our Will, as long as we are given over to the pressing throng of desires with their constant hopings and fearings, as long as we are the subject of the Will, we can never have lasting happiness or peace. It makes no essential dif-ference whether we pursue or flee, fear calamity or strive after sen-sual enjoyment; the care for the constant demands of the Will, irrespective of the form in which*

ohne Ruhe aber ist durchaus kein
wahres Wohlsein möglich. So
liegt das Subjekt des Wollens
beständig auf dem drehenden Rade
des Ixion, schöpft immer im Siebe
der Danaiden, ist der ewig
schmachtende Tantalus. (WV,
279–80)

these reach us, continually fills
and moves our consciousness. But
without rest, no authentic well-
being is at all possible: thus, the
subject of the Will lies unceas-
ingly on the revolving wheel of
Ixion, scoops water perpetually
with the sieve of the languishing
Danaids, is the eternally lan-
guishing Tantalus. (WI, 253–54)

These passages of Schopenhauer's provide an astoundingly accurate picture of K.'s initial manner of life. K. is a kind of perverse Tantalus who, far from being condemned to eternal frustration, is actually attracted by the superhuman and the exceptional precisely because these are beyond his grasp. K. strives towards the inaccessible far distance because what exists there seems much more attractive than what is close at hand. Seen from a distance in the first chapter, the Castle seems to K to be characterised by a soaring sense of ease and freedom. When he comes closer to it, however, it appears to be a random conglomeration of buildings, and as such, far less inspiring. Conversely, at the outset of his stay in the village, K. has no interest whatsoever in the possible, the purely human and the ordinary which are spread out before him. Thus, even though, as has been shown,[8] K knows that he is no land-surveyor and can never be one in the village, he insists on maintaining the fiction of his self-bestowed identity and rejects the post of janitor which is offered to him by the village authorities. More particularly, in the second chapter, K. says to himself that although he is prepared to enter the Castle by night, through a back entrance, and on the arm of a Barnabas he takes to be superhuman, he has not the slightest desire to enter the Castle by day, according to the proper procedure, and on the arm of a Barnabas who is all too human:

Mit dem Sohn dieser Familie
aber, zu der er völlig gehörte und

But to go in broad daylight, on
the arm of the son of this family,

[8] See pp. 56–8 above.

mit der er schon beim Tisch saß, mit einem Mann, der bezeichnenderweise nicht einmal im Schloß schlafen durfte, an seinem Arm am hellen Tag ins Schloß zu gehen, war unmöglich, war ein lächerlich hoffnungsloser Versuch. (48)	*to whom he completely belonged and with whom he was already sitting at table, on the arm of a man who, significantly enough, was not even allowed to sleep in the Castle, was impossible. Such an attempt was laughably futile. (36)*

K. has absolutely no evidence, after so short a time in the village, on which he could possibly base such far-reaching and seemingly authoritative conclusions. Consequently, the irony of the last five German words is striking. Although K. is entirely accurate in his estimate of the uselessness of relying on Barnabas, he does not take it to heart since it represents, at this juncture, nothing more than a baseless rationalisation of his unwillingness to consort with Barnabas the mere man.

Similarly, when, one page later, K. imagines that he can gain entry to the *Herrenhof* without any difficulty, he is not attracted by the project, but as soon as Barnabas' family intimates that he will, in all probability, not be permitted to go inside that inn, we hear that K.:

. . . bestand doch dringend darauf, mitzugehen, ohne sich aber die Mühe zu nehmen, einen verständlichen Grund für seine Bitte zu erfinden. (49)	*. . . nevertheless insisted emphatically upon going with her [Olga], without bothering, however, to invent an intelligible reason for his request. (37)*

Thus, when K. reaches the *Herrenhof*, he plagues the landlord for permission to stay there overnight, contrary to the regulations, even though he has accommodation in the *Brückenhof*. From the hints which Kafka obliquely drops,[9] it seems that the impossible venture to stay the night in the *Herrenhof* is as attractive to K. the man as was the attempt to climb the impossible wall to K. the child. Then

[9] See p. 86 above.

again, although K. behaves extremely boorishly and condescend-
ingly towards Barnabas' family when he first meets them, as soon as
he discovers that they are a taboo subject in the village for reasons
that no one will explain to him, he hastens to get to know them
better—even at the risk of losing Frieda. Likewise, although K.
clamours for an interview with Klamm, as soon as the possibility of
one is held out to him by Momus, his only official connection with
Klamm in the village, he rejects it; and when Gardena promises to
try and arrange him an interview with Klamm, he still refuses to
give up his own futile struggles to see the official. Lastly, when
Hans Brunswick tells K. that an interview with *his* mother is out of
the question, K., although he has no reason whatsoever to suppose
that such an interview would benefit him in any way, goes to immense lengths of casuistry and scheming in order to try and achieve
this impossible end. Throughout the novel, the pattern is the same.
Whenever K. meets with something that appears to be impossible,
he desires it to the neglect and detriment of that which he already
has. And if he loses interest in that impossible goal, or if, by some
accident, it proves to be attainable after all, then he immediately
invents new impossible goals for himself. K. does not want satisfaction, he wants eternal striving, wants to keep Ixion's wheel turning even if this crushes what is near at hand. Thus, Kafka could
have been thinking specifically of K.'s frame of mind when he remarked to Janouch during the years when *Das Schloß* was taking
shape:

Unsere übermenschliche Gier und
Eitelkeit, die Hybris unseres
Machtwillens. Wir ringen um
Werte, die keine wirklichen Werte
sind, um achtlos Dinge zu zer-
trümmern, an die unsere ganze
menschliche Existenz gebunden
ist. Das ist eine Verwirrung, die
uns in den Kot zerrt und um-
bringt. (G, 108)

Our superhuman greed and vanity,
the hubris of our will to power. We
wrestle for values which are no
real values, in order heedlessly to
smash things to pieces to which
our whole human existence is
bound. That is a form of confusion which drags us into the
mire and kills us. (C, 73-4)

And Schopenhauer paints a comparable picture of the same aspect
of the Faustian mentality in the following words:

Daher kommt es, daß wir der Güter und Vorteile, die wir wirklich besitzen, gar nicht recht innewerden noch sie schätzen, sondern nicht anders meinen als eben, es müsse so sein: denn sie beglücken immer nur negativ, Leiden abhaltend. Erst nachdem wir sie verloren haben, wird uns ihr Wert fühlbar: ... (WV, 438)	*Thus it comes about that we are not properly aware of and fail to prize the goods and advantages that we really possess, but take them for granted—for they provide us with a negative happiness only, by keeping suffering at bay. Only when we have lost them do we become sensible of their value: ... (WI, 412)*

K.'s Faustianism causes him to overlook the fact that he has been
given a home, a wife and a job to which he has no entitlement as
'gifts of grace'. Only when it is too late does he realise the value of
'the goods and advantages' which he has forfeited by his love of the
impossible.

K.'s tendency to desire the impossible is closely connected with
his propensity to struggle and his love of 'motion forwards'. Early
on in the book, just after K. has made the fallacious claim to be a
land-surveyor and has received apparent confirmation of this claim
over the telephone, he thinks to himself:

Das Schloß hatte ihn also zum Landvermesser ernannt. Das war einerseits ungünstig für ihn, denn es zeigte, daß man im Schloß alles Nötige über ihn wußte, die Kräfteverhältnisse abgewogen hatte und den Kampf lächelnd aufnahm. (10)	*So the Castle had appointed him as land-surveyor. On the one hand, that was unfortunate for him, for it indicated that the people in the Castle knew everything relevant about him, had weighed up the balance of forces and were taking up the struggle with a smile. (12)*

No one has said anything about a struggle—indeed, the telephone
conversation has suggested that no struggle is necessary. Consequently, the notion can only have originated, quite gratuitously, in

K.'s own mind. Given the probable fallaciousness of K.'s claim to
be a land-surveyor and the frequent suggestions that he enjoys
'motion forwards' for its own sake, it begins to look as though a
tendency to engage in obstinate and pointless struggle as an end in
itself is a major feature of K.'s make-up. This suspicion is reinforced when K. ponders Klamm's first letter in the second chapter,
and concludes from the three words 'as you know' that Klamm is
intimating that it was he, K., who had had the temerity to initiate
the struggle. Looked at objectively, there is no apparent reason why
K. should draw this conclusion from Klamm's words. Klamm's
letter thus seems to have acted as a kind of Rorschach test, per-
suading K. to reveal aspects of his motivation which would otherwise have remained concealed.

K.'s attraction to struggle is the obverse of his love of the impossible. Only by setting himself impossible goals can K. assure
himself that his struggles will last for ever. This reciprocal relationship is made plain above all in that crucial passage where K. thinks
back to the wall-climbing episode of his youth. There was no need
for him to climb the wall, for it was possible to gain access to the
graveyard by a 'kleine Gittertür', a 'little trellis-work gate',[10] and
anyhow, what lay on the far side of the wall was no secret to him:

Nicht Neugier trieb sie dazu, der Friedhof hatte vor ihnen kein Geheimnis mehr. (44)	*It wasn't curiosity that drove them to do this, the graveyard was no mystery to them any more. (34)*

Hence, K. tackles the wall partly because it is known to be impossibly difficult to climb and partly because the attempt to 'conquer'
('bezwingen') the wall involves violent struggle, certain failure and
the consequent necessity of beginning the struggle all over again.

A further feature of K.'s personality, closely connected with his
desire for the impossible and his love of struggle for its own sake,
is a will to power. In the pursuit of his own obsessive ends, K.
unconsciously seeks power over others by compelling them to serve

---

[10] 'A little trellis-work gate.' For the connotations of the word 'Gitter', see p. 84
above.

those ends, conform to his preconceptions and acquiesce in his fictions. And if, paradoxically, K. were to achieve the impossible, the exhilaration of having done so would involve a sense of domination. Thus when, impossibly, the young K. did manage to scale the graveyard wall, he felt a surging sense of power when he reached the top. For one impossible moment, K. was 'King of the Castle', able to feel that 'here and now, no one was greater than he' (34). Walter Sokel possibly obscures the megalomaniac aspect of K.'s drive to achieve the impossible by force for he speaks of this urge as a 'burning desire for the ecstatic-mystical happiness of having scaled the heights'[11] and describes the experience of conquest as a 'mystical triumph'.[12] In view, however, of the attitude taken by mystical adepts to men like K. who attempt to take heaven by storm, one cannot help wondering whether Professor Sokel's characterisation puts the incident into too positive a light. All major mystical writers warn their students *against* struggling to attain mystical insight by force and counsel them to wait patiently for the appropriate time when insights are granted to them independently of their volition. Similarly, all major mystical writers warn their students *against* such feelings of intoxication as those experienced by K. on top of the churchyard wall. First, such feelings are said to represent a very low and deceptive form of mystical experience, and second, such feelings are said to be a particularly insidious temptation to pride in what has apparently been achieved by subjective effort. Kafka, who was mystically inclined in an agnostic way, knew this, and seems to be saying as much when he sets the feelings of absolute power that K. experiences on top of the wall against the 'little flag' which he plants there and which seems to reflect more accurately the true status of K.'s 'victory'. Furthermore, the fact that K. is very soon dislodged from his perch and ignominiously hurt in the process suggests that the sense of triumph which crowns this incident indicates not an authentic triumph, but a sham triumph such as he will later experience in the *Herrenhof* courtyard. Here, as in the wall-climbing episode of his youth, K.'s feelings of sweetness are short-lived and K.'s sham victory ends in the inner hurt of despair.

---

[11] Sokel, *Franz Kafka: Tragik und Ironie*, p. 403.
[12] Sokel, *Franz Kafka: Tragik und Ironie*, p. 407.

To adapt one of Kafka's letters to Milena,[13] K., who 'in the great game of chess' is not even a 'pawn of a pawn', desires, 'against all the rules of the game and to the confusion of the game, to occupy the place of the King himself and even the whole board ...' (LM, 73).

In attempting to gain power over others, K. is also seeking to gain power over those parts of his own personality which he cannot or will not accept. In attempting to impose his fiction of being a victimised land-surveyor on the world outside himself, K. is also trying to impose an inauthentic personality upon the self that he most truly is. Just as the world must react convulsively against him, so too, the deepest powers of K.'s being must react in a similar way. Because of this inner conflict, the satisfaction which K. achieves by his wilfulness is, like the satisfaction achieved by Schopenhauer's man under the control of the Will, short, unfulfilling and deceptive. It serves as the stimulus to new strivings in order to escape a convulsive crisis and as the source of new frustrations when it is realised that such a crisis is ultimately inescapable. The freedom which K. attains both in the wall-climbing episode and in the *Herrenhof* courtyard is spurious. It is not the authentic, unemotional state of freedom which flows from an unself-conscious harmony between the subject, the external world and the power which lies behind it, but the artificial and temporary feeling of exhilaration which ensues when the subjective will has been imposed upon the external world. Again, Kafka could have been thinking explicitly of K. when he said to Janouch:

Die falsche, nur durch äußere Maßnahmen angestrebte Schein-freiheit ist ein Irrtum, ein Durch-einander, eine Wüste, wo außer den bitteren Gräsern der Angst und Verzeiflung nichts gedeihen kann. Das ist natürlich, denn was einen wirklichen, beständigen Wert	*The false mock-freedom which has been striven for by external means alone is an error, a confusion, a waste land where nothing can thrive apart from the bitter herbs of anxiety and despair. That is only to be expected, for whatsoever is of real and perma-*

[13] Milena Jesenská, the Czech translator of some of Kafka's early stories. Kafka met her for the first time in March 1920 and broke with her, after a passionate and tragic love affair, in May 1922. Max Brod draws a certain parallel between Milena and Frieda, and between Klamm and Milena's husband—to whom she was unhappily married.

hat, ist immer ein Geschenk von innen. Der Mensch wächst ja nicht von unten nach oben, sondern von innen nach außen. Das ist die Grundbedingung aller Lebensfreiheit. (G, 60)

nent value is always a gift from within. Man does not grow upwards from below, but outwards from within. That is the basic condition of all freedom in life. (C, 35–6)

Because 'man does not grow upwards from below', it is useless for K. to climb the wall. When he reaches its summit by wilful striving, the momentary exhilaration soon disappears and K. is precipitated once more into the 'waste land' of 'anxiety' and 'despair'. Only when K. comes to see that all such victories are defeats because they have been won at the expense of reality can he begin to take account of those 'gifts from within', in the acceptance of which lies true victory and genuine freedom.

Dasselbe zeigt sich endlich auch in den menschlichen Bestrebungen und Wünschen, welche ihre Erfüllung immer als letztes Ziel des Wollens uns vorgaukeln; sobald sie aber erreicht sind, sich nicht mehr ähnlich sehn und daher bald vergessen, antiquiert und eigentlich immer, wenngleich nicht eingeständlich, als verschwundene Täuschungen beiseite gelegt werden; glücklich genug, wenn noch etwas zu wünschen und zu streben übrigblieb, damit das Spiel des steten Überganges von Wunsch zur Befriedigung und von dieser zum neuen Wunsch, dessen rascher Gang Glück, der langsame Leiden heißt, unterhalten werde und

Finally, the same thing manifests itself in human strivings and desires which always fool us by presenting their satisfaction as the final goal of the Will. As soon as they are attained, however, they no longer seem as they did, and they are therefore soon forgotten, outmoded, and indeed, even if this is not admitted, always discarded as vanished illusions. We are fortunate enough if there still remains something to desire and strive after so that the game of constant transition from desire to satisfaction and from satisfaction to new desire (the rapid play of which is called happiness and the slow play of which is

nicht in jenes Stocken gerate, das sich als furchtbare, lebenserstarrende Langeweile, mattes Sehnen ohne bestimmtes Objekt, ertötender languor zeigt.—Diesem allen zufolge weiß der Wille, wo ihn Erkenntnis beleuchtet, stets was er jetzt, was er hier will; nie aber was er überhaupt will: jeder einzelne Akt hat einen Zweck; das gesamte Wollen keinen: ... (WV 240–1)

called suffering) can be kept up and does not result in that final state which manifests itself as frightful, life-paralysing boredom, lifeless yearning without a definite object, deadening languor.—In accordance with all this, the Will always knows, when enlightened by insight, what it wants here and now; but it never knows what it wants overall: every individual act has a purpose, but the whole business of willing has none at all: ... (WI, 214–5)

In the above passage, Schopenhauer makes the penetrating comment that although the man who lives under the blind impulsion of the Will may be able to explain what immediate aim he is pursuing, he will be unable to give an account of the nature of his final goal. This particularly applies to K. Although K. appears to be capable of giving a coherent account of his short-term aims, a close analysis of his words reveals on the one hand, that this coherence is more apparent than real, and on the other hand, that he never manages to say what he really wants in the long term.

When all is said and done, what does K. want to achieve? Entry into the Castle? But this answer still leaves open the question of what K. wants to achieve when he gets there. Is it, as he suggests within the first six pages of the novel, that he wants to discover the nature of the surveying work which he has to do? But if this is so, then it is strange that K. should never again give this as his reason for seeking entry to the Castle, and that, in the second half of the novel, he should make relatively few references to his assumed position as land-surveyor. Is it that K. wants to be accepted as a land-surveyor? K. never explicitly tells us the answer to this question, but if this is his only reason for wanting to gain entry to the Castle, then it is an odd one. The Castle recognises him as land-surveyor over the telephone on the first evening of his stay in the village and its officials never at any time give K. reason to assume that they do not regard him as a land-surveyor. Furthermore, if this desire is at the root of K.'s attempt to enter the Castle, then, after his interview with the Village Superintendent, he might just as well spare himself any more trouble, for he knows by then that he is not entitled to the job and that even if he were, he could never be given work in this particular village simply because there is no call for any land-surveying work to be done there. Although the insistent quality of K's striving remains constant up to his interview with Bürgel, his goal does not. For the first few chapters, K. seems to imply that he wants to enter the Castle in order to discover something or other about his work or position as a land-surveyor. After about the fourth chapter, however, K. implies more and more that he wants to enter the Castle in order to see Klamm about his relationship with Frieda. Here again, it does not become clear just what he wants to ask Klamm about Frieda. So does K. want to gain entry to the Castle in order to discover some metaphysical truth about the lords of the Castle or the meaning of existence? Again, K. never says. But when the opportunity comes of asking Bürgel *the* metaphysical question which could tear the Castle into pieces, he does not do so. This indicates putative will to truth that his is not sufficiently strong to overcome his tiredness.

Because K. never gives a convincing reason for wanting to penetrate the Castle and because none of his actions imply any such reason, his language becomes highly inexplicit and vague whenever his talk or his thoughts turn to final ends. In the second chapter, for instance, K. says that he hopes 'to attain something in the Castle'— a turn of phrase which seems to mean nothing more than 'to get into the Castle', and in Chapter Thirteen, he says to himself:

Das alles war nicht allzu schmerzlich, es gehörte in die Reihe der fortwährenden kleinen Leiden des Lebens, es war nichts im Vergleich zu dem, was K. erstrebte, und er war nicht hergekommen,	*All that wasn't too painful, it was part of the persistent succession of life's petty irritations; it was nothing compared with that which K. was striving to attain, and he hadn't come here in order to lead*

um ein Leben in Ehren und	*an honoured and trouble-free life.*
Frieden zu führen. (223)	*(146)*

Although this passage seems convincing and purposive enough at
first sight, a closer inspection reveals that it says nothing concrete
whatsoever about K.'s final ends. Similarly, the language of the
despairingly absurd letter which K. dictates to Barnabas for Klamm,
although purposeful on the surface, has the same abstraction and
aimlessness about it. Then again, although, at the end of the four-
teenth chapter, K. describes his greatest and only wish as the wish:

Meine Angelegenheiten mit den	*. . . to sort out my affairs with the*
Behörden in Ordnung zu bringen	*authorities. (161)*
. . . (248)	

he never indicates what substance, if any, this classic bureaucratic
cliché might have in his mind. During his interview with the
Village Superintendent, K. never tells him what he wants from the
authorities and when the Superintendent asks K. *how* he intends to
assert the rights which he claims to have, K. can only reply with the
cryptic: 'I can't give that away.' Similarly, when K. is asked whether
he will pay the Superintendent another visit if anything new emerges,
K. replies with the vacuous: 'I don't want any gifts of grace from
the Castle, but my rights.' What precisely *does* this mean? It sounds
very impressive, but K. *has* no rights because he is no land-surveyor
and has never been employed as one by the local authorities, and if
by 'rights', K. means that he wants the basic rights of a home, a
wife and a job, then he has these already, ironically enough, as
'gifts of grace from the Castle'!

   If it is not possible for the reader to define with any certainty the
nature of K.'s final goal, even though he makes frequent reference
to the 'greatness of his aim', then that is an inability which is shared
by all the characters in *Das Schloß* who have anything to do with K.
Gardena refers to K. in the fourth chapter as one 'whose intentions
are unknown', and Frieda, in the thirteenth chapter, reports her as
saying that she does not understand what he wants from Klamm.
Frieda says 'I don't know what you want' when she meets K. for the

very first time, and towards the end of the thirteenth chapter, she admits that although she knows that Klamm is no longer his goal, she cannot say exactly what his goal now is. Even Pepi, temperamentally the most similar character to K. of all the characters in *Das Schloß*, is unable to say what K. really wants and twice tells him as much:

... *denn was will er, was ist er für ein sonderbarer Mensch? Wonach strebt er, was sind das für wichtige Dinge, die ihn beschäftigen und die ihn das Allernächste das Allerbeste, das Allerschönste vergessen lassen? (421)*	... *for what does he want, what sort of a strange person is he? What is he striving for, what are those important things that concern him so and that make him forget what is closest to him, what is best of all, what is most beautiful of all? (274)*
Ja, woran denkt denn K.? Was hat er für besondere Dinge im Kopf? Wird er etwas Besonderes erreichen? Eine gute Anstellung, eine Auzseichnung? Will er etwas Derartiges? Nun dann hätte er von allem Aufang an anders anstellen müssen. (430)	*Yes, what has K. got in mind? What special things does he have in his head? Will he achieve something out of the ordinary? A good position? An award? Is he after something of that nature? Well then, he ought to have gone about things in a different way right from the very start. (280)*

In the fourth chapter, the landlady listens to K.'s insubstantial reasons for wanting to see Klamm:

... *es genügt mir, wenn ich den Eindruck sehe, den meine Worte auf ihn machen, und machen sie keinen oder hört er sie gar nicht, habe ich doch den Gewinn, frei vor einem Mächtigen gesprochen zu haben. (75)*	... *it is sufficient for me if I can see the impression that my words make on him, and if they don't make any impression, or if he doesn't listen to them, then I shall at least have the satisfaction of having spoken freely before a powerful man. (53)*

She then, in bewilderment, asks him: 'but tell me then, what is it that you want to speak to Klamm about?' To this K. replies: 'about Frieda of course'. Now this is a nonsensical thing to say, considering that there is nothing K. needs to know about Frieda which he does not know already, and that, as he himself goes on to say in the very next paragraph, there is no way in which his relationship with Frieda could remotely affect Klamm. Then again, during her interview with K. in the sixth chapter, Gardena twice asks K. about his reason for wanting to see Klamm. At first, K. avoids giving a direct answer to these questions; then he admits to being very uncertain of his aims ('but what I want from Klamm is difficult to say'); and finally he gives three reasons which are again very implausible:

Zunächst will ich ihn in der Nähe sehen, dann will ich seine Stimme hören, dann will ich von ihm wissen, wie er sich zu unserer Heirat verhält. Worum ich ihn dann vielleicht noch bitten werde, hängt vom Verlauf der Unterredung ab. Es kann manches zur Sprache kommen, aber das wichtigste ist doch für mich, daß ich ihm gegenüberstehe. Ich habe nämlich noch mit keinem wirklichen Beamten unmittelbar gesprochen. (127)	*First of all I want to see him close to, then I want to hear his voice, then I want to find out what his attitude to our marriage is. What I shall ask him after that depends upon how the interview goes. Lots of things may get discussed, but the most important thing for me is to stand in front of him. You see, I haven't yet spoken face to face with a real official. (86)*

As K. has already seen and heard Klamm, the first two reasons for wanting an interview with him would seem to be somewhat thin. And in view of the fact that Gardena, who K. accepts as an authority on these matters, has just told him that Klamm completely forgets those who he no longer summons, there would seem to be very little point in asking Klamm about marriage to a woman who Klamm, almost certainly, will not remember. Apart from these three reasons, K. has no very clear idea why it is so imperative for him to see Klamm, and during the course of this same chapter, even his assertion that the most important thing for him is to meet Klamm face to face becomes less than convincing when he concludes his conversation with Gardena by saying:

»Daß ich dann nebenbei auch deu Beamten mir gegenüber haben werde, werde ich gern hinnehmen, aber es ist nicht mein erstes Ziel.« (127–28)	'If then I should find myself face to face with [Klamm] the official as well, I would accept that gladly, but that's not my primary aim.' (86)

In the same way, Frieda, at the end of the thirteenth chapter, provokes K. out of bewilderment into explaining why he wants to see Hans Brunswick's mother so badly:

»... und diese Frau kommt vom Schloß, sie selbst hat es mir gesagt, als ich mich am ersten Tag zu Lasemann verirrte. Was lag näher, als sie um Rat oder sogar um Hilfe zu bitten; kennt die Wirtin ganz genau nur alle Hindernisse, die von Klamm abhalten, dann kennt diese Frau wahrscheinlich den Weg, sie ist ihn ja selbst herabgekommen.« (235)	'... and this woman comes from the Castle, she told me so herself when I strayed into Lasemann's house on my first day here. What is more natural than to ask her for advice or even for help: if the landlady only knows the precise nature of the obstacles which keep one from Klamm, then this woman probably knows the way to him— for she has, after all, come down that way herself.' (154)

Frieda, not surprisingly, does not understand what exactly K. means by 'the way', and asks him: 'the way to Klamm?' To this K. replies: 'to Klamm of course, where else did you think I meant?' Despite the assurance with which this answer is given, K.'s logic is badly at fault. K. has absolutely no reason to suppose that Hans' mother is in any way connected with Klamm, and it is even more illogical to argue that if the landlady simply knows 'the obstacles', then Hans' mother will probably know 'the way'. Furthermore, if K. is serious at this point in his attempt to see Klamm, why has he said previously that he was not struggling to get to Klamm so much as to get past Klamm and into the Castle?

Summing up, K. argues as follows. Sometimes he says that he wants to see Klamm even though he can give no convincing reason for doing so. Sometimes he says that he wants to see Klamm in order to get into the Castle even though he has no reason to assume either that the second follows from the first or that the first is necessary for the second. Sometimes he says that he wants to get into the Castle even though he cannot explain what it is that he hopes to attain there. Whichever way one looks at it, K.'s rationalisations and logic are riddled with inconsistencies and implausibilities. It is therefore not at all surprising that, in the above incident, immediately after he has answered Frieda's last question, K. jumps up without warning. Then, as if to cover his confusion at finding himself in so awkward and untenable a position or to prevent Frieda from questioning him more closely, he rushes off to fetch the teacher's breakfast. Like Schopenhauer's man under the control of the Will, K. is unable to give any indication of his ultimate end, even though, at any given moment, he seems to be able to explain what he wants immediately. As has been suggested, K.'s struggle is the important thing—not his goal.

Throughout the secondary literature which surrounds *Das Schloß*, one comes across statements which impute clear intentional aims to K. Wilhelm Emrich, for example, writes:

K. unternimmt das ungeheuerliche Wagnis, die überpersönliche Macht, die „unsichtbar", geheimnisvoll und proteushaft in allen menschlichen Liebesbegegnungen, ja vielleicht in allem Lebendigen wirkt, als eine personale Macht Auge in Auge zu bestehen, ja diese Macht zum Bewußtsein seines „Selbst" und seiner Beziehung zu ihr zu bringen.[14]

K. dares the immense venture of confronting face to face and withstanding the supra-personal, protean power which operates 'unseen' and secretly in all human love-relationships, and even, perhaps, in everything that lives. Indeed, he dares to bring this power to the consciousness of his 'self' and of his relationship to it.

[14] Wilhelm Emrich, *Franz Kafka*, 7th ed., Frankfurt and Bonn, 1970, p. 313.

But in view of what has just been said, it seems likely that this paragraph attributes too much reflective deliberateness to K. K. wants to see Klamm, that much is beyond doubt, but he wants to see Klamm because he knows that such a thing is impossible rather than for any specific of clearly definable reason. For all K.'s talk of aims and goals, he is a compulsive wanderer rather than a conscious seeker. He does not know what he really wants; he arrives at a destination despite rather than because of his will to do so; and when he gets there, he discovers that the end of all his strivings is not domination but freedom from the dispensation of the Castle.

Similarly, Walter Sokel maintains:

K. ordnet alles Menschliche dem Ziel unter. Nichts geschieht bei ihm ohne Absicht. Spontaneität, unmittelbares, unbedachtes Handeln ist ihm unbekannt.[15]	K. subordinates everything human to his goal. Nothing happens unintentionally as far as he is concerned. He is ignorant of spontaneity and immediate, unconsidered actions.

But if it is true that K. suffers from a fundamental aimlessness, then it is worth asking just how true this is. K. would indeed like us to think that he is absolutely rational and that he is working according to a carefully thought-out design. Because of the absence from K.'s life of clearly definable ends, however, it is arguable that the rational gloss on his actions provided by his intellect conceals an urge which is irrational and unconsidered. Even though K. asks himself when he meets people just how useful they will be to him, this kind of question seems to arise from a momentary instinct. Because it does not form part of an overall strategy, K. rarely follows up an initial utilitarian impulse. K.'s ability to conceal his aimlessness with an apologetic intellect is shown most clearly when he is standing in the snow after being ejected from Lasemann's house in the first chapter.[16] K. would fall into despair were he not able to persuade himself that his ejection had happened as a result of his conscious intentions, when in fact, it had happened to him

---

[15] Sokel, *Franz Kafka: Tragik und Ironie*, p. 421.
[16] See p. 71 above.

against his will, by accident almost. *Pace* Walter Sokel, K. *does* react instinctively and spontaneously all the time, but his instinctual spontaneity, like that of Barnabas' father, is that of a man who is obsessively divided against himself, who hides this division from view with superficially plausible rationalisations, and who therefore runs the risk of letting his intellect atrophy and become powerless to direct his affairs. K.'s instinctual spontaneity is the neurotic spontaneity of the man who is fleeing from reality and from himself, not the healthy, childlike spontaneity of the man who is at one.

Kafka once wrote to Milena of himself:

In meinem Fall kann man sich drei Kreise denken, einen innersten A, dann B, dann C. Der Kern A erklärt dem B, warum dieser Mensch sich quälen und sich mißtrauen muß, warum er verzichten muß, ... warum er nicht leben darf. ... C, dem handelnden Menschen wird nichts mehr erklärt, ihm befiehlt bloß B. C handelt unter strengstem Druck, in Angstgeschweiß. ... C handelt also mehr in Angst als in Verständnis, er vertraut, er glaubt, daß A dem B alles erklärt und B alles richtig verstanden und weitergegeben hat. (BM, 246 and 247)

In my case, one can think of three circles, an innermost one A, then B, then C. The centre A explains to B why this man has to torture and distrust himself, why he has to renounce, ... why he may not live. ... To C, the acting person, nothing is any longer explained, it only takes orders from B. C acts under most severe pressure, in a sweat of fear. ... Thus, C acts more from fear than from understanding. He trusts, he believes that A has explained everything correctly to B and that B has understood and passed on everything correctly. (LM, 218)

Although it would be wrong to suggest that Kafka and K. are the same person, Kafka's picture can be applied almost exactly to K.'s personality. Because there is a rift between A (K.'s deepest self) and B (K.'s wilful nervous energies), C (K.'s intellect) acts 'in a cold sweat of fear' as an apologist who ostensibly believes (but in fact secretly doubts) that the rest of the personality is working in a state of reconciliation and harmony. Similarly, Schopenhauer suggests that the intellectual faculties of the man who is dominated by the Will are reduced to a state of impotence when he writes, in striking anticipation of K.'s disposition and situation:

Man gleicht einem, der um ein Schloß herumgeht, vergeblich einen Eingang suchend und einstweilen die Fassaden skizzierend. (WV, 156)	*One is like a man who goes round and round a castle, seeking in vain for an entrance, and sketching the façades in the meantime. (WI, 128)*

Up to the transformation which takes place after his interview with Bürgel, K. 'goes round the Castle', focuses (as in the first and eighth chapters) on its 'outline' ('Umrisse'), is fascinated by people's clothes, 'sketches façades', discovers 'relationships' and creates a surface of intentionality with an apologetic intellect that is dissociated from the care of his personality. Consequently, K. fails to find an entry to the world of the village and Castle. Only when his deepest self suffuses and integrates his nervous energies and rationalising intellect can K. discover that reconciliation with the Castle depends upon the free operation of that self. When K.'s intellect ceases to be an additional means of walling himself up within his solipsistic obsessions and becomes a channel between his inner world and the outer world, K. discovers that inner and outer are one, that entry into the apparently closed world of the Castle is synonymous with entry into the deepest regions of the self. When Kafka wrote:

Wer sucht, findet nicht, aber wer nicht sucht, wird gefunden. (H, 94)	*He who seeks does not find, but he who does not seek will be found. (W, 90)*

he could have been thinking of K. When K. gives up pretending to know what he is doing and learns to sit still, he is discovered by a meaning which allows him to accept himself and the world on its own terms.

Up to that point of enlightenment, however, Kafka repeatedly makes the point that a person who is dominated by an obsessive will is less than human and almost animal. When K. and Frieda make love for the second time, frenetically and without being able to accept each other, they are compared to dogs digging in the ground. When K. is at his most defiantly wilful, during his long wait in the *Herrenhof* courtyard, his approach towards Klamm's sledge is compared with the movement of a cat. Amalia, who is the most wilful character in the novel and who, on the surface at least, is a model of cool rationality, is referred to, surprisingly, as a 'proper wildcat'. And it is Gisa's cat, the symbol of K.'s bestial energies, that frightens Frieda and precipitates the succession of incidents which ends in the expulsion of the assistants and the breakdown of K.'s marriage. To paraphrase a remark of Kafka's to Janouch, K., for much of *Das Schloß*, seems to be trying to return to a state of animality because it is easier to live as an animal than as a full human being.[17]

Having tried to provide a description of the major characteristics of K.'s Faustian personality, it is worth pointing out that at least one commentator sees only a limited parallel between K. and Faust:

Beider, Fausts und K.s Ziel liegt jenseits der unbedingten Hingabe an die Welt, wie sie ihr im Augenblick begegnen können. Beide sind ihrem eigenen Streben unaufhebbar verpflichtet. Es bestimmt sie ganz. Auch K.s Ziel führt ihn über die Beruhigung im jeweils Erreichten der unmittelbaren Gegenwart hinaus auf ein für ihn quasi absolutes Ziel. Damit aber ist die Gemeinschaft Fausts mit K. auch schon erschöpft; . . .[18]

The aim of both Faust and K. lies beyond unconditional commitment to the world as they can encounter it in the present moment. Both are irrevocably bound to their own striving. Both are completely determined by it. K.'s aim leads him too out beyond a state of quiescence in what has been reached in the immediate present, towards a goal which for him is virtually an absolute. But with that, the similarity between Faust and K. is at an end; . . .

---

[17] Compare G, 44.
[18] Philippi, p. 49.

As it has been suggested throughout this book that there is a more than superficial similarity between K. and Faust, it is worthwhile paying closer attention to the distinctions between K. and Faust which Dr. Philippi then goes on to make:

Nicht nur durch die weit größere Distanz des Zieles und seinen anderen Charakter hebt sich K. von Faust ab, sondern auch durch sein Verhältnis zu den Mitteln, mit denen er es zu erreichen sucht. K. braucht ein Vehikel nach dem anderen, und in dem Maße, wie er sie nach seinen Vorstellungen einsetzen will, erweisen sie sich als untauglich. . . . Auf ein entferntes Ziel konzentriert, scheitert er [K.] schon im Vordergründigen, an seinen Mitteln, nicht an seinem eigenen Erfolg oder seinem inneren Unbefriedigtsein auf dem Höhepunkt des jeweils zu Erreichenden wie Faust. K. strebt nicht über jedes Ziel hinaus, sondern strebt, weil er nie sein Ziel erreicht.[19]

K. is distinguishable from Faust not only because his goal is much farther off and because its character is different, but also because he relates in a different way to the means by which he tries to reach his goal. K. uses one vehicle after another, and to the extent that he tries to make use of them according to his preconceptions, they prove to be useless. . . . Because he concentrates on a far-off goal, he [K.] comes to grief over things which are right in the foreground, comes to grief because of the means he uses and not, like Faust, because of his own success or his inner state of dissatisfaction even when he has reached the summit of what he is striving for. K. does not strive past every goal, he strives because he never reaches his goal.

To present the opposing case, the discussion of the wall-climbing incident suggests that K. does 'come to grief' on his own success. The discussion of the scene in the *Herrenhof* courtyard suggests that K. does 'come to grief' on the futility of the climax of his endeavours. The discussion of K.'s love of the impossible suggests that K. does strive past all mediate aims into the indistinct distances. The discussion of K.'s tendency to struggle suggests that a profound

[19] Philippi, p. 50.

dissatisfaction underlies all K.'s actions. Finally, Faust, like K., surely does use 'one vehicle after another'—which is why, in *Wald und Höhle*, he says:

So tauml' ich von Begierde zu Genuß,/ Und im Genuß versch- macht' ich nach Begierde.	*Thus do I reel from desire to sensual enjoyment, and in the midst of sensual enjoyment, I languish for desire.*

Essentially, I would suggest, both K.'s and Faust's temperaments are the same, and if a distinction does exist between them, then it concerns the consciousness with which the two men strive. Whereas Faust *deliberately* wagers that he can never be satisfied, *deliberately* demands everything because he knows that his wish can never be fulfilled, K. makes the same wager and the same demand *instinctually*, without knowing that he has done so. But the result of both wagers is the same. K., as much as Faust, fears that he will be led into saying to the moment:

Verweile doch, du bist so schön . . .   Stay, thou art so fair . . .

which is why, whenever K. senses the deep satisfaction of silence and stillness coming over him, he experiences it as a threat and struggles to resist it.

B. The Psychology of Faustian Man—the Basis

In the first part of this chapter, a description of K.'s behaviour was offered and the suggestion made that K.'s personality suffers from what Kierkegaard called a 'disrelationship'.[20] The self which K. wills to be is not the self that he really is. From this 'disrelationship' flow a profound sense of guilt and an all-pervading sense of fear, and because he wants to escape from these two annihilating sensations K. engages in that frenetic and aimless struggle which was described above.

From K.'s knowledge that he is not what he ought to be, there

[20] In *The Sickness unto Death*.

results a sense of guilt[21] which K. simultaneously projects onto the nearest authority and seeks to eradicate by a process of struggle with and self-justification before that authority. When K. enters the gloom of Lasemann's house, a voice whose source he cannot identify asks him who he is, whereupon K., attempting to justify himself it is said, replies that he is the Count's land-surveyor. After that, K.'s actions and reactions throughout the first four-fifths of *Das Schloß* amount to a wordless reiteration of this tacit admission of guilt and a sustained attempt at self-justification. Because, however, this response contains a contradiction within itself, K. cannot sustain it indefinitely. Because K.'s sense of guilt derives from himself, he is unable to eliminate it by struggling with the Castle. Indeed, the only result of K.'s attempt to escape his sense of guilt by struggle is a gradual increase in the tension within his personality between A, his deepest self, and B, his wilful self, until that point is reached when K.'s wilful self is broken open and assimilated to the self which he truly is.

The counterpart of K.'s sense of guilt towards the Castle authorities is a sense of *Angst* towards the inhabitants of the village. K. mistrusts Gerstäcker's offer of help in the first chapter; he reads his own aggressiveness and suspicion into other people's actions; he resents being laughed at; he sees enemies lurking everywhere and he is neurotically sensitive to the slightest hint of criticism. When Jeremias says to K. that the basis of his rejection of the assistants is fear, he has identified a major trait of K.'s personality and could have taken his diagnosis several stages further. K. is afraid of other people because they represent the hidden powers of his personality which he cannot or will not accept and which therefore threaten the security of his ego. K. struggles and strives in order to escape from his fear and from those hidden powers which perpetually threaten to surge back. And because such a struggle is fore-doomed to failure, there comes a point when K. has to resort to violence in order to sustain that struggle and keep his corrosive sense of *Angst* at bay. Such violence, however, also has an effect on K.'s inner life. The violence which K. uses on the assistants is also instrumental in

---

[21] See, for instance, the discussion of K.'s response to Klamm's first letter on pp. 55–6 above.

breaking open his ego and destroying the false identity which he has asserted. Thus, it allows that 'indestructible element' which is the source of his true identity, to emerge after his interview with Bürgel.

At a deeper level still, K.'s sense of guilt towards the Castle and sense of fear towards other people are symptomatic of an inability or refusal to come to terms with the fact of death. For most of *Das Schloß*, K. is not prepared to allow death its rightful place in his personality, is not prepared for a false and childish part of himself to die so that the best and most mature part of his personality may emerge, is not prepared to concede that he is mortal. K.'s flight from his dual sense of *Angst* and guilt is also a flight from the destructive potential of those sensations. Thus, that flight is in turn a flight from the painful experience of death and rebirth. So, in the very first chapter, K. refuses to be drawn symbolically to his death by Gerstäcker, 'the wretched-looking yet inexorable driver' and refuses to understand the meaning of the bell which threatens and yet promises him the fulfilment of that which he was only dimly conscious of wanting. K's flight from death is, however, most evident in his memory of the wall-climbing incident. K. refuses to go into the graveyard through the small 'Gittertür', a leitmotiv which, as we have seen, is linked throughout the novel with the symbolism and experience of crucifixion. And he climbs the wall, it is suggested, in order to eliminate death, in order to see the crosses in the graveyard 'disappearing' into the earth. But because such a flight cannot succeed, K. is forcibly reminded of his own mortality and the rights which death has over his personality by being brought down from the wall and injured. It is possible for K. to overcome death only if he admits that it has a proper place in his life, recognises the relativity of his own ego, accepts that he is as other men, develops a sense of self-irony. For the first four-fifths of the novel K. is unwilling to make these admissions. Instead, he prefers to create a false security for himself by engaging in a pointless struggle with a giant figure of his own devising and by holding other people at arm's length. Once he allows his fear and guilt to corrode his will, however, death invades his personality, a crisis ensues and he emerges from the experience purged of his fear and guilt and reconciled with the fact of death. After K. has fallen into that deep sleep before Bürgel, metaphorically died, he begins to sense that his fear of others and his sense of guilt towards the Castle were the symptoms of a struggle to absolutise his own ego, and assert his own immortality over and against the world. Paradoxically, K. is most threatened by death when he thinks that he has overcome it and least threatened by it when he tacitly admits its power. By allowing himself to undergo a death, K. affirms that there is an 'indestructible element' within him which is stronger than death, and as that power is allowed to emerge from its hiding-place, so K. is brought from a state of striving to a state of stillness.

Amalia is engaged in a flight from herself, from others and from death which is similar to, but ultimately more dangerous than K.'s. As recently as 1960, Hermann Pongs could write of Amalia:

Von Amalia aber heißt es bewundernd, und dieses Wort gilt nur für sie: „Aug in Aug mit der Wahrheit stand sie und lebte und ertrug dieses Leben damals wie heute." *Amalia repräsentiert einen sittlichen Wert.*[22]	But of Amalia it is admiringly said, and this statement is valid for her alone: 'She stood and lived face to face with truth, and bore this life then just as she does now.' Amalia stands for a moral value.

But it is doubtful whether it is still possible to see Amalia in such a positive light. Although she has preserved an icy moral purity by refusing to answer Sortini's summons, at a deeper level, the narrative suggests that Amalia is guilty of a sin which is much more subtle and much more deadly than sexual promiscuity. Like K., Amalia is summoned to leave her wilful solitude, to die to her will and to participate in the great festival of procreation around the phallic fire-pump ('Spritze') so that those vital energies which her will holds in check may be released in her. Various signs suggest the necessity for Amalia to undergo this metaphorical death. She is dressed in white lace for the festival (a material which, throughout *Das Schloß*, has overtones of shrouds and funeral garments). Around her neck hangs a 'Granatenhalsband', literally a 'necklace

---

[22] Hermann Pongs, *Franz Kafka: Dichter des Labyrinths*, Heidelberg, 1960, p. 82.

of garnets', but the German word 'Granat' also suggests the idea
of the 'pomegranate', the fruit of which Persephone ate while she
was in the realm of Hades. Amalia is summoned by Sortini, the god
of lots and chance, whose face is covered with wrinkles which run
like horns to the roots of his nose. When Sortini first sees Amalia,
he is sitting on the shafts of the fire-pump with his arms crossed
over his chest in the attitude of a corpse, and his presence is sig-
nalled by wild apocalyptic trumpets. But to all of this, Amalia remains impervious. It is said that she alone refused to unbend and
join in the communal celebration, and in the light of this refusal, it
is significant that she should say to K. at one point:

»*Sei ruhig* . . . *ich bin nicht einge-*   '*Don't get excited* . . . *I'm not*
weiht, nichts könnte mich dazu   *initiated and nothing could in-*
bewegen, mich einweihen zu lass-   *duce me to let myself be initiated* . . .'
en . . .« (*249*)   (*162*)

Although Amalia means in this context that she is not 'initiated'
into the secrets of Barnabas' work in the Castle, the second half of
the above quotation seems to have a much more general significance.
Amalia has refused to become 'initiated' into village society by
means of the festival of procreation, and there lies the root of her
crime.

   There is therefore a sense in which the Sortini episode, far from
causing Amalia any real moral indignation, merely gave her the
supreme excuse to do something which her whole manner of life
suggests she had wanted to do all along. It enabled her to cut herself
off once and for all from other people by denying the existence within
herself of those vital energies which are common to everyone—by
implicitly making the claim that she, of all her community, was
exempt from death. Dr. Gray calls Amalia's refusal 'sincere and
honourable' and claims that: 'no one could have been more justified
than she was . . .',[23] but if one is to judge the moral status of Amalia's
action, then one has to take care not to look at it in isolation. Rather,
it has to be examined in the context of the *mores* of the village,
Amalia's motives, its disastrous effect on her family and her negative

[23] Gray, p. 117.

attitude to the feast of procreation where Sortini first saw her. In the village, it is perfectly normal for the girls to sleep with officials, indeed, they regard it as a privilege to be invited to do so and they expect, accept and understand the officials' rudeness. This means that in the terms of the village world, Amalia is not asked to do anything reprobate or shocking and that it is her refusal to go to Sortini which represents the deviation from the local moral norm. Then again, Amalia's refusal is not simply an isolated action, rather, it is *the* symbolic action which gives expression to and ratifies once and for all that wilful pride and refusal to be human which had always been salient features of Amalia's personality. Thus, Olga mentions that Amalia's 'dark glance' (which, she implies, had always been the particular mark of Amalia's sense of superiority and will to dominate) became a permanent feature of her face ever since the day when she rejected Sortini's advances. At this point, it is perhaps worth stressing that on this reading, Amalia's rejection of Sortini's bed does not necessarily amount to an allegory of a refusal of divine grace. Amalia's rejection of Sortini was another version of her refusal to take part in the feast of procreation, and her refusal to take part in that feast was in turn a more particular manifestation of her refusal to live by the life forces within her personality. Long before Sortini summoned her, Amalia had committed the sin of hubris and her reactions to Sortini simply demonstrate the extent to which her personality had become permeated by that hubris.

Finally, the effects of Amalia's refusal on her family cannot be forgotten. From what Olga tells us, the whole of Barnabas' family knows that the root cause of their predicament and their despair lies with themselves and their indulgence of Amalia—not with the Castle authorities. Olga tells K. that they only have to return to their former way of life in order to restore themselves to favour in the village:

Wenn wir also nur wieder hervorgekommen wären, das Vergangene ruhen gelassen hätten, durch unser Verhalten gezeigt hätten, gleichgültig auf welche	*So, if only we had come forward again, let the past rest in peace, shown, in any way we cared to, that we had got over the whole affair and thus convinced public*

Weise, und die Öffentlichkeit so
die Überzeugung gewonnen hätte,
daß die Sache, wie immer sie
auch beschaffen gewesen sein mag,
nicht wieder zur Besprechung
kommen werde, auch so wäre alles
gut gewesen; überall hätten wir
die alte Hilfsbereitschaft gefund-
en, selbst wenn wir die Sache nur
unvollständig vergessen hätten,
man hätte es verstanden und
hätte uns geholfen, es völlig zu
vergessen. (304)

opinion that the matter, whatever
the truth of it might have been,
would never be mentioned again,
everything would have been all
right. We would have found the
old readiness to help wherever we
looked, and even if we had man-
aged to forget the incident only
incompletely, people would have
understood this and helped us to
forget it once and for all. (196)

But, Olga implies, for this to have happened, it would have been necessary for Amalia, who, by the time of K.'s arrival, holds her family in an iron grip, to make the first move, and this is precisely what she has become incapable of doing. If Amalia were able to make a gesture of reconciliation towards the community, she would be implying that she no longer saw herself as an exception, that she had come to recognise her oneness with the village community, that she was prepared to 'die'. In view of all this, it is difficult to see the justification for blaming the plight of the Barnabas family onto the Castle authorities. Like K., Barnabas' family project their own inability onto the Castle and turn it into a malignant divinity who cannot be placated.

It is therefore difficult to accept the hypothesis of Amalia's 'moral worth'. Whereas there is an unwitting innocence about K.'s hubris, megalomania and scorn for others, Amalia's cold incisiveness indicates that although she knows the meaning of her defiance and sees its effects on its family, she is prepared to persist in it. Whereas K. unself-consciously projects his guilt and fear onto others, Amalia is under no illusions and refuses to believe that anyone else is responsible for her state of being. If K.'s despair is the hidden despair of a man who is not given to introspection and therefore does not understand his own state of soul, Amalia's despair is the potentiated despair of someone who is quite clear about the violence which she is doing to herself and to others but who refuses to change her way of life. If K. suffers from the despair which Kierkegaard described as the 'despair over possibility' and takes refuge from this despair in fantasy, then Amalia suffers from the despair which Kierkegaard described as the 'despair which is conscious of being despair, as also it is conscious of being a self wherein there is after all something Eternal...'[24] K. is open to those vital powers which can resolve his despair because he is unaware of their existence, but Amalia is closed to those powers because she is aware of them, and, out of a sense of wilful irony, refuses to admit them into her conscious life. Thus, where K.'s despair can erupt into creative self-doubt, Amalia's cannot, precisely because her self-consciousness enables her to be aware of this possibility and to resist it. Where K.'s personality is riven by a conflict which involves the possibility of resolution, Amalia's personality has hardened into a state of rigid defiance which involves no such possibility.

B. F. M. Edwards, writing on the relationship between Kafka and Kierkegaard, remarked:

Neither in Kafka's biography nor in the lives of his heroes is there anything that could reasonably be described as sinful, immoral or even anti-social. No single execution or suicide in Kafka's work can be considered as humanly or ethically justifiable; each represents a judgement passed upon the self by a human being, over-sensitive to personal guilt to the point of disease, a judgement which would have been denied and abhorred by all accepted canons, secular or religious.[25]

It is perfectly easy to see how such a conclusion could be reached in connection, for instance, with *Das Schloß*. Because the reader sees everything in the first place through the mind of K. and only later comes to suspect that K.'s point of view is incomplete and distorted, and because K. is not given to introspection, it is not at all difficult to overlook K.'s hubris, self-delusions and guilt. Neverthe-

[24] In *The Sickness unto Death*.
[25] B. F. M. Edwards, 'Kafka and Kierkegaard: A Reassessment', *German Life and Letters*, 20 (1966-7), pp. 222-3.

less, I hope that the preceding analysis of the personalities of K. and Amalia has indicated that Mr. Edwards's conclusion may be somewhat premature. If anything, K. is under-sensitive rather than over-sensitive to the existence and nature of his guilt and all his experiences in the village conspire to make him see this. For Kafka, who once claimed to know more about original sin than any other man, the concept of 'sinfulness' did not relate to the morality of particular acts measured against a scale of norms, but to the extent to which the personality as a whole was divided against itself. For Kafka, who once wrote:

Eines der wirksamsten Verführungsmittel des Bösen ist die Aufforderung zum Kampf. (H, 40)	*One of the most effective means of seduction which evil has at its disposal is the challenge to struggle. (W, 39)*

the 'sinful' man is the man who struggles against the world because he is divided against himself, because he is not what he ought to be. Thus, although neither K. nor Amalia, in whom K. unconsciously divines a parallel to himself, has committed any particularly blatant crime or obviously unethical act, both are profoundly guilty. Both have engaged in struggle against themselves and the world, opted for a selective and therefore false identity, attempted to forego the humiliation and responsibility of being human. Clearly, there is no way of proving definitely that K.'s and Amalia's natures are deeply dislocated. Nevertheless, the hypothesis of an unconscious conflict does explain the presence of those characteristics (aggression, fear, guilt and tension) which seem strangely at variance with the surface of rational order, intentional purposefulness and moral uprightness which both, in their different ways, present to the world.

Although Kafka offers a very searching, even shocking analysis of the state of K.'s being, he does not do so to reject or condemn K. Paradoxically, Kafka seems to suggest throughout *Das Schloß* that K. has to go wrong and experience the effects of his errancy to the full before he can ever hope to break out of his self-created prison and become reconciled with himself and the external world. K., it is suggested, needs to climb the wall so that he may discover the futility of doing so. Just as Kierkegaard said in *The Sickness unto Death* that the person who exists in a state of despair is both infinitely near to and infinitely far from salvation, so Kafka seems to suggest the same of K. Perhaps the clearest indication of this is Klamm's second letter. This reaches K. quite soon after he has prevented Klamm from leaving the *Herrenhof* in his sledge—in other words, at a point in the novel when one would expect Klamm to be violently angry with K. But, strangely enough, there are no signs of anger in Klamm's letter. While this letter can be read as a piece of gratuitous sarcasm, many signs in the novel point to the conclusion that Klamm is not, ultimately, a malevolent power.[26] Indeed, if, as has been done already, Klamm's second letter is read in a positive light, then its last five sentences suggest that K. must necessarily carry on as he has been doing so that a 'fortunate conclusion' may be reached. If K. is a lesser Faust, then Klamm is perhaps a distant relation of the Lord who appears in the *Prolog im Himmel* of Goethe's play and who says to Mephistopheles that a good man, even when he is impelled by dark forces, is always conscious of 'the right way'. In this connection, it is worth reproducing an entire passage from a letter which Kafka, quoting verbatim from Kierkegaard, sent Max Brod in 1918:

Nun will sich allerdings das religiöse Verhältnis offenbaren, kann das aber nicht in dieser Welt, darum muß der strebende Mensch sich gegen sie stellen, um das Göttliche in sich zu retten, oder, was das gleiche ist, das Göttliche stellt ihn gegen die Welt, um sich zu retten. So muß die Welt vergewaltigt werden von Dir wie von Kierkegaard, hier mehr von Dir, hier mehr von ihm, das sind Unterschiede bloß auf der Seite der vergewaltigten Welt.

Now, at any rate, the religious relationship seeks to reveal itself but cannot do so in this world. For this reason, the striving human being must set himself against the world in order to save the divine element within himself, or, what amounts to the same thing, the divine element sets him against the world in order to save itself. Thus, the world must be assaulted by you as it is by Kierkegaard—more by you here, more by him there—those are

[26] See, for instance, the colour symbolism discussed on pp. 200-1 below.

Und die folgende Stelle ist nicht aus dem Talmud: »Sobald ein Mensch kommt, der etwas Primitives mit sich bringt, so daß er also nicht sagt: Man muß die Welt nehmen wie sie ist, . . . sondern der sagte: Wie die Welt auch ist, ich bleibe bei einer Ursprünglichkeit, die ich nicht nach dem Gutbefinden der Welt zu verändern gedenke: im selben Augenblick, als dieses Wort gehört wird, geht im ganzen Dasein eine Verwandlung vor sich. Wie im Märchen, wenn das Wort gesagt wird, sich das seit hundert Jahren verzauberte Schloß öffnet und alles Leben wird: so wird das Dasein lauter Aufmerksamkeit. Die Engel bekommen zu tun und sehen neugierig zu, was daraus werden wird, denn dies beschäftigt sie. Auf der andern Seite: finstere, unheimliche Dämonen, die lange untätig dagesessen und an ihren Fingern genagt haben, springen auf und recken die Glieder, denn, sagen sie, hier, worauf sie lange gewartet haben, gibts etwas für uns u.s.w.« (B, 239)[27]

differences simply from the point of view of the world which is being assaulted. And the following passage doesn't come from the Talmud: 'As soon as a person comes along who has some primitive quality about them, and who therefore says not: "One must accept the world as it is" . . . but: "No matter how the world is, I shall abide by my originality and do not intend to change it as the world thinks fit"—in the same instant that this word is heard, a transformation comes about in the whole of existence. As in the fairy-tale, when the word is spoken and the castle which has lain under a spell for a hundred years is opened and everything comes alive again, so, similarly, the whole of existence becomes sheer attentiveness. The angels get something to do and watch with curiosity to see what will happen—for this matter is of concern to them. On the other side, dark, sinister demons, who have sat there idly for a long time biting their finger-nails, jump up and stretch their limbs—for they say that there is something here for them, something that they have been awaiting for a long time, etc.'

[27] The passage in quotation marks is taken verbatim from one of Kierkegaard's journal entries dating from the late autumn of 1854. See: *Søren Kierkegaard's Papirer,*

K. is just such a person who 'sets himself against the world'. He refuses to give up his 'originality' or adapt himself to the world, and if the angels are to have their say in deciding his fate, then it is necessary for him to be delivered over for a time to the dark demons, to experience the implications of his Faustianism to the full so that 'das Göttliche', the 'divine element', may triumph in his personality. Were K. a more conscious and introspective person, he might, like Kafka, have remarked to himself:

Manchmal das Gefühl fast zerreißenden Unglücklichseins und gleichzeitig die Überzeugung der Notwendigkeit dessen und eines durch jedes Anziehen des Unglücks erarbeiteten Zieles ... (T, 466; dated 13.iii.1915)	*Occasionally I feel an unhappiness which almost rips me apart, and at the same time, I am convinced of its necessity and of the existence of a goal to which one works one's way by undergoing every kind of unhappiness... (D2, 118)*

but he does not. Throughout most of the book, his conscious mind will not admit that the root of his unhappiness, his guilt and his fear is a flight from himself, from others and from death.

C. The Necessity of Transcendence

Besides providing a description of Faustian man, Schopenhauer also offers insights into the possibility of transcendence. A point may come when a human being under the control of the Will undergoes a radical transformation and becomes someone entirely different:

In ihren Mienen, besonders den Augen, sehn wir den Ausdruck, den Widerschein der vollkommensten Erkenntnis, derjenigen näm-	*In their countenances, and especially their eyes, we see the expression and reflection of the most perfect knowledge, namely*

eds. P. A. Heiberg, V. Kuhr and E. Torsting, Vol. XI², Copenhagen, 1969, pp. 50–51, entry entitled: *Man mas tage Verden som den er (One must take the world as it is)*. Kafka probably found the passage in question in: Søren Kierkegaard, *Buch des Richters: Seine Tagebücher 1833–1855*, ed. and trans. Hermann Gottsched, Jena and Leipzig, 1905, p. 160. See also Kafka's diary entry for 21.viii.1913.

lich, welche nicht auf einzelne Dinge gerichtet ist, sondern die Ideen, also das ganze Wesen der Welt und des Lebens vollkommen aufgefaßt hat, welche Erkenntnis in ihnen auf den Willen zurück-wirkend, nicht wie jene andere Motive *für denselben liefert, sondern im Gegenteil ein* Quietiv *alles Wollens geworden ist, aus welchem die vollkommene Resignation, die der innerste Geist des Christentums wie der indischen Weisheit ist, das Aufgeben alles Wollens, die Zurückwendung, Aufhebung des Willens und mit ihm des ganzen Wesens dieser Welt, also die Erlösung hervor-gegangen ist. (WV, 327)*

of that knowledge which is not directed to particular things but which has fully comprehended the Ideas, and thus the entire essential nature of the world and of life. And this knowledge, reacting back within those people on to the Will, does not, like that other mode of knowledge, provide motives for the Will, but is, on the contrary, something which stills all motives of the Will. From this stilling there proceeds that perfect resignation, which is the innermost spirit of Christianity as well of Indian wisdom. This resignation is the renunciation of all volition, conversion, the super-cession of volition and consequently the abolition of the entire nature of this world—in short, it is redemption. (WI, 301)

Die echte Güte der Gesinnung, die uneigennützige Tugend und der reine Edelmut gehn also nicht von abstrakter Erkenntnis aus, aber doch von Erkenntnis: nämlich von einer unmittelbaren und intuitiven, die nicht wegzuräsonie-ren und nicht anzuräsonieren ist, von einer Erkenntnis, die eben weil sie nicht abstrakt ist, sich auch nicht mitteilen läßt, sondern jedem selbst aufgehn muß, die daher ihren eigentlichen adäquaten Ausdruck nicht in Worten findet, son-

Genuine goodness of disposition, disinterested virtue and pure nobility do not proceed therefore from abstract knowledge, but from a different kind of knowledge: namely from a direct and intuitive mode of knowledge which can neither be abolished nor arrived at by reasoning, from a mode of knowledge which, precisely because it is not abstract, cannot be communicated, but which every person must discover for himself; which therefore finds

dern ganz allein in Taten, im Handeln, im Lebenslauf des Menschen. (WV, 503)

its appropriate and adequate expression not in words, but solely in deeds, in the conduct and course of the life of man. (WI, 477-8)

Es ist nicht der unruhige Lebensdrang, die jubelnde Freude, welche heftiges Leiden zur vorhergegangenen oder nachfolgenden Bedingung hat, wie sie den Wandel des lebenslustigen Menschen ausmachen; sondern es ist ein unerschütterlicher Friede, eine tiefe Ruhe und innige Heiterkeit, ein Zustand, zu dem wir, wenn er uns vor die Augen oder die Einbildungskraft gebracht wird, nicht ohne die größte Sehnsucht blicken können, indem wir ihn sogleich als das allein Rechte, alles andere unendlich überwiegende anerkennen, zu welchem unser besserer Geist uns das große »sapere aude« zuruft. (WV, 529-30)

It is not the restless pressure of life, the exultant joy which has violent suffering as its preceding or succeeding condition—two states which usually accompany the life of the man who loves existence. But it is an unshakable peace, a deep state of repose and inner serenity, a state of mind on which we cannot look without the greatest longing when it is brought before our eyes or our imagination because we at once recognise that it alone is right and infinitely surpasses everything else—whereupon our better self calls out to us the great 'sapere aude'. (WI, 503-4)

Although K. does not realise it for most of his time in the village, beyond his strivings, his obsessions, his rationalisations, his fear and his guilt, there lies a profound longing for the 'knowledge' which is not 'abstract knowledge' about relationships, but an 'indestructible peace', or as Kafka himself once put it, an 'incomprehensible grace'. Beyond K's spurious quest for an undefined goal there lies a quest for peace of mind which is so secret, so unknown to K. himself, that when he finds it after his interview with Bürgel, he does so by accident and seems not to realise that he has discovered what, in reality, he was looking for all along. Indeed, it is probably more accurate to say that peace of mind finds K. rather than that K. finds peace of mind. To quote Marthe Robert:

Le fait est que les trois romans et les principaux récits de Kafka ont pour thème une recherche difficile dont l'objet, comme toujours dans une recherche véritable, est mal connu et par là même passionnant.[28]

The fact is that Kafka's three novels and principal stories have as their theme a quest of great difficulty whose object, as always in a true quest, is only partially known and for that very reason, inspires passion.

This should not be taken to mean, however, (as Marthe Robert later says that it does)[29] that K. finds nothing simply because he is vague about the true object of his quest. As will be argued, the peace of mind which K. discovers is very real, and it cannot be attained *by* struggle but only *after* struggle, when the futility of struggle has been realised and overcome, when the experience of death has been accepted and undergone. To use Kafka's own words, in order to attain this state of mind:

Es ist nicht notwendig, daß du aus dem Hause gehst. Bleib bei deinem Tisch und horche. Horche nicht einmal, warte nur. Warte nicht einmal, sei völlig still und allein. Anbieten wird sich dir die Welt zur Entlarvung, sie kann nicht anders, verzückt wird sie sich vor dir winden. (H, 54)

It isn't necessary for you to leave your house. Stay seated at your table and listen. Don't even listen, simply wait. Don't even wait, be completely still and solitary. The world will offer itself to you like something about to emerge from a chrysalis; it can't do anything else, enraptured it will writhe into life before your eyes. (W, 53)

K., as has been shown, perpetually rejects the 'table' and flees from those moments of stillness which threaten his Faustianism, even though, in the first chapter, he obliquely sees at one point that stillness increased his powers of judgement. But, within *Das Schloß*, he meets people who have learnt to 'sit still at their tables', who have reached perfection in the sense that they no longer 'reach out

---

[28] Robert, p. 195.
[29] Robert, p. 232.

for anything beyond their sphere',[30] and who, in consequence, have acquired something of that essential 'knowledge' which K. secretly and unconsciously desires. Of these, the person who most consistently lives in this state of stillness and peace is, as her name suggests, Frieda. To quote Walter Sokel:

Diese Mädchengestalt ist nicht wie alle ihre Vorgängerinnen im Werk Kafkas (mit der Ausnahme Grete Samsas) Chiffre im Machtkampf des Ich-Helden mit der Vatergestalt oder bloße Projektion seiner Gefühle. Sie ist eigenständige Persönlichkeit, . . .[31]	*Unlike her predecessors in Kafka's works (with the exception of Grete Samsa), this girl is not a cipher in the struggle for power which goes on between the first-person hero and the father-figure, or a mere projection of his feelings. She is a personality in her own right, . . .*

Although this would seem to be the case, although Frieda *does* seem to have a calm self-possession and a capacity for self-giving which brings out the best in K., it needs to be said, and this modifies the picture of Frieda which is drawn by some commentators, that she is far from an ideal or a superhuman figure. She is blind to Olga's positive qualities and allows herself to be prejudiced against her by the local taboos. In comparison with Olga's human and motherly estimate of the Castle and its officials, Frieda's is over-deferential and childlike. She is over-susceptible to Gardena's influence, and, despite her own intuitions, she almost allows herself to be convinced by Gardena's excessively harsh estimate of K. Finally, Frieda permits her relationship with K. to be ruined by her prejudice against the Barnabas family, nostalgic love for a playmate of her childhood and the exploitation of the weaknesses of that relationship.

At a deeper level still, Frieda's relationship with K. is strangely ambiguous. Although Kafka clearly suggests that Frieda is a source of life, a person who wants to relate to K. in a creative and adult way, he also suggests, by means of the symbolism already discussed,[32]

[30] Compare Kafka's diary entry for 24.xi.1914.
[31] Sokel, *Franz Kafka: Tragik und Ironie*, p. 424.
[32] See p. 76 above.

that there is a deathly quality about her which makes her want to
relate to K. in a way that leads to the grave of which she dreams in
the thirteenth chapter. Kafka seems to have been attempting to
make a general statement about the ambiguity of any love-relation-
ship when he wrote:

Die sinnliche Liebe täuscht über	*Sensual love deceives as to the*
die himmlische hinweg; allein	*nature of divine love. On its own,*
könnte sie es nicht, aber da sie das	*it would not be able to do so, but*
Element der himmlischen Liebe	*as it has unconsciously within it-*
unbewußt in sich hat, kann sie es.	*self an element of divine love, it is*
(H, 48)	*able to do so. (W, 47)*

While K.'s and Frieda's sexual relationship preserves an element of
'divine love', the 'cloth remains on the table', but when the element
of *Agape* is obscured by naked *Eros,* 'the cloth is removed from the
table' and the sensual relationship becomes daemonic. Thus, when
K. and Frieda make love for the second time, they are at first
depicted as rapacious animals digging their own graves, but when
the elements of 'stillness' and 'gratitude' come back into their love-
making, they become human beings again. Similarly, their relationship is disrupted in the school-room by Gisa's large grey cat, the
symbol of uncontrolled animal *Eros,* which finally wounds K.
physically. K. seems to acquire some insight into the ambiguous
potential of love, for he says to Frieda that they can relate to each
other either as animals or as human beings and asks her for her
estimation of their relationship in the light of this distinction:

Wenn es aber nicht der arge Fall	*But if that isn't the vicious fact*
ist und nicht ein schlaues Raubtier	*of the matter, and if it wasn't a*
dich damals an sich gerissen hat,	*cunning beast of prey that seized*
sondern du mir entgegenkamst,	*you for itself that night, but if*
sowie ich dir entgegenkam und	*you came towards me just as I*
wir uns fanden, selbstvergessen	*came towards you and if we*
beide, sag, Frieda, wie ist es denn	*found each other, both oblivious*
dann? (232)	*of ourselves, tell me Frieda, how*
	would things stand then? (152)

Although Frieda is herself aware of the destructive and bestial elements in her relationship with K., she shows herself to be incapable of accepting and dealing creatively with them, and it is from this inability that her desire for death derives. She fears and is ashamed of the 'lascivious assistants' who personify the animal urges and gives herself to the 'passionate' Jeremias only when he has become sick and ailing. She seeks at one point to deal with the carnal elements of human nature by suppression and violence (she whips Klamm's lustful servants out of the *Herrenhof*) and her general incapacity enables the assistants to come, quite literally, between K. and her during their night in the school-room. Although one part of Frieda wants to wake K. up, to inflame his carnal energies and to relate to him fully as a woman to a man, another part of her wants to keep K. in a state of passive slumber or virtual death so that she will not have to deal with those sexual drives of which she is so afraid. Because of this ambiguous attitude, she cries out at one point:

Laßt K. schlafen! Stört ihn doch nicht! (182)

Let K. sleep! Don't disturb him! (120)

and tells K. during the thirteenth chapter:

Einmal fürchte ich, daß du auf-wachen wirst und alles zu Ende sein wird, und dann wieder springe ich auf und zünde die Kerze an, damit du nur schnell aufwachst und mich beschützen kannst. (204-5)

One minute I'm afraid that you'll wake up and that everything will be over, and the next instant I'm jumping up again and lighting the candle so that you'll wake up quickly and can protect me. (135)

In *Das Schloß*, Kafka shows that a fully developed love relationship, involving a 'fraternal union' between Apollo and Dionysos, spiritual powers and carnal urges, brings a twofold risk. When the carnal forces become predominant, daemonism ensues, but when the carnal forces are suppressed in the way that Frieda is continually tempted to suppress them, the wasting death of debiliation and emotional childishness inevitably results. *Das Schloß* is not normally mentioned in the same breath as *Der Zauberberg (The Magic Mountain)* or *Women in Love*, but it is quite remarkable how Kafka manages to reach the same conclusions about the love relationship as do Lawrence and Mann, while avoiding the posturings of the former and the long-windedness of the latter.

K. must be held in large measure responsible for Frieda's failure. Frieda is not one of those to whom 'grace' and 'peace' have come easily, and when K. first speaks to her, he notices that for all the indefinable depth which she possesses, her voice reverberates not with her victories but with the 'infinite disillusionments' of her life. Frieda is a sad, undernourished figure. She perpetually transmits the sense of knowing that her stillness and self-effacing self-possession are almost an effrontery in the bleak world of the Castle where spring and summer last no more than a few days. And in her 'general love for people', she seems to have recognised all the sufferings of the world as her own. If K. needs Frieda's qualities to reconcile him with the world of the village, then Frieda needs K.'s strength and determination to enable her to overcome that deathly temptation to resign herself to the childish impulses in her nature. K., however, does not see just what an effort it is for the weary Frieda to deal with his carnal energies, fails to attempt to make her task any easier, and consequently loses her.

In his diaries, Kafka noted:

Die Wirkung eines friedlichen Gesichts, einer ruhigen Rede, besonders von einem fremden, noch nicht durchschauten Menschen. Die Stimme Gottes aus einem menschlichen Mund. (T, 346; dated 20.xii.1913)

The effect of a peaceful face, of calm speech, especially when they belong to a strange person who one hasn't yet seen through. The voice of God out of a human mouth. (D1, 324)

and:

So wenig ich sein mag, niemand ist hier, der Verständnis für mich

Insignificant as I may be, there is no one here who understands me

im Ganzen hat. Einen haben, der dieses Verständnis hat, etwa eine Frau, das hieße Halt auf allen Seiten haben, Gott haben. (T, 475; dated 4.v.1915)

in my entirety. To have someone possessed of such understanding, a wife perhaps, would mean to have support from every side, to have God. (D2, 126)

For all her shortcomings, Frieda does seem to speak in these terms to K., even if he begins to understand what she is saying only when it is too late. Although K. at first sees Frieda merely as a means of reaching Klamm, and although he ceases to look at her in this way relatively late in the novel, another element enters his estimate of her fairly early on, with the result that he begins, unconsciously, to appreciate her value as a person in her own right. It is she who brings out in him those qualities of tenderness and self-forgetfulness which were mentioned earlier, and it is she who has the magic ability to make even the most unpromising situation habitable. At the beginning of the seventh chapter, K. sees how she has turned the squalid attic where the maids lived into a clean and airy room, and she even manages to lend an aura of homeliness to the schoolroom. Later still, after he has spent a good time with Pepi, her caricature, K. realises the extent to which he had taken Frieda's rare qualities for granted. Where Frieda's 'clothes' fit her exactly, Pepi's are both too big and too ornate for her because she has 'reached out for something beyond her sphere'. Where Frieda is natural and unself-conscious, Pepi is artificial and self-conscious. Where Frieda is 'experienced, cool and collected', Pepi rushes around making a great fuss about things which Frieda did automatically. Whereas Frieda is able 'to put up with herself calmly, without being precipitate' and 'to live as she must', Pepi 'chases her tail like a dog'.[33] Whereas Frieda has the ability to look deeply into people and to give her entire attention to the other person, Pepi tends to see only their surface attributes, to notice only what suits her and to exploit such insights as she obtains in order to gossip with the other maids or to generate feelings of superiority. Whereas Pepi is concerned to acquire status, respect and power, Frieda's ability to give herself to other people (she is said to work at a 'Schenktisch',

[33] Compare Kafka's diary entry for 9.xii.1913.

lexically, a 'bar', but the German word literally means 'giving-table') permits her to acquire a personal status and authority of which she is unaware, but which are far superior to those crude facsimiles which Pepi desires. What Frieda acquires by her calm self-acceptance, Pepi and K. try to acquire wilfully, and when they fail in their aim, they are tempted to destroy everything out of the ensuing sense of frustration and despair.

Above all, Frieda offers K. something which Kafka perhaps prized above all else: a home. The high value which Kafka placed on the family emerges at every turn in his letters and his diaries:

Als der Doktor im Vorlesen des Vertrages zu einer Stelle kam, die von meiner möglichen künftig-en Frau und den möglichen Kind-ern handelte, bemerkte ich mir gegenüber einen Tisch mit zwei großen Sesseln und einem kleiner-en um ihn herum. Bei dem Gedanken, daß ich niemals im-stande sein werde, diese oder beliebige drei Sessel mit mir, meiner Frau und meinem Kind zu besetzen, bekam ich ein von allem Anfang an so verzweifeltes Ver-langen nach diesem Glück, daß ich aus dieser gereizten Aktivität meine während des langen Vor-lesens einzig bleibende Frage an den Doktor stellte, die sofort mein vollständiges Mißverstehen einer größeren gerade vorgelesen-en Partie des Vertrages enthüllte, (T, 150; dated 8.xi.1911)

When the lawyer, in reading the agreement to me, came to a pass-age concerning my possible future wife and possible children, I saw across from me a table with two large chairs and a smaller one around it. At the thought that I should never be in a position to seat in these, or any other three chairs, myself, my wife and my child, there came over me a yearning for this happiness which was so despairing from the very start that in my excitement I asked the lawyer the one question I had left after the long reading, which at once revealed my com-plete misunderstanding of a rather long section of the agreement that had just been read out. (D1, 141)

Das unendliche, tiefe, warme er-lösende Glück, neben dem Korb

The infinite, deep, warm, redemp-tive happiness of sitting beside the

seines Kindes zu sitzen, der Mutter gegenüber. (T, 555; dated 19.i.1922)	cradle of one's child opposite its mother. (D2, 204)

Indeed, the very explicitness with which Kafka longed for a wife and a family was one of the major factors which vitiated his relationships with women, for it perpetually seemed to him that he was manipulating and using them for his own gratification. K., in contrast, at the outset of *Das Schloß* at any rate, places no such hopes on marriage. As distinct from Kafka himself, K. is capable of appreciating the fulfilment and peace that marriage with Frieda might bring him only when that has become an impossibility. Thus, because he does not normally understand the value of family life, he twice turns down the invitation to sit at the Barnabas 'family table'. Similarly, although he is momentarily attracted by the 'good coffee' which Frieda fetches, and thinks 'gratefully' of Frieda during the episode in the *Herrenhof* courtyard when he eats the sandwiches which she had packed up for him, he begins to glimpse what Frieda is offering him only when he can say to Olga:

... *ich habe, so geringfügig das alles ist, doch schon ein Heim, eine Stellung und wirkliche Arbeit, ich habe eine Braut, die, wenn ich andere Geschäfte habe, mir die Berufsarbeit abnimmt, ich werde sie heiraten und Gemeindemitglied werden,* ... *(289–90)*	... *insignificant though it all is, I already have a home, a position and proper work to do; I'm engaged to a woman who, when I have other business to see to, takes some of my professional work off me. I'm going to marry her and become a member of the community here,* ... *(187)*

Even then though, K.'s change of heart is not complete, for a few pages before this admission it is said that he regards the corner where the Barnabas family table was standing with 'repugnance' ('Widerwillen'), and immediately after this admission, he describes the gifts which had been bestowed upon him through Frieda's agency as 'Machtmittel', 'means of acquiring power'. Similarly, instead of jumping up there and then and returning home to Frieda, he forfeits her by staying on in the Barnabas house.

Because K. does not understand what marriage can mean, for most of *Das Schloß* he proves to be incapable of exercising the tolerance, good humour, self-restraint and patience which it demands. Consequently, as Walter Sokel points out, when, with the assistants as his substitute children, he is placed in the position of husband and father, he cannot rise to the challenge, lets Frieda down in front of the teacher and eventually drives out the assistants who have been entrusted to him.

What K. experiences most intensely with Frieda, he experiences to a lesser extent with several other people. Schopenhauer wrote that it is possible to recognise by their eyes those people who have made the transition from an existence under the domination of the Will to a state of transcendent peace, and in *Das Schloß*, the reader can look for the same sign. Just as Frieda's eyes speak of her elusive depth, so Olga's blue eyes suggest that her gentleness, humour, calm and humility are of far more value than all Amalia's lovelessness and self-assertive pride. At the same time, however, it should be noted that Olga, like Frieda, is not presented as an idealised figure. Although she sees that Barnabas' strivings are achieving nothing, she encourages him to persist in them. Although she knows that her family needs only to give up its attempt to justify itself before the Castle and return to its old way of life in order to be accepted back into the village community, she indulges her parents and brother and helps bring then deeper into despair. Furthermore, Olga's ability to give herself comes, at times, very close to being a desire for martyrdom. At that point when she should have said 'thus far and no farther', she allows herself to become a virtual prostitute, even though she knows that this can be of no help to anyone. Nevertheless, K. twice experiences a feeling of peace when he is with her. The first of these moments occurs in the second chapter when he is walking with her from the Barnabas house to the *Herrenhof*, and the second comes at the beginning of Chapter Fifteen. Neither experience produces the intense peace which K. knows when he is with Frieda, but both are real and both reflect very positively on the blue-eyed Olga. Finally, a brief mention must be made of the blue eyes of the man who K. glimpses with his family at the end of the sixth chapter. Although K. does not

pay much attention to this man, his eyes speak of a friendly tolerance and a patient ability to still his family's hunger which K. himself would do well to acquire.

If K. encounters several people who, through a quality of peace
and grace, implicitly show him the possibility of transcending
his Faustian way of life, he also encounters people who have a
negative and corrosive influence upon him. And of these, the most
important are, of course, the assistants and Amalia. As has already
been pointed out, the assistants objectify those parts of K.'s personality which he cannot accept. They personify that unself-
conscious childlikeness which all the gracious characters in *Das
Schloß* possess and that erotic animality of whose presence within
himself, K. the rationaliser is only momentarily aware. Thus, the
major task of the assistants is to persuade K. to accept these aspects
of himself, and this in turn means that K. must, somehow or other,
be persuaded to stop taking himself seriously, to see the fatuity of
the identity which he is striving to maintain and to learn that 'other
laughter' which comes when the subject is freed from servility to
things and institutions.[34] K., however, has the greatest difficulty in
learning this laughter for he is a terrible self-dramatiser. As Galater
tells the assistants, K. thinks that his arrival in the village is a great
event, whereas in reality it is nothing at all. Because of this, K. is
unable to accustom himself to the idea that his point of view is
simply relative, one among many, and everything that he encounters
turns into a demon against which he has to defend himself. If K.
can be persuaded to laugh at himself, he will also learn to laugh
at the Castle authorities, cease to be mesmerised by his image of
them and thus be able to live in the village without reference to
them. Perhaps an incident from Kafka's own experience sheds light
upon the change that would be wrought in K.'s attitude to the
world if only he could learn to laugh at himself. In a letter to Felice
Bauer in 1912 or 1913 (BF, 236–40), the style of which is more that
of one of his short stories than that of a letter to a girl-friend, Kafka
tells how once, during a formal ceremony on the occasion of his
promotion in the insurance firm where he was employed, he had
been overcome by a fit of uncontrollable laughter at the President's:

---

[34] Compare Kafka's letter to Elli Hermann of the autumn of 1918 (B, 341).

12

...übliche, längst vorher be-
kannte, kaiserlich schematische,
von schweren Brusttönen begleit-
ete, ganz und gar sinnlose und
unbegründete Rede, ... (BF,
238)

...usual speech, which we all
knew long in advance, which was
imperially schematic, accompa-
nied by portentous rumblings from
the presidential chest, and completely lacking in sense and
foundation, ...

As a result of this, the whole pompous ceremony broke up in em-
barrassment. At the beginning of the description of this incident,
the President is described as a person whom the normal official
regards as a more-than-earthly, quasi-imperial being. Thus, there
is an unmistakable analogy between the relationship of the normal
official (among whom Kafka counts himself) to the President, and
the relationship of K. to the Castle authorities. Correspondingly
then, if only K. could break into laughter at these all-too-human
Greek gods who squeak when chased, like a girl who is pinched, he
would be able to live in the village in peace. K. is a man who covers
up the conflict at the heart of his personality by building castles in
the air which bear only a limited resemblance to the reality of the
Castle. If only K. could admit the comic absurdity of his fantasies
and accept the existence of his inner conflict, then, paradoxically,
that conflict would begin to resolve itself of its own accord.

Where Frieda and Olga show him what he might be and the
assistants try to goad him into becoming what he is, Amalia shows
him what he will become unless he undergoes a radical change of
heart. Where Frieda's glance promises infinite peace, Amalia's
glance is 'dull' and 'lifeless'. Where Frieda tolerates out of a sense
of human unity, Amalia scorns out of cold pride. Where Frieda
looks into people in order to discover and release what is hidden
within them, Amalia looks past people, and ministers to her parents
with the uninvolved chilliness of duty. Where both Frieda and Olga
can understand that the coarseness of the officials' demands derives
from their preoccupation with official business and their inexperi-
ence of the world of men, Amalia can make no such allowances for
the crudeness of Sortini's letter. When K. learns to know the Barnabas family better, he sees that both Barnabas and Amalia are refus-

ing to admit their doubts, refusing to allow those negative pressures into the forefront of their personalities which could turn them from their misguided way of life. Thus, having attained this insight, K. is that much more ready himself to be broken open and transformed.

From his positive, negative and parodistic encounters, from his lyrical moments and his disillusionments, K. gradually becomes dimly aware that his personality must undergo a radical change. The hold of his defiant will must be broken, so that, to use the metaphor provided by the third quotation which prefaces this chapter, the young spring greenness may begin to become visible behind the dead foliage. Gradually, K. becomes aware that the confines of his fearful ego need to be burst open by love, and it is to this process of 'bursting-open' that we must now turn.

D. Death and Rebirth

Kafka's posthumously published *Fragmente* include the following strange little story:

Ich habe eine Tür in meiner Wohnung bisher nicht beachtet. Sie ist im Schlafzimmer in der Mauer, die an das Nachbarhaus grenzt. Ich habe mir keine Gedanken über sie gemacht, ja ich habe gar nicht von ihr gewußt. Und doch ist sie recht wohl sichtbar, ihr unterer Teil ist zwar von den Betten verdeckt; sie aber ragt weit hinauf, fast keine Tür, fast ein Tor. Gestern wurde sie aufgemacht. Ich war gerade im Speisezimmer, das noch durch ein Zimmer vom Schlafzimmer getrennt ist. Ich war sehr verspätet zum Mittagessen gekommen, nie-

I have never taken any notice before now of a door in the flat where I live. It is in the bedroom wall which separates my flat from the house next door. I've never thought about it—indeed, I've never known about it. And yet it's plainly visible. Admittedly, its lower part is hidden by the beds, but it towers up towards the ceiling, and it's almost more of a gateway than a door. Yesterday it was opened. I was just in the dining-room which is separated from the bedroom by one other room. I had come into lunch very late, no one was at home, and

mand war mehr zu Hause, nur
das Dienstmädchen arbeitete in
der Küche. Da begann im Schlafzimmer der Lärm. Ich eile sogleich hinüber und sehe, wie die
Tür langsam geöffnet wird und
dabei mit riesiger Kraft die Betten
weggeschoben wurden. Ich rufe:
»Wer ist das? Was will man?
Vorsicht! Achtung!« und erwarte
einen Trupp gewalttätiger Män-
ner hereinkommen zu sehn, aber
es ist nur ein schmaler junger
Mann, der, sobald der Spalt nur
knapp für ihn reicht, herein-
schlüpft und freudig mich be-
grüßt. (H, 233–4)

only the maid was working in the
kitchen. Then the row began in
the bedroom. I immediately hurry
over there and watch how the door
is slowly opened, and how, as this
happens, the beds are pushed aside
with considerable force. I call out:
'Who's there? What d'you want?
Careful! Look out!' and expect
to see a troop of powerful men
come in. But it is only a slim
young man, who, as soon as the
door is just wide enough ajar for
him, slips in through the crack
and greets me joyously. (W,
227–8)

If one understands this story as a parable of the human psyche, then
it is possible to say that after K.'s interview with Bürgel, a hitherto
'unnoticed door' opens in his mind through which there comes a
'slightly-built young man' who represents the self which he had
repressed or of whose existence he was ignorant. Although the forgotten door in K.'s consciousness opens after immense inner tur-
moil and pandemonium, the self who emerges through it is quiet
and modest—superficially less impressive than the old K., but,
like the young man in the parable, with a quality of peace about
him.

It needs to be made quite clear, however, first, that this transformation does not come about without warning, and second, that
even when it has taken place, K. is never fully aware of it. Thus, if
one looks carefully at the narrative of *Das Schloß*, slight but significant changes of tone, emphasis and attitude can be detected
throughout which prepare the reader for K.'s final transformation.
For instance, the K. who consciously defended himself against the
feelings of well-being which he experienced with Olga in the second
chapter is content to accept the same experience without resistance

at the beginning of Chapter Fifteen. When, at the beginning of Chapter Four, K., briefly and untypically, learns to accept his dependence on Frieda and enjoy the 'good coffee' which she has brought him, the assistants obey his order to leave the room. This is the only time in the novel that the assistants obey K. without demur or prevarication, and the narrator clearly suggests that they make this exceptional gesture towards K. because K., uncharacteristically, has issued his order:

... mehr aus behaglicher Laune als in der Hoffnung auf Erfolg ... (68)   *... more out of an impulse of good humour than in the hope of success ... (48)*

In Chapters One and Four K. appreciates the openness of Lasemann and Gardena respectively, and this instinctive willingness to recognise this particular value in others will, in the end, enable K.'s total experience to make a fundamental difference to his own personality. In Chapter Six, the normally aggressive K. talks 'softly' to Gardena. By Chapter Ten, K. is beginning to accept the incomprehensibility of the Castle authorities, and after the storm has broken, he becomes perceptibly more gentle and even allows the assistants to do as they like on the way home. In Chapter Thirteen, K. resolves, briefly, to be more appreciative of and concerned about Frieda. When he indulges in fantastic hopes after his conversation with Hans Brunswick, he has acquired enough self-detachment to see that these hopes are improbable and baseless, and later on in the same chapter, he actually begins to do his job as a janitor for a while. The K. who, at the beginning of the book, needs no one, is ready, at the beginning of the ninth chapter, to admit that he wants to see human faces, hurries towards the two lights which he sees bobbing along the road and is even glad to see the despised Barnabas. The K. who listens to Olga's long story, thanks her for telling it when she has finished and appreciates her for what she is in herself, is not the arrogant, egocentric K. who twice rejected the Barnabas family table and condescended to Olga in the second chapter. The K. who listens so patiently to Olga's story has almost ceased to assert the fiction that he is a land-surveyor, and instead of emphasising what he hopes to attain by his own efforts, he begins to be thankful for what has been given him undeservedly through the agency of Frieda. Indeed, by the end of Chapter Fifteen, the extent to which a transformation has already taken place in K.'s personality is evident from the symbolic rôle which the assistant plays there. Jeremias is, when he knocks on the Barnabas family door, described, very suggestively, as 'der späte Besucher', 'the late visitor'. He, like the young man in the parable, causes the door to be opened, tries to push his way forcefully into the room and when he fails, attempts to shine his lantern into the 'curtained'[35] room. Olga, the less wilful of the two sisters, is unable to hold Jeremias back and it takes all Amalia's will-power to prevent him from making his entry. In short, this little episode seems to symbolise the imminent resurgence of all those insights, experiences and energies which K. has done his best to ignore but which have had their effect on his unconscious life and his discernible attitudes. Thus, the K. who struggled so wilfully at first is able, immediately before his interview with Bürgel, to offer a frank and tender account to Frieda of his own failings and of what has gone wrong between them, to make the symbolic statement: '. . . laß' also 'die Fäuste ruhen'.[36] From time to time during the course of Das Schloß, a 'thin little stream' which is 'impossible to seek out' breaks through to the surface of K.'s personality. It manifests itself in occasional flashes of insight, untypical gestures and uncharacteristic tones of voice, and its name is 'love'.[37]

Because the reader sees and hears almost everything through the mind of K., there is no one who can draw his attention explicitly to this process of gradual change. Furthermore, because K. himself tends to rationalise it in terms of a growing sense of tiredness and is even unaware of it after it has reached its climax, it is very easy to overlook. Indeed, critic after critic has failed to register it or has denied its existence. Klaus-Peter Philippi, for example, implies that no process of change takes place when he says:

[35] The word used here for 'curtained' is 'verhängt'—which also suggests 'fateful', 'fated'.
[36] See pp. 87–8 above.
[37] Compare Kafka's diary entry for 5.vii.1916.

Der feste Wille, in das geahnte oder gewußte Schloß zu gelangen, ist allein sicher, weil K. bis zum Schluß des Romans immer noch danach strebt.[38]	*The resolute will to get inside the Castle whose existence is either suspected or known, is only certain because K. is still striving to do this right up to the conclusion of the novel.*

and:

Kafka bietet für die entwickelten Probleme keine Lösung an, . . .[39]	*Kafka offers no solution to the problems which have been unfolded, . . .*

Although Marthe Robert maintains that K. does achieve something through being in the village,[40] she also says, more definitely, that:

. . . les épisodes de son [K.'s] histoire se juxtaposent sans augmenter d'intensité et, par suite, sans se rapprocher jamais d'un éventual dénouement.[41]	*. . . the episodes of K.'s story are placed next to one another, but they do not increase in intensity and consequently do not get any nearer to a possible conclusion.*

Heinz Politzer writes:

> *From the moment of his arrival K. is denied any chance to develop or to acquire the personal growth which would inform his end with the dimension of tragedy. . . . He does not get wiser; only the days grow longer.*[42]

And Erich Heller is even more emphatic:

> *. . . the most oppressive quality of Kafka's work is the unshakable stability of its central situation. It takes place in a world that*

[38] Philippi, p. 61.
[39] Philippi, p. 226.
[40] Robert, pp. 275–6.
[41] Robert, p. 232.
[42] Politzer, p. 251.

*knows of no motion, no change, no metamorphosis. . . . There is,
in fact, no pilgrimage to be watched in* The Castle, . . .[43]

In contrast, Ronald Gray, of all the critics of *Das Schloß*, maintains most consistently and explicitly that a transformation does take
place in K.'s personality:

*It is in K.'s fundamental disposition that the change has taken place,
the change whereby he is persuaded of good will not only in the
castle but in everyone around him. He cannot be said to have
deserved the transformation or to have wrested it from the castle
by his own efforts.*[44]

and:

*So long as he [K.] imagined that his goal was in the castle or
beyond, he waited against his will. The moment he gave up completely, a miracle transformed his reality.*[45]

While the present writer does not agree with Dr. Gray's suggestion
that his argument 'only makes sense so long as the castle and its
officials are taken to represent the relationships of men with the
supernatural world'[46] and does not see that there is any need to
make use of explicitly Christian terminology in order to describe
the transformation which K. undergoes, he does find himself in
agreement with Dr. Gray on the reality of the transformation which
takes place in K.'s manner, in K.'s dealings with other people and
in K.'s attitude to the Castle bureaucracy.

To begin with, during the interview with Bürgel, K. sees quite
explicitly 'the uselessness of all his struggles'. This is something
entirely new. Up to that point, K. had only been able to see the
uselessness of other people's struggles. Then again, even before K.
had reached Bürgel, he had virtually ceased to maintain the fiction
that he was a land-surveyor, and during the interview, when one

[43] Heller, p. 193.
[44] Gray, pp. 78–9.
[45] Gray, p. 81.
[46] Gray, p. 121.

would expect this subject to be in the forefront of his mind, he never even mentions it—presumably because it no longer has very much interest for him. Similarly, when, two pages before the end of the book, K. is asked who he is, he replies that he is a land-surveyor in one word only, does not justify himself or evade the issue, and when the landlady accuses him of not telling the truth, he tacitly admits as much[47] without becoming angry or excited. When K. leaves Bürgel's room and goes out into the corridor, similar changes in his attitudes become apparent. At a point when the old K. would probably have forced his way into the officials' rooms, the new K. is content to efface himself and watch their dealings with a sympathetic appreciation of their efforts that is entirely different from his old obsessive curiosity. Where the old K. talks as though he understood the system, the new K. is prepared to admit that it passes his comprehension. Whereas the old K. would have assumed, without any apology whatsoever, that the one last bit of paper on the servants' trolley referred to his case, the new K., when he catches himself entertaining this thought, is prepared to regard it, rightly, as 'arbitrary' and 'laughable'. Whereas the old K. would probably have blocked the landlord's way, condescended to him or remonstrated with him before allowing him to pass, the new K. stands back against the wall in all innocence to let him pass. Because he wants 'to understand what the gentleman is saying' and 'to understand the exact nature of his guilt', he allows himself to be led out of the corridor without protestation. Whereas the old K., knowing that he had done something wrong, would have voci-ferously denied any guilt, because the new K. in all innocence does not realise what he has done wrong, he apologises for his mistake, makes the amazing admission that he is inexperienced in matters concerning the Castle and the village, and tells the landlord and landlady that he would never have remained in the corridor during the distribution of the documents if he had known that this was not permitted. Furthermore, K.'s new respect for what he does not understand is so patent that it persuades the *Herrenhof* landlord to allow him to sleep in the bar.

The transformation persists and becomes even more apparent

[47] See p. 58 above.

during the conversation with Pepi which takes place after K.'s long
sleep. Although K. is more conscious than ever of Pepi's shortcomings, he no longer despises her because of them, for now he can
see that her shortcomings are his own as well. He listens to her
attentively, without moralising in the way that he tended to while
Olga was telling her story, and without assertively trying to prove
his superiority over her by scoring points. Although K. is convinced from the start that Pepi's account of Frieda is distorted, he
is now magnanimous enough to realise why Pepi is making these
distortions, and when he reproves her, he does so with compassion.
Instead of pushing himself and his ideas forward, he effaces himself
in order to listen. Instead of insisting on his rights, he frankly
admits how much he owes to others. Instead of offering advice, he
goes so far as to ask the formerly despised Pepi for her advice. Instead of giving the impression that he can explain everything, he
admits that he is not completely clear about the reason for the
break-up of his relationship with Frieda. Instead of clinging to his
first impressions, he now shows that he is prepared to revise these
under the influence of new evidence or new experience. Instead of
seeking to dominate and be distinguished, he is now prepared to
class himself among the 'common people'. Instead of talking as
though his point of view were absolute, his hesitant manner now
indicates that he is aware of the relativity of his perspective. Instead
of 'calculating what he should become', he begins to 'see what he
is'.[48] Indeed, so profound a transformation has he undergone, and
so polite and deferential has his manner become, that the *Herrenhof*
landlady cannot believe her ears, and it is recorded that on hearing
K. speak, she looks at him 'with a glance as though she were dreaming' and even goes so far as to smile at him! Consequently, when she
begins to bully him, K., instead of becoming flustered, irritated,
defensive or assertive, answers her with candour and courtesy.
As Dr. Gray puts it, whereas the old K. was 'filled with distrust,
malice, hatred, yearning, dissatisfaction, introspection', the new K.
is 'certain, sympathetic, charitable, forgiving, self-forgetful'.[49]

Furthermore, K.'s entire attitude to the Castle has undergone a

[48] Compare Kafka's diary entry for 27.viii.1916.
[49] Gray, p. 80.

considerable change. Because K. has rid himself of his 'wollenes Umhängetuch'[50] and discovered that he 'cannot force his way into the world' but must 'learn to lie quietly, receive, spread out within him what he has received and the step quietly forth',[51] he ceases to flee from himself and shows himself willing to sit still. Thereupon, a healing element breaks into his personality, and as it does so, his fear and guilt are dissolved, he no longer needs to project his fantasies onto the Castle and he is no longer obsessed with striving frantically to reach an impossible and undefined goal. Throughout the novel, K. was afraid of sitting still because he knew that stillness represented the antithesis of his Faustianism. After his interview with Bürgel, however, a quality of stillness, which is by no means apathy, blank passivity or indifference enters into his dealings with others and erodes his curiosity about the Castle. Although K.'s critical faculties are as sharp as ever after his interview with Bürgel, and although K. has not been reduced to a state of subservience by his bout of sleep, he is now prepared to accept that there are things which he cannot know about the Castle. Whereas previously the Castle and its representatives had been endowed in K.'s mind with a massively oppressive and malevolent authority, they now appear to him as mysterious beings whose ways, be they good or evil, are inscrutable. To quote Dr. Gray once more: 'K. gets certainty when he has given up wanting it . . . The important point is not whether K.'s case is concluded but that he is no longer concerned to know.'[52]

To put it another way, after the dominance of K.'s will has been broken, he discovers that it is possible to live a good life in the village as though the Castle bureaucracy did not exist, accepting it simply as a necessary fiction. Surprising though this conclusion may seem, several pieces of evidence point to it. First of all, no one of any importance seems to mind Schwarzer performing his duties in a casual manner so that he can devote most of his time and energy to his life with Gisa. Second, it is suggested that Gardena's life has

[50] The leitmotiv of the 'wollenes Umhängetuch' or 'Wolltuch' occurs two or three times in *Das Schloß*. Considered literally, the expression means 'woollen wrap' or 'woollen shawl'. But looked at with an eye for the apposite pun (a device of which Kafka was especially fond), the expression can also be rendered as 'enveloping garment of will', 'husk of will'.

[51] Compare Kafka's diary entry for 20.i.1915.

[52] Gray, p. 72.

been ruined precisely because she has allowed herself to be hypnotised by the memory of a relationship with the Castle and in consequence, neglected the possibility of a full and happy life with her husband. Third, although K. does not have an official position in the village, no one prevents him from remaining there and his experience as a whole suggests that the authorities, in their oblique way, would like him to settle down with Frieda. Finally, although Barnabas' family know that they only need to return to their old pattern of life in the village for the curse that hangs over them to be lifted, and although Olga is quite clear that the influence of the Castle was *least* in evidence at the time when the village community was drawing back from them, they wear themselves out in their attempts to justify themselves before the very authorities who are powerless, as officials, to do anything for them. In short, it begins to look as though the Castle has official power only over those who allow it to have that power, and once K. finds himself and exorcises the image of an all-powerful official bureaucracy which he has built up, the malignant fascination which the Castle has had for him vanishes. After his interview with Bürgel, K.'s attitude to the Castle authorities is the detached admiration of the kind which one adult might feel for the hard work and expertise of other adults. Before that interview, K.'s attitude to the authorities had been the ambiguous respect of the kind which a child might feel for the father on whom he wants to be dependent and from whom he desires, simultaneously, to be free.

In the Fourth Octavo Notebook, Kafka wrote of Kierkegaard's Abraham:[53]

Abraham ist in folgender Täuschung begriffen: die Einförmigkeit dieser Welt kann er nicht ertragen. Nun ist aber die Welt bekanntlich ungemein mannigfaltig, was jederzeit nachzuprüfen ist, indem man eine Handvoll Welt nimmt und näher ansieht.

Abraham has been caught in the following delusion: he cannot bear the monotony of the world. But, as is well known, the world is uncommonly variegated—and this one can verify at any time by taking a handful of world and looking at it more closely. Abraham

[53] The central figure of *Fear and Trembling*.

Das weiß natürlich auch Abraham. Die Klage über die Einförmigkeit der Welt ist aber eigentlich eine Klage über nicht genügend tiefe Vermischung mit der Mannigfaltigkeit der Welt. (H, 125)	knows that too, of course. The complaint about the uniformity of the world is in fact a complaint about insufficiently deep involvement with the variegated nature of the world. (W, 118)

K., like Abraham in Kafka's estimation, had decided that the world was uninhabitable and begun to climb his version of Mount Moriah. During his never-ending climb, however, K. discovers that the splendour which he secretly seeks is not to be found away from the world, with the elusive beings who inhabit the Castle, but within himself, 'veiled from view, deep down, invisible, far off.'⁵⁴ Thus, K. has to change his direction, and in order to do this, he has to learn the secret word which could release that splendour, bring the 'young man' out of his attic hiding-place and turn his 'peep-hole perspective' into an ability to appreciate the world for what it is in itself.

The question which must now be asked is therefore: did K. *learn* that word or was it *taught* to him? Are the Castle authorities in any way instrumental in arranging K.'s fate and bringing about the change in his disposition? The next chapter is devoted to this question. But before moving on, it must be noted that K.'s change of heart has been bought at a great cost. Frieda, K.'s Gretchen, has aged prematurely and deteriorated because of his neglect. There is no 'Stimme von oben' ('voice from above') in *Das Schloß* which could intervene to free her from her final prison of emotional childishness, and no concluding scene in which she is seen to be among the blessed, interceding for the man who ruined her. Similarly, just as Jeremias, the assistant who seems to externalise K.'s sexual energies, appears to be sick and wasting away by the end of the novel, so too, K. seems to have been drained of his erotic urges. When, in the final chapter, K. makes a pass at Pepi, there is nothing of his former carnality but only fatigue in the gesture. Earlier in the novel, K. had been offered the possibility of undergoing a change of

---

⁵⁴ Compare Kafka's diary entry for 18.x.1921.

heart while maintaining his sexual vitality within a family context. Now, however, he has destroyed that context and dissipated his vitality to such an extent that he can tell Pepi that he desires to attain a state of even more total inactivity. Furthermore, as the novel closes, K. is left with Gerstäcker, one of the death-figures, tugging at his sleeve. *Pace* Heinz Politzer, K. *is* the hero of a tragedy, and one of the most poignant features of that tragedy is that its hero acquires his insight, his ability to accept and a sense of reconciliation too late to prevent Frieda's destruction and his own death. K.'s transformation is precisely that of the classic tragic hero: it is achieved in the midst of suffering and at a cost which is almost too great to be justifiable.

CHAPTER FOUR

The Status of the Castle Authorities

Daß er [mein Vater] mein Feind ist und ich seiner, so wie es durch unsere Natur bestimmt ist, das weißt Du, aber außerdem ist meine Bewunderung seiner Person vielleicht so groß wie meine Angst vor ihm. (BF, 452; dated 24.viii.1913)

You know that he [my father] is my enemy, and I his, as is determined by our temperaments, but apart from this my admiration for him as a man is perhaps as great as my fear of him.

Ich lese im Ganzen nicht viel, das Leben auf dem Dorf ist mir so entsprechend. Hat man erst einmal das Gefühl mit allen seinen Unannehmlichkeiten überwunden, in einem nach neueren Prinzipien eingerichteten Tiergarten zu wohnen, in welchem den Tieren volle Freiheit gegeben ist, dann gibt es kein behaglicheres und vor allem kein freieres Leben als auf dem Dorf, frei im geistigen Sinn, möglichst wenig bedrückt von Um- und Vorwelt. (B, 181; letter to Felix Weltsch of early October, 1917)

On the whole, I don't do very much reading because village life here suits me so much. As soon as one gets over the feeling, with all its unpleasant implications, of living in a zoo built according to the most up-to-date principles, in which the animals are given complete freedom, then there is no more comfortable and, more particularly, no more unhampered life than village life—and when I say unhampered, I mean that in the spiritual sense, oppressed as little as possible by environment and the past.

Nun bist Du ja im Grunde ein gütiger und weicher Mensch, . . . aber nicht jedes Kind hat die Ausdauer und Unerschrockenheit, so

Now, you are basically a good-natured and tender-hearted person . . . but not every child has the perseverance and undauntedness

lange zu suchen, bis es zu der   to go on searching until he reaches
Güte kommt. (H, 166; letter to   the goodness. (W, 161)
his father of November, 1919)

The question of the status of the Castle authorities in Kafka's
novel is fraught with difficulties. It is not necessary to go very
far into the immense amount of secondary literature to discover
that these difficulties have caused commentators on *Das Schloß* to
take a bewildering variety of attitudes to the mysterious Castle and
its elusive occupants. So, before an attempt is made here to come
to any conclusions about this intricate problem, it is useful to be
clear about the questions which are asked about the Castle authorities and to consider the various answers which have been given to
them. On the whole, two questions tend to be asked: Is the Castle
an allegory of God? and: Are the Castle authorities benevolent or
malevolent? More often than not, however, these two questions
become merged, and because this elision makes the whole problem
of the Castle more difficult than it need perhaps be, they will be
dealt with separately here.

The possibility that the Castle stands for God was first suggested
by Max Brod in his afterword to the first edition to *Das Schloß*:

K. sucht die Verbindung mit der   By trying to put down roots in the
Gnade der Gottheit, indem er sich   village at the foot of the Castle,
im Dorf zu Füßen des Schlosses   K. is seeking union with divine
einzuwurzeln sucht . . .[1]   grace.

and:

Sollte man nun die von K.   If one thinks that the relationships
erlebten und vermuteten Bezieh-   which K. learns and senses exist
ungen zwischen den Frauen und   between the women and the
dem »Schloß« also der göttlichen   'Castle'—divine Providence—are
Lenkung, rätselhaft und vor allem   an enigma and if, above all
die Sortini-Episode unerklärlich   else, one thinks that the Sortini
finden, in der der Beamte (der   episode, in which the official

[1] Brod, *Nachwort*, p. 530.

Himmel) sichtlich etwas Unmoralisches und Schmutziges von dem Mädchen verlangt, so sei auf Kierkegaards »Furcht und Zittern« hingewiesen—ein Werk überdies, das Kafka sehr geliebt, oft gelesen und in vielen Briefen tiefsinnig kommentiert hat. Die Sortini-Episode ist geradezu ein Parallelstück zu Kierkegaards Buch, das davon ausgeht, daß Gott von Abraham sogar ein Verbrechen, die Opferung seines Kindes, verlangt, und in dem dieses Paradox zur siegreichen Feststellung verhilft, daß die Kategorien der Moral und die des Religiösen durchaus nicht als einander deckend vorzustellen sind. —Die Inkommensurabilität irdischen und religiösen Tuns: das führt direkt ins Zentrum von Kafkas Roman.[2]

(heaven) visibly demands something immoral and dirty from the girl, is inexplicable, then let me draw attention to Kierkegaard's Fear and Trembling. *Kafka was very fond of this work, read it frequently and made penetrating comments on it in many of his letters. The Sortini episode forms an exact parallel to Kierkegaard's book, for this book starts out from the premise that God goes so far as to demand the commission of a crime by Abraham—namely, the sacrifice of his son. And, during the course of Kierkegaard's book, this paradox allows the triumphant conclusion to emerge that the categories of morality and the categories of religion cannot be thought to coincide with each other.—The incommensurability of earthly and religious action: that takes us right into the heart of Kafka's novel.*

Not a few critics have, in one way or another, taken a similar view. Herbert Tauber, for instance, writes:

This messenger [Barnabas], one of the deepest and most beautiful motifs in the novel, is the symbol of the communication between above and below, between the Castle and the village, between God and the world.[3]

and:

[2] Brod, *Nachwort*, p. 534.
[3] Tauber, p. 170.

13

The reality of the Castle and its officials gets lost behind a veil of contradictory suppositions. The man who wants to take guidance from it as a fixed point finds himself confronted as it were with a grey mass that swims away into the endless. But nevertheless this Castle remains the essence of all appointing of ends and of all values.[4]

Similarly, Ronald Gray concludes his work on *Das Schloß* by saying:

All this argument, however, only makes sense so long as the castle and its officials are taken to represent the relationships of men with the supernatural world.[5]

This view of the Castle authorities was once fairly widespread, and it is not difficult to see why this should have been so. The Castle authorities do seem to possess an omniscience which enables them to anticipate every move that K. makes and an omnipotence which enables them to lead K. providentially into situations from which he will benefit directly or indirectly. The Castle appears in the novel not as a dead and distant authority but as an inscrutable force which penetrates everywhere, even, as K. remarks at one point, into his bedroom. When, at the beginning of Chapter Eight, K. looks up at the Castle buildings, he sees them not as a rickety and dilapidated shell, but as a living personality who sits there with all the self-possession of a dreaming god. Within the village, the Castle and its representatives have an absolute and quasi-divine authority. They preside over festivals of purgation and procreation, they are associated with elemental powers such as fire and water, and elemental experiences such as copulation and death. The officials are unpredictable, inaccessible, elusive and almost invisible to the mortal eye for they rarely permit themselves to be seen. Nobody really knows what Klamm looks like, as he seems to be able to change his appearance at will, and he, like all the other senior officials, has surrounded himself with contradictory myths and a host of angelic and priestly

---

[4] Tauber, p. 170.
[5] Gray, p. 121.

beings. *Prima facie*, there would seem to be at least an arguable case for identifying the Castle bureaucracy with a divinity.

Nevertheless, a very powerful corrective to this general understanding of the Castle authorities was provided by Erich Heller, who, in an incisive outburst of angry wit, wrote:

The Castle *is as much a religious allegory as a photographic likeness of the Devil could be said to be an allegory of evil.*[6]

and:

This [Max Brod's reading of Das Schloß] *is, for the believer, downright blasphemy, and a critical insult to the intelligence of a reader able to read for himself the Bible, Kierkegaard, and Kafka. The comparison between Kierkegaard and Kafka would indeed be relevant. It might bring home, even to a modern reader, the difference between Purgatory and Hell. For this is the precise relationship between Kierkegaard's* Fear and Trembling *and Kafka's* Castle. *The sacrifice of Isaac a parallel to Sortini's designs on Amalia? But this means, without any polemical exaggeration, to ascribe to the God of Abraham a personal interest in the boy Isaac worthy of a Greek demi-god. Moreover, He, having tested Abraham's absolute obedience, did not accept the sacrifice. Yet Sortini (who conveys to Max Brod the idea of divine guidance and Heaven itself) can, to judge by the example of his colleagues, be relied upon not to have summoned Amalia to his bedroom merely to tell her that one does not do such a thing.*[7]

This kind of argument cannot be circumvented, and Professor Heller might well have poured even more cold water on Max Brod's somewhat simple parallel between *Fear and Trembling* and *Das Schloß* by pointing out that Kafka's relationship with Kierkegaard the man[8] and with the book of Kierkegaard's in question[9] was far

---

[6] Heller, p. 179.

[7] Heller, p. 197.

[8] In whom he saw a parallel to himself. See Kafka's diary entry for 21.viii.1913.

[9] Whose hero he described as monstrous. See his letter to Max Brod of early March, 1918 (B, 23–6).

from straightforward. But even without these marginal reservations, Heller's criticism of Max Brod's interpretation seems to have had the effect of drawing attention forcibly to the all-too-human features of the Castle officials which earlier critics had played down. This line of argument, together with the growing influence of Marxian thought in academic circles over the last decade, seems to have moved critics away from religious interpretations of the Castle and towards more immanentist readings. Accordingly, since about the early sixties, interpreters of *Das Schloß* have tended to say that the Castle is a humanly created absolute, God-like, but not divine in itself, a socially determined edifice which has acquired unquestioned authority within the world of the village and the minds of the villagers, but which, at the same time, is of human origin. Correspondingly, Marthe Robert describes the Castle authorities as anomalous 'ancient hierarchies' which still exercise control over men's lives even though they have been emptied of content.[10] In a similar vein, Walter Sokel writes of the Castle:

Darüber hinaus aber ist es jeder vom Feudalismus ausgegangene bürokratische und hierarchische Staat, der, von Traditionen sanktioniert, das Leben der Bauern und Handwerker beherrscht und dessen Spiegelung wir im Schloß wiederfinden. Dem System liegt ein von Ehrfurcht und Gewohnheit getragener Irrationalismus zugrunde, der die Macht heilig spricht. Die Beamten stehen über allen menschlichen und moralischen Maßstäben.[11]	*But over and above that, what we find reflected in* Das Schloß *is every bureaucratic and hierarchical state that has descended from the feudal system. It rules over the lives of the peasants and artisans with the authority of tradition and the whole system is based on an irrationalism which sanctifies power and is underpinned by respect and custom. The officials stand above all human and moral standards.*

Wilhelm Emrich writes:

[10] Robert, p. 243.
[11] Sokel, *Franz Kafka: Tragik und Ironie*, p. 397.

Offenbar ist also gerade der religiöse, transzendierende Aspekt aus diesem Schloß und Dorf vertrieben oder stark eingeschränkt.[12]

Clearly, the transcendent, religious dimension has either been driven out of the Castle and the village or else has been greatly diminished there.

and Klaus-Peter Philippi refers categorically to the Castle as:

... die leere Hülse eines verlorenen Wertes ...[13]

... the empty husk of a lost value ...

and:

... kein für den Menschen erkennbares Wertsystem ... sondern ein bloßes Funktionieren sinnlos erscheinender Vorgänge ...[14]

... not a system of values which could be recognised as such by human beings ... but a mere functioning of processes which appear to be meaningless ...

Clearly, there is a considerable amount of evidence within the novel which supports this view as well. Klamm and his colleagues appear, as human beings, either monstrously cold or wantonly aggressive (especially in their dealings with women), and as officials, they frequently seem to be neurotically and unnecessarily industrious, perversely pedantic, farcically ineffectual or childishly vulnerable. There is an inescapable similarity between the Castle authorities and the shambling imperial Austrian bureaucracy with which Kafka himself was only too familiar, and once this suggestion is ventured, then gaps and cracks begin to appear in the supposedly so infallible Castle apparatus. When they are bored, the officials pick up telephones in order to play jokes on the person who is ringing up. A simple case like the appointment of a land-surveyor accretes administrative attention until the work generated far exceeds the importance of the original case. Contrary to the best

[12] Emrich, p. 311.
[13] Philippi, p. 217.
[14] Philippi, p. 224.

interests of infallible efficiency, inspection systems are created for the inspection of inspection systems. The whole apparatus is so overloaded that the chancelleries resound with the crash of falling stacks of documents. The Village Superintendent's filing system is a mockery of divinised bureaucracy. The two assistants seem to parody this bureaucracy during K.'s interview with the Superintendent and when his wife Mizzi kneels in an attitude of prayer before an empty filing cabinet on which a candle stands as though upon an altar, she seems to be indicating the unreality and ghostly nature of the Castle administration. Several pages later, she drops a similar hint to K. when she makes a little boat out of Klamm's letter, thereby suggesting that the entire administrative system is nothing but an insignificant, man-made bark, floating on the chaotic flux of Becoming. When K. says to Momus, shortly before his interview with Bürgel, that the Castle officials only think of themselves, Momus implies that the Castle bureaucracy is primarily a self-perpetuating organism, for he replies:

An wen sollen wir denn denken?   *Of whom then should we think?*
Wer ist denn sonst noch hier?   *Who is here apart from us? (227)*
(352)

Then again, when K., on the first day of his time in the village, looks at the Castle and the school-house (which is one of the chief institutions in the village through which the Castle propagates the idea that it is divine), these buildings appear quite clearly as decaying, rambling, earthly buildings. The Castle itself is described as 'a right wretched little town' whose paint had flaked off and whose masonry appears to be crumbling away, and the school is described as 'a long, low building' which gives the ambiguous impression of being very old and yet temporary at one and the same time. Similarly, when K. sees the portrait of the official in the first chapter, the face is virtually invisible, being merged with the black background of the painting, the man's hand is unable to raise his head, and that head is bowed so deeply that the eyes, a symbol of life and vitality in *Das Schloß*, are barely visible. This suggests that the Castle which the official represents is all but dead as well. As has been mentioned above,[15] the colours of the dresses of the *Herrenhof* landlady which K. sees in the final chapter and the colours which are most characteristic of the village and the Castle are brown, black and grey. Thus, when K. remarks to himself that the landlady is overdressed, he seems to be saying implicitly that the Castle is 'overdressed' as well, that its authority is nothing more than an extremely impressive illusion concealing something that is far less impressive. But perhaps the most decisive piece of evidence which points to the contingent nature of the Castle authorities is the fact that in the course of K.'s dream during his interview with Bürgel, the Castle authorities are compared with Greek gods who can be made to squeal like girls. Given the special status of the dream in *Das Schloß*, this comparison suggests that this is indeed the case, that the officials *are* of human origin. And, as if he wished to confirm this suspicion, Bürgel himself says to K. that if K. were to ask a specific question ('By what authority?'), he, Bürgel, would have to answer it, even if this action were to reveal the nothingness of the Castle authorities and caused the entire Castle edifice to tear apart at the seams. In one of his *Betrachtungen*, Kafka wrote:

Es wurde ihnen die Wahl gestellt, Könige oder der Könige Kuriere zu werden. Nach der Art der Kinder wollten alle Kuriere sein. Deshalb gibt es lauter Kuriere, sie jagen durch die Welt und rufen, da es keine Könige gibt, einander selbst die sinnlos gewordenen Meldungen zu. Gerne würden sie ihrem elenden Leben ein Ende machen, aber sie wagen es nicht wegen des Diensteides. (H, 44)	*They were given the choice of becoming either kings or the kings' messengers. After the fashion of children, they all wanted to be messengers. For that reason, there is nothing but messengers. They chase through the world, and, as there are no kings, they shout the messages (which have become meaningless) to one another. They would be very glad to put an end to their wretched lives, but they do not dare to do so because of their official oath. (W, 43)*

And there is an unmistakable sense in which the Castle officials

[15] See pp. 54–5 above.

are just such children, rushing self-importantly through the world, calling messages to one another which have become meaningless because of the non-existence of the king.

While this de-mystification of the Castle authorities is undoubtedly a necessary corrective to over-simple interpretations of them as an allegory of God, it seems, paradoxically enough, that neither the extreme transcendental position adopted by Max Brod, nor the extreme sociological reductionism of Klaus-Peter Philippi does justice to the facts of the case as they appear in *Das Schloß*. Despite the contingent character of the Castle, a quality of transcendence haunts that institution, and even after one has argued for the all-too-human character of the officials, a strangely irreducible quality does, I would suggest, still pervade the world which they govern.

Perhaps then, it is worth noting the ambiguity which attaches to the name of the Lord of the Castle, Graf Westwest. Interpreters have pointed out that the sun sets in the 'west' and that the count's name suggests the verb 'verwesen' ('to decay' or 'to decompose'). But, at the same time, the Count's name also suggests the noun 'Wesen' ('essence') and this ambiguity indicates the paradoxical possibility that the Lord of the Castle is both dead and alive, a mere man and yet something more, a humanly created fiction that is in a state of advanced decay and yet the bearer of a metaphysical essence.

This ambiguity is also suggested by an implication of the narrative at the point when K. contemplates the Castle buildings for the first time after his arrival at the village. Here, the text reads as follows:

Und er verglich in Gedanken den Kirchturm der Heimat mit dem Turm dort oben. Jener Turm, bestimmt, ohne Zögern geradewegs nach oben sich verjüngend, breitdächig, abschliessend mit roten Ziegeln, ein irdisches Gebäude— was können wir anderes bauen?— aber mit höherem Ziel als die nied-

And in his mind he compared the church tower at home with the tower up there. The former tower, firm in line, soaring unfalteringly upwards to its tapering point, with a broad roof and topped with red tiles, an earthly building— what else can we build?—but with a loftier goal than the low throng

rige Häusermenge und mit klarerem Ausdruck, als ihn der trübe Werktag hat. (15)	*of houses and with a more clearly expressed meaning than the dismal workaday world possesses. (15)*

The transition from the *er/he* of the first line to the *wir/we* of the sentence in parenthesis is highly significant, for it means that at this point of the narrative, the narrator is leaving his normal detachment from K. and moving extremely close to him in order to associate himself with K.'s thoughts. Thus he addresses the reader indirectly. But the form of words which the narrator chooses in order to make this indirect address is that of an open-ended question, and this in turn suggests that although the Castle is, in one sense, an 'earthly building', there may be something more to it besides. At this one point in the novel when the narrator could tell us something relatively definite about the Castle, could tell us that the Castle is nothing but a crumbling human structure, he chooses to insert a parenthetical aside which leaves the matter open.

The second of our two questions seems at first to lead to a similar ambiguity. As might be expected, those writers who look to the Castle authorities for a religious allegory or see them in religious terms, tend to regard them as benevolent. Herbert Tauber, for instance, writes:

> *The 'cheering up' of K., which is the assistants' appointed task, is intended to reconcile the former to finiteness, to bring him to a trusting attitude towards the Giver of this finiteness, impenetrable fate.*[16]

Throughout his book, Ronald Gray suggests that the power behind the Castle is a benevolent one, working for K.'s good, even if K. is normally too blind to see this. Surprisingly perhaps, Professor Sokel takes this view as well and writes:

Indem er für die Eindeutigkeit der Ereignisse, die zwischen ihm und Frieda stattgefunden, eintritt, be-	*By maintaining that the incidents which have taken place between him and Frieda have a clear-cut*

[16] Tauber, p. 158.

schützt K. nicht nur Friedas Ruf und Würde, sondern auch die objektive, eindeutig feststellbare Menschlichkeit und Erreichbarkeit der Schloßbeamten.[17]

meaning, K. is not defending Frieda's reputation and dignity alone, but also the objective, unequivocally verifiable humanity and approachability of the Castle officials.

and:

Könnte er diese Botschaft, die die Gehilfen mit ihrer kindlichen Ausgelassenheit verkörpern, begreifen lernen, würde er sowohl Frieda behalten als auch die Erwartungen des Schlosses erfüllen. Das Schloß will ihm nichts Übles.[18]

If he could learn to grasp the message which the assistants embody in their childish exuberance, he would keep Frieda and fulfil the expectations of the Castle as well. The Castle has no evil designs upon him.

A considerable body of evidence supports this conclusion. Metaphorically speaking, planks are held out to K. throughout the novel so that he may extricate himself from the deep snow. K.'s experience is so consistently structured for his ultimate good that someone or another does seem to have a positive interest in his fate. The authorities try to bring about a change of heart in K. by parody (the assistants), gifts (Frieda), instruction (Gardena and the teacher) and revelation (the Village Superintendent). Furthermore, it also looks as though Klamm has had a hand in arranging K.'s interview with Gardena during which, as has been shown,[19] K. comes very near to learning the truth about himself and his situation in the village. When K. comes in to see Gardena, he sees her 'white and red'[20] bedspread shimmering in the darkness of her room. Now, red and white are also the colours of the face of Momus, Klamm's village secretary. So, given the special status of colours in *Das*

[17] Sokel, *Franz Kafka: Tragik und Ironie*, pp. 459–60.
[18] Sokel, *Franz Kafka: Tragik und Ironie*, p. 488.
[19] See pp. 40–1 and 60–2 above.
[20] For some reason which is unknown to me, the 'weiß-rote' of the German text is rendered by 'purple' in the Muir translation.

Schloß, Kafka probably wants the reader to make certain connections between the two incidents where those colours occur together, and that connection, is, I suggest, the hand of Klamm. Kafka's use of leitmotivs, parallelisms and mythic events also suggests a similar conclusion. K. continually finds himself confronted with people, objects and situations which say something positive to him about himself and his relationship with the external world. Although it may simply be accidental that K.'s experience has a hidden consistency about it, K. himself dimly senses at times that there is a secret power shaping and directing his experience which emanates from or works through the Castle authorities. Furthermore, although the beneficence of the Castle authorities seems to be denied by the fact that many of K.'s experiences are negative in character, K., it must be noted, is confronted with such experiences (ejection from the *Brückenhof*, dereliction in the *Herrenhof* courtyard, the confusion which is caused by Klamm's second letter, punishment in the school-room, deprivation of Frieda) only when he has failed or refused to profit from gentler and more positive encounters. And even then, those negative experiences contribute positively to that change in K.'s personality which is undeniably for the better.

Erich Heller, of course, takes the diametrically opposed view to this:

> *I do not know of any conceivable idea of divinity which could justify those interpreters who see in the castle the residence of 'divine law and divine grace'. Its officers are totally indifferent to good if they are not positively wicked. Neither in their decrees nor in their activities is there discernible any trace of love, mercy, charity, or majesty. In their icy detachment they inspire certainly no awe, but fear and revulsion.*[21]

Correspondingly, the Kafka critics of the sixties, tending to see the Castle as a purely immanent institution, tend also to regard it as a grandiose version of the repressive father figure, which transmits either no grace at all, or only the faintest glimmerings of grace to those whom it governs. Marthe Robert, for example, accuses the

[21] Heller, p. 196.

Castle of terrorism,[22] says that K.'s almost paranoiac mistrust of the authorities is entirely justified[23] and accuses Klamm of having cruelly chased love out of the village.[24] Wilhelm Emrich suggests that the Castle authorities are lifeless and sick[25] and that Klamm intervenes in the life of K. only in his capacity as a private person.[26] And Klaus-Peter Philippi, adopting the position that the Castle authorities are totally ossified and lifeless, suggests, by implication, that no help of any kind can be expected from them.

Again, there is a certain amount of evidence to support this line of argument. There is undeniably a certain cold and detached in-difference about Klamm. His treatment of Gardena and K. can be seen as actively callous. The Castle's treatment of Amalia and the Barnabas family can be regarded as monstrous. Many of the officials who K. meets or hears about during the course of the novel seem sick or ineffectual, and the effect which the Castle has on the simple village-folk could well be described as deadening, repressive or conducive to keeping them in a state of bestiality.

But, having said all that, the reader has to ask himself very care-fully whether the evil and frustrations which he hears about in *Das Schloß* are due to an inherent malice on the part of the authorities or to a failure of response and insight on the part of the 'victim'? The whole point of the preceding chapter was to show how K.'s frustrations are largely the result of a wilful refusal on his part to accept 'the gifts of grace' that he is offered, and the same is true of Gardena's 'sickness of heart'. Klamm appears to have had a hand in providing her with a good husband, a home and a job, but instead of concentrating on and being grateful for these, she, like K., chases after illusions and wounds herself deeply in the process. Likewise, as Herbert Tauber also argues,[27] it is the inability of the Barnabas family to overcome their dispiritedness that brings about the extremity of their ruin, and Olga confirms this by saying that if they had returned to their old way of life, as other families had

[22] Robert, p. 244.
[23] Robert, p. 273.
[24] Robert, p. 283.
[25] Emrich, p. 325.
[26] Emrich, p. 321.
[27] Tauber, p. 166.

done on previous occasions (303), the whole Sortini affair would have been forgotten as soon as possible. Then again, as has been discussed at some length, it is questionable whether Sortini's treatment of Amalia can be ascribed simply to malevolence on his part, and possible that the real evil lies in Amalia's hubritic attitude to people in general. Finally, although the Castle does seem to exercise considerable repression over the inhabitants of the village, they seem, for the most part, to accept the situation as though they were in general happy to live in 'a zoo built according to the most up-to-date principles'. As Frieda says to Jeremias towards the end of the novel: supposing that K. had negated everything, what would have been gained? Apart from the Castle, there appears to be nothing in the village, and the villagers, who are perpetually compared to children, seem to need the Castle to still their metaphysical hunger just as the children round the table at the end of the sixth chapter need their blue-eyed father to help them forget their physical hunger. The innermost voice of the Castle sounds to K. through the telephone like the collective song of children, and that song may need the total, if dilapidated structures of the Castle if it is to be sung at all. Such arguments have, of course, been used to justify the worst excesses of fascism and all kinds of obscurantism, but the Castle authorities do not seem to be viciously fascist. They seem to have no police or soldiery at their disposal, they can tolerate the huge waste of time and effort which their system involves, and they do not seem to be worried by Schwarzer's continual dereliction of duty for the sake of his affair with Gisa.

All of which seems to lead to a doubly and irreducibly paradoxical conclusion. On the basis of what the reader is told, the Castle appears to be all-too-human and yet endowed with divine powers of observation and intervention; to be both benevolent and malevolent. Because the Castle is so complex and ambiguous a phenomenon, it is not surprising that some commentators seem to compound confusion when they try to define its status. Thus, Marthe Robert, apparently unaware that she is contradicting herself, claims that the Castle is actively malevolent[28] and yet implies that it is in some respects benevolent seeing that it does not chase K. out of the

28 Robert, p. 273.

village even though he has no official right to stay there.[29] She claims that the Castle exercises a secret power over the villagers' lives[30] and yet concludes in the last few pages of her book that it is a *Neutrum*:

Le Château est neutre, il entérine les initiatives individuelles, prend note de ce qui se passe et se fait, mais n'intervient pas dans le cours des événements . . .[31]	*The Castle is neutral, it ratifies individual initiatives, takes note of what happens and what is done, but it does not intervene in the course of events . . .*

Walter Sokel too can talk of the Castle, again without appearing to sense the contradiction, both as a repressive social edifice and as a benign quasi-divinity.[32] Other commentators, less aware than Mme Robert or Walter Sokel of the complexities surrounding the Castle, ignore what does not accord with their interpretation and simply opt for one aspect of the paradox. Similarly, it must have seemed at times as though the present writer was entangling himself in the same contradictions, for within this book, the Castle has been spoken of both as human and as divine, both as a benevolent presence and as a destructive force.

Consequently, it appears that the reader of *Das Schloß* is faced with three equally unsatisfactory and frustrating alternatives for understanding the status of the Castle. It appears that he can choose either finely balanced ambiguity, or pointless contradictoriness, or over-simplification. Nevertheless, there is a way out of this apparent *impasse*, and the discovery of this way is inseparable from an appreciation of the peculiar narrative structure of *Das Schloß*—a characteristic of the novel which critic after critic (Erich Heller, for example) either ignores, or registers and then forgets. To put it briefly, the reliability of information about the Castle is inseparably bound up with the way in which it reaches the reader. It is therefore illegitimate to assume that any given item of information is comparable, without more ado, with any other item of information or to talk

[29] Robert, p. 196.
[30] Robert, p. 243.
[31] Robert, p. 294.
[32] See footnotes 11 and 17 of this chapter.

about the Castle in the abstract without paying close attention to the source from which the information in question has come.

The reader of *Das Schloß* knows the Castle under three aspects. He knows it as K. experiences it; he knows it as K. interprets that experience; and he knows it as K. hears about it from other people. Or, to put it another way, the reader knows the Castle as K. encounters it directly; he knows it as K. projects his own preconceptions upon it; and he knows it, via K., as the object of local folklore. Again, Marthe Robert's work implies that she understands these distinctions, but because her very stimulating analysis of *Das Schloß* pays relatively little attention to narrative structure, she turns distinctions between categories of information into unresolved contradictions. Thus, she can look at the officials as gods,[33] yet speak of the Castle administration as though it were nothing but a man-made organisation and affirm that the Castle is simply a product of K.'s fantasy.[34]

K.'s interpretation of his experience of the Castle differs from the reality of his experience of the Castle in two ways. On the one hand, as has been argued,[35] K. evolves an image of the Castle as a malevolent, super-efficient and monolithically purposeful bureaucracy which is not legitimised by his actual experience of the Castle authorities. And on the other hand, K. is blind to the mythic dimension of the Castle authorities to which frequent reference has been made. Thus, despite the image of the Castle which exists in K.'s mind, no one tries to eject him from the village or deprive him of anything that is not properly his, and nobody engages in any struggle with K. which he has not initiated himself. Indeed, it is possible to go further and to say that for all K.'s grandiose mental picture of the Castle, that institution, as a bureaucratic machine, is singularly ineffectual. Administratively, it rarely intervenes in K.'s life, and when it does so, its interventions are usually pointless. Thus, from the point of view of administrative efficiency, Klamm's first letter is vague to the point of uselessness and his second letter meaningless. The choice of Barnabas as messenger is, administratively, a

[33] Robert, pp. 224–5.
[34] Robert, pp. 248 and 307.
[35] See pp. 63–5 above.

mockery and the assistants do anything but assist in their official capacity. From the point of view of officialdom, it seems immaterial whether K. co-operates with Momus or not. The Village Superintendent's office is one huge muddle. Erlanger's directive that Frieda should return to the *Herrenhof* tap-room comes at a point when she has already done so. And just before K.'s interview with Bürgel, Frieda is said to be amazed that K. keeps talking instead of taking her by the arm—an indication perhaps that even at this late stage in the narrative, K. could have carried off Frieda again without any interference from the officials.

Furthermore, although the officials present themselves to K.'s experience as mythic beings who invite him to undergo elemental experiences of death and rebirth, K. is consistently blind to that aspect of his experience and neglects it when he has to interpret his experience. As has been argued, there is a pattern in K.'s experience of which K. himself is ignorant. Throughout the novel, the authorities seem to be trying to tell K. how it is possible to live fully and creatively within the Castle world, to be using official channels or everyday experience in order to communicate a message whose import is more than official and more than immediate. Thus, although Klamm's letters are administratively absurd, both of them tell K. something about himself as a person. Although the assistants and Barnabas are useless from an official point of view, both have something vital to say to K. Although Erlanger's directive is futile, what K. hears about Erlanger communicates something to him about the real meaning of his descent into the *Herrenhof*. Although K. learns little or nothing that is reliable about the workings of the Castle administration during his interview with the Village Superintendent, there are elements in his experience during that interview which impart much more fundamental information to K. about the status of the Castle bureaucracy.

Throughout *Das Schloß*, the officials present themselves to K. under two complementary aspects to both of which K. is blind. They are simultaneously the ineffectual administrators of a man-made bureaucratic system and *agents not allegories* of a power working actively for K.'s good. K.'s prejudices, however, prevent his interpretation of the Castle authorities from doing justice to their twofold nature and it is only when K. has died to his prejudices, rid himself of his obsessive image of the Castle that he becomes capable of developing an attitude towards the Castle which is appropriate to its ambiguous nature. Only after K. has penetrated to the 'goodness' which lies behind his image of a massive father-figure, does K. learn to be indifferent towards the officials as the executives of an administration and respectful towards them as 'the impenetrable executives of Providence'.[36]

Many of the villagers whom K. meets seem similarly incapable of appreciating that the Castle operates at two levels. Indeed, some, notably Frieda and Gardena, are caught in the vicious trap of paying the kind of respect to the officials as men which is properly due to them only in their capacity as agents. Because Gardena is mesmerised by her memory of Klamm the man, she fails to see how Klamm, in his capacity as an agent of Providence, is working to free her from himself. Because Frieda has excessive respect for the institutions and taboos of the Castle world, she fails to see that the Castle may desire to liberate her, through a relationship with K., from those selfsame institutions and taboos. Because the village girls are flattered by the attentions of the officials as men, Amalia is censured for not sleeping with Sortini the man, and the real significance of Amalia's act, her implied rejection of the mythic experience of death and rebirth, seems to get overlooked. (Incidentally, this same confusion underlies Max Brod's interpretation of the Amalia episode. Because Sortini the man and Sortini the demi-god are merged in Brod's mind, the refusal of Sortini's bed becomes *in itself* the refusal of divine grace. In contrast, it might have been more helpful to regard Amalia's refusal of Sortini's bed simply as one indication among many that Amalia is refusing to be human.) Because Mizzi regards the Castle administration as a necessary but man-made fiction and seems to serve it out of that spirit, she can only tell K. of the emptiness of that fiction. What she cannot do is tell K. of a creative power from beyond which works through that fiction. Finally, because the teacher's respect is directed to the officials as men and to their institutions as human institutions, he, like the *Herrenhof* landlady, is aggressive and authoritarian in his

<hr>

[36] Compare Tauber, p. 133.

14

guardianship of those institutions. If Count Westwest, the all-too-human divinity, is dead, then the children must not know of it, for in the view of the teacher, besides the institutions whose central figure he is, there is nothing. Thus, if the world of the Castle and village looks bleak because of K.'s failure to comprehend adequately what he sees, then that world is made doubly bleak by the persistent failure of others of its inhabitants to understand that a power of good may flow through it secretly and work through them obliquely.

Surprisingly enough, in view of his damning judgement on the Castle, Erich Heller seems to have recognised something of that secret power which flows through the Castle and its executives. Having suggested that Kafka's fictional world is the symbol of a real world which 'has been all but completely sealed off against any transcendental intrusion',[37] and having demolished any suggestion that the Castle authorities can be equated with God, he goes on to say:

> . . . although the cursed rule of the castle is the furthest point of the world to which his wakeful mind can reach, there dawns, at its extreme boundaries, a light, half suspectingly perceived, half stubbornly ignored, that comes from things outside the scope of Klamm's authority.[38]

The choice of the word 'light' is particularly apposite, for the light of which Heller speaks here is the light which appears from behind the Law in Kafka's parable *Vor dem Gesetz (Before the Law)* and the light which K. perceives in the blue of the sky behind the Castle buildings when first he sees them:

Nun sah er oben das Schloß deutlich unrissen in der klaren Luft und noch verdeutlicht durch den alle Formen nachbildenden, in dünner Schicht überall liegenden Schnee. (14)	*Now he could see the Castle above him clearly outlined in the clear air, its form made even more distinct by the thin layer of snow which lay everywhere, forming a crust over everything. (15)*

[37] Heller, p. 188.
[38] Heller, pp. 199–200.

Der Turm hier oben . . . war ein einförmiger Rundbau, zum Teil gnädig von Efeu verdeckt, mit kleinen Fenstern, die jetzt in der Sonne aufstrahlten . . ., und einem söllerartigen Abschluß, dessen Mauerzinnen . . . sich in den blauen Himmel zackten. (15)	*The tower up above him here . . . was uniformly round, and, mercifully, concealed in part by ivy, pierced by small windows which were glittering now in the sun . . ., and topped by a kind of garret, the crenellation . . . of which stood out jaggedly against the blue sky. (15-16)*

But, having noticed that, it is possible to go further than Erich Heller is prepared to, and to say not simply that that light and that blueness are visible *behind* the Castle, at the farthest corner of the Castle world, but also that they are to be found *within* the world of the village. For instance, when K. reaches his point of greatest dereliction at the end of the eighth chapter, the narrator says explicitly that even after all the electric lights had been extinguished in the *Herrenhof* courtyard, a faint gleam of light still remained visible from the wooden gallery above, providing a certain point of stability for K.'s wandering gaze. Although K. then overlooks this one remaining gleam of light, its very existence seems to suggest that even after K. has done his utmost to antagonise the Castle authorities to the limit of their endurance and has cut off all official connections with them, they still refuse to break off all unofficial contact with him. Throughout *Das Schloß*, K., when he is out in the open and away from the harsh artificial glare which illuminates the inside of many of the village buildings, encounters similar 'guiding lights'. The assistants above all are associated with lanterns, and although their lanterns are described as 'schwankend' ('bobbing', 'swaying', 'unsteady'), the very nature of these lanterns seems to symbolise the fluctuating, sporadic and secret ways in which positive influences are at work on K.'s personality and within the world of the village. Similarly, it is perhaps not too much to suggest that the blue which K. sees in the eyes of Olga and the man who sits at table with his children at the end of the sixth chapter is also the blue which he had seen behind the jagged turrets of the Castle.[39]

---

[39] Surprisingly enough, we never hear the colour of Frieda's eyes.

Admittedly, it takes K., 'the man from the country', a long time to sense the presence of the 'beyond' amid the 'self-sufficient finitude' of the Castle world. Consequently, it takes the reader an even longer time to develop the same sense. Nevertheless, it is possibly that sense which caused Wilhelm Emrich to add the qualification 'oder stark eingeschränkt' ('or greatly diminished') to his statement quoted above[40] and Marthe Robert to concede at one or two points that the Castle may not be entirely evil.

It is often assumed that the fact that K.'s perspective monopolises the foreground of *Das Schloß* is a cause for despair, an indication that nothing can be said about the world of the village and Castle with any certainty. If, however, the reader is prepared to devote close study to the text, then that very limitation may become an advantage. K. sees more than he is aware of seeing, and if the reader can accustom himself to looking for those elements in K.'s experience which K. himself overlooks or leaves out of account, then there appears, behind and through the mind of K., a world of mythic beings and archetypal events which work together for the benefit of those people who are open to their power. Perversely paradoxical though the claim may seem, Klamm, the assistants, Sortini and the rest are, in their strange ways, the agents of a power that is benevolent at the same time as they are, respectively, the bureaucrat who helps mesmerise the villagers, the tormentors of K. and the lecherous pursuer of the village women. Outrageous though the claim may seem, a power which invites people to become what they are meant to be is working upon K. through the labyrinthine medium of the ossified Castle bureaucracy, upon Frieda through her relationship with the stronger K. and upon Amalia through the apparently destructive medium of Sortini's lust. Absurd though the claim may seem, the neurotic, childish and frequently inhuman officials are the executives of a power of enlightenment, even if that light is, as often as not, obscured by the neuroses, infantilism and apparent inhumanity through which it has to travel before it can reach its fore-ordained destination.

The foregoing analysis should, if nothing else, have helped to modify the idea that it is a question in *Das Schloß* of a simple

[40] See footnote 12 of this chapter.

opposition between a 'good' heroic K. and a 'bad' Castle authority, or between a malevolently assertive K. and a godlike and benevolent Castle authority. In reality, the relationship between K. and the Castle authorities is much more complicated, and it is with a brief consideration of this relationship that this chapter will conclude.

If the preceding argument holds good, then K. should not be regarded as an existential hero on the Sartrean model, or rather, if he is regarded as such, this should be taken as an indication of the mistakenness of his way of life rather than its commendability. In a recent article in which he relates Kafka to Sartre's existential philosophy,[41] Walter Sokel describes Sartre's picture of the 'human condition' and Kafka's image of man thrown into a world of tortured uncertainty, and concludes that there is a:

. . . *Gleichstimmigkeit der beiden Autoren und ihrer Seh- und Darstellungsweise der menschlichen Realität.*[42]	. . . *close similarity between the two authors and between the way in which they see and depict reality.*

According to Sokel, K. is the archetypal existential hero, who, compelled to make sense of a world in which there is nothing given, no essence and no *a priori* meaning to existence, does so by creating an identity for himself:

K., von dessen Vergangenheit und Motivierung wir nichts Bestimmtes kennen und daher auch nichts ihn Bestimmendes, ist identisch mit seinem Vorhaben. Abgesehen davon ist K. nichts.[43]	*We know nothing determinate about K.'s past and motivation: we therefore know nothing about the circumstances which have determined him. K. is identical with his intention and nothing apart from that.*

[41] Walter H. Sokel, 'Kafka und Sartres Existenzphilosophie', *Arcadia* 5, 1970, pp. 262–77.
[42] Sokel, *Kafka und Sartre*, p. 265.
[43] Sokel, *Kafka und Sartre*, p. 271.

Er muß sich selbst eine Funktion, eine Stellung als Stelle, er muß sich selbst Natur und Wesen geben. Auch bei ihm geht Existenz der Essenz voran.[44]	*He has to give himself a function, a position as a place in life; he has to provide himself with a nature and an essence. For K. too, existence precedes essence.*

By now, the weakness of this position should be obvious. Sokel talks here as though K.'s perspective were identical with Kafka's: as though Kafka were endorsing K.'s way of seeing and doing things. In contrast, this book has tried to show that K.'s vision is initially much narrower than that of the narrator who stands behind him, and that, as the novel progresses, K. comes to realise that the world around him which he had assumed was a featureless nothingness has a secret life of its own, is full of hidden signs which could reveal to him, among other things, who he really is. Where Sartre and K. posit 'le néant', Kafka posits 'le tout'. Then again, it is not true to say that K. is identical with his intention. As has been shown, K. is more than an amalgam of conscious mind and intentional will, and as the novel progresses, so K. begins to discover something of that *a priori* essence whose existence Walter Sokel seems to doubt. Indeed, *Das Schloß* could be said to represent the complete rebuttal of Sartrean existentialism. Using as his central character a man whose assumptions, it is true, are remarkably like those of the Sartre who wrote *L'Etre et le Néant*, Kafka proceeds to demonstrate the inadequacy of those assumptions.

Nor is K. a Prometheus who has consciously come to free an oppressed community from a collection of omnipotent but flippant gods. K. arrives in the village with a propensity for struggle. He therefore projects his own aggressiveness onto the Castle and villagers without any justification for doing so. The result of this is that he derives a neurotic and precarious 'negative identity' from his fantastic struggle with a Castle which is, to a great extent, the product of his own imagination. Despite K.'s cryptic remarks about his final aims and his general air of messianic purposiveness, the fact is that K., far from wanting to break the hold of the Castle over himself and the villagers, actually needs to believe in the mono-

[44] Sokel, *Kafka und Sartre*, p. 274.

lithic oppressiveness of the Castle so that his false identity as a victimised land-surveyor and his obsessive struggles may be legitimised and perpetuated. Out of this spirit, K. says to himself towards the end of the second chapter that he preferred those villagers who sent him away or were afraid of him to the Barnabas family who offered him hospitality. Whereas the antagonism of the former helped him to concentrate his powers, the friendliness of the latter diverted him and contributed to the dissipation of those powers. Appearances to the contrary, it actually makes life simpler for K. if he demonises the Castle, for by so doing, he can avoid seeing the complexity of the experiences which he undergoes in the village. This vicious circle, in all its childish simplicity, is only broken because the Castle authorities, being more than the 'subjective projection' of an 'absolute' aim of K.'s own',[45] act as the agents of a power from beyond themselves which cuts into K.'s wilfulness and opens up what appears to be a hopeless situation.

Nevertheless, the Promethean, messianic image which K. presents to the world is convincing enough to worry some of the villagers and encourage others. The landladies and the teacher, those guardians of the myth of the Castle's absolute and unassailable authority, are seriously agitated by the implications of K.'s behaviour, for they know that if he is what he appears to be and persists in his struggles, then he will destroy Castle society. What they fail to realise, however, is that K. needs the Castle, that he has arrived in the village without any real purpose and that he himself is unaware of the threat which his behaviour poses to the system. K.'s unawareness shows itself fairly early on in the novel when he sees that he has disturbed Gardena in some way and begins, metaphorically speaking, to 'open the door' to some ultimate knowledge about the frailty of the apparently impregnable Castle authorities:

».. . was fürchten Sie also? [sagte K.] Sie fürchten doch nicht etwa —dem Unwissenden scheint alles möglich«, hier öffnete K. schon die

'. . . so what are you afraid of? [said K.] You're surely not afraid —everything seems possible to an ignorant man', at this point K.

[45] Philippi, p. 223.

Tür—, »*Sie fürchten doch nicht*   *was already opening the door*—,
etwa für Klamm?« *(84)*   'You're surely not afraid for
                                        Klamm?" *(59)*

But Gardena does not admit that this is so, and because ultimate
knowledge is not K.'s aim, he does not pursue the point and carries
on much as he had done before. Similarly, in Chapter Nine, Gardena mentions that everyone is afraid 'um Klamm', 'for Klamm',
and does their best to protect him. Then again, right at the end of
the book, the *Herrenhof* landlady betrays her fear of K. and tries to
elicit from him, by asking him about her clothes, just how far he is
conscious of the implications of his earlier conduct. K., she says,
is either a fool or a child or a very wicked, dangerous person. And
although he may be nothing but the former, the possibility remains
that he may be the latter, that he may be dedicated to discovering
that the Castle is in one sense nothing and to liberating the village
from its frail authority by means of that knowledge. But the *Herrenhof* landlady need not have worried, for one of the great ironies of
Das Schloß is that K., despite his appearance of messianic assertiveness, is no messiah and all but completely innocent of the depth of
fear that he has the power to cause in the minds of the guardians
of the myth.

Conversely, during his stay in the village, K. meets several people
who seem to need a messiah figure to liberate them from the con-
strictions of village society. Although Frieda has been sent by
Klamm to 'still K.'s hunger' (during their first night on the *Herrenhof* floor, she sings a little song to K. just as the collective voice of
the Castle sings a song down the telephone and the blue-eyed father
sings to his children), she discovers that she needs K. to exorcise her
childishness just as much as K. needs her love, and immediately
before their final parting, K. remarks to Frieda on his ability to free
her from illusions. The Barnabas family, too, regard K. as a kind of
saviour. From the outset, this family, alone of the villagers, welcome
K., and Olga tells him that he has come to mean almost more to
her than all of Barnabas' work in the Castle. To quote Wilhelm
Emrich:

K. hat die Aufgabe, Olga und Amalia ins Leben zurückzuführen, ohne ihre höhere kritische Bewußtseinsstufe zu opfern.[46]	*K. has the task of bringing Olga and Amalia back into life without sacrificing their higher critical faculties.*

During the interview with Gardena, K. cuts through the self-deceptions and illusions with which she has palliated her inner pain for years in a way that none of the villagers could, and young Hans Brunswick implies that he regards K. as a man who will do great things. When K. first looks at the peasants in the second chapter, he feels that they want something which he does not understand, and although it may be a delusion, it is just possible that they half-expect K. to act as a kind of saviour in Castle society. Furthermore, more than one hint is given that the officials themselves would like K. to tear down the dead structures of the Castle in the same way that the messengers in Kafka's *Betrachtung* would like someone to put an end to their meaningless official lives.[47] Bürgel describes the possibility of the destruction of the Castle apparatus with something of the lascivious eagerness of a voluptuary contemplating an orgasm, and concludes:

. . . wie wird es aber nachher sein, wenn es vorüber ist, die Partei, gesättigt und unbekümmert, uns verläßt und wir dastehen, allein, wehrlos im Angesicht unseres Amtsmißbrauches—das ist gar nicht auszudenken! Und trotzdem sind wir glücklich. Wie selbstmörderisch das Glück sein kann! (390)	*. . . but how will it be afterwards, when it is all over, when, sated and free of care, the applicant leaves us and we stand there, alone, defenceless in the face of our misuse of official power—that does not bear thinking about! And yet we are happy. How suicidal happiness can be! (253)*

When K. finds himself in the corridor outside after this interview, one of the officials begins to crow like a cock, a sound which perhaps means that the officials are both celebrating K.'s awakening *and*

---

[46] Emrich, p. 373.
[47] See p. 197 above.

pointing to the possibility that they have been betrayed. The man who can cause them so much discomfort has, in the end, failed to destroy them. But, despite the hints that are given him, K. is as impervious to the fact that the village needs a kind of messianic figure as he is to the fears of the landladies that he may be one. Because he is obsessed by his egocentric struggle with an opponent who is largely imaginary, K. is unaware of the wider possibilities inherent in that struggle. Another of the great ironies of *Das Schloß* is that the village seems to need a man of K.'s intelligence who could pierce the mystification which surrounds the Castle authorities, but K. has neither the vision to see the necessity of that task, nor the sense of responsibility to those who would suffer as a result of such surgery, nor the compassion towards those who need a healing herb that is not 'bitter'.[48] Thus, the bowed heads and averted eyes which K. uncomprehendingly encounters as he moves through the world of the Castle[49] perhaps signify respect for him as a potential messiah, fear of him as a potential destroyer of the system and shame for him as one who is ignorant both of his potential ability and of his potential destructiveness.

The relationship between K. and the world of the Castle seems therefore to have two levels. At one level, because the Castle is the indirect agent of a benevolent power, its representatives seek to turn K. from his aimless, solipsistic striving and to reconcile him with himself and the village. But, because the Castle is, at a second level, a decrepit human institution, its officials secretly desire K.

[48] The reference is to K.'s long conversation with Hans Brunswick, during which it transpires that K. has considerable abilities as a doctor and was known as 'the bitter herb' before he came to the village. Although there is no direct connection between Kafka and St. John of the Cross, the following extract from the Spanish mystic's *Spiritual Canticle* may, in view of the comments in the preceding sections on K.'s wilfulness, shed some indirect and coincidental light upon K.'s strange nickname:

The wormwood, a most bitter herb, refers to the will, because to this faculty belongs the sweetness of the possession of God. When this possession is lacking, the will is left in bitterness.

The Collected Works of St. John of the Cross, E. T. K. Kavanagh and O. Rodrigues, London, 1966, p. 427.

[49] For instance, the peasants run from K. with averted faces in the first chapter. Lasemann bows his head before K. later on in the same chapter. The landlord at the *Brückenhof* bows his head before K. at the beginning of the sixth chapter. Barnabas lowers his eyes before K. in the tenth chapter.

to become aware of the revolutionary implications of his conduct and to destroy their bureaucratic system which is, by any standards, rotten. These two levels interpenetrate throughout the novel. On the one hand, the Castle does not exist and K. is an adult in a world of children because his conduct suggests, deceptively as it turns out, that he realises this metaphysical truth. On the other hand, the Castle does exist and K. is a child in a world of adults because he wilfully refuses to see the transcendent quality of bene-volence which operates obliquely, through the Castle authorities and the institutions of the village.

Marthe Robert writes of *Das Schloß*:

Entre toutes les possibilités que lui offre le Château, Kafka ne sait pas plus que K. ce qu'il décide de choisir: il reste en suspens, aussi clairvoyant qu'irrésolu, condamné à tout comprendre sans jamais prendre un parti. De là vient la beauté si captivante de son œuvre, mais aussi le sens réactionnaire, si ce n'est politiquement dan-géreux de son message.[50]

Kafka has no more idea than K. which of the possibilities offered him by the Castle he will decide to choose. He remains in suspense, as clear-sighted as he is irresolute, condemned to understand every-thing without ever committing himself to anything. From that arises not only the captivating beauty of his work but also the reactionary and even politically dangerous tendency of its message.

Although it is not all difficult to see why Mme Robert should have passed this judgement on the novel, it may be somewhat misplaced. K., it is true, chooses nothing, but there is a very real sense in which events and experiences choose K. in order to bring about a change in his personality, and an equally real sense in which the agents of this change are the elusive beings who inhabit the Castle. If then *Das Schloß* is, politically speaking, a conservative and even a reactionary novel, it needs to be understood that its conservatism is of a very peculiar order. During his career as a writer, Kafka de-veloped a very subtle sense that, despite all evidence to the contrary, the world as it stood had a life of its own, that there was, in the end,

[50] Robert, p. 194.

a rightness about the way in which the world was moving, and that the greatest mistakes a man could make were to ignore or to impede that movement. Hence the question mark which finally hangs over *Das Schloß*. There is a sense in which the world of the Castle is in need of a social revolution, and yet, Kafka seems to suggest, perhaps that action would have the effect of irreparably destroying the channels through which a kind of grace still flows. The village community is in need of a messianic figure—but it needs someone who, unlike K., understands the secret workings of that community, knows that a revolutionary movement might disrupt or interfere with those workings and is prepared to accept the responsibility which such knowledge brings. In an indirect way, *Das Schloß* is about the problem of revolution and the strange conclusion that Kafka seems to reach is that revolution can only take place on the basis of a willingness to accept what already exists. K., for most of the novel, does not possess this quality of acceptance and learns it only when he is near his death. Thus, for the want of a revolutionary who understands the depths of the problem of revolution,[51] the Castle, ramshackle yet transparent, all-too-human and yet the executive of a kind of Providence, is permitted to stand.

[51] An illuminating parallel to Kafka's apparent position on the subject of revolution is provided by Albert Camus, who, in *L'Homme révolté (The Rebel)* distinguishes between 'rebellion' and 'revolution', the 'rebel' and the 'revolutionary'. According to Camus, the revolutionary fails to acknowledge history by attempting to impose ideas upon his situation which are alien to that situation but which, he mistakenly assumes, will bring a final solution to that situation. The rebel, on the other hand, acknowledges history by utilising the forces for revolutionary change which are already at work within his situation and is prepared to overthrow the new situation in turn when that becomes ossified. Whereas the rebel 'starts from a negative supported by an affirmative', the revolutionary starts 'from absolute negation and is condemned to fabricate an affirmative which is dismissed until the end of time'. (Albert Camus, *The Rebel*, London, 1962, p. 217.) Thus, K. can be described as a 'revolutionary' who, by the end of *Das Schloß*, is beginning to see that the implication of his way of life is total nihilism, the negation of everything out of attachment to a pre-existent set of ideas which cannot do justice to the complexities of reality.

APPENDIX

Das Schloß – *A brief chronology*

Kafka himself says next to nothing about the history of *Das Schloß*. What follows, represents an attempt to summarise the findings of recent research into the origins and chronology of *Das Schloß*.

11.vi.1914 (Diary entry) A short sketch entitled *Verlockung im Dorf (Temptation in the Village)*. Although it would be too much to say that this fragment amounted to a preliminary sketch for *Das Schloß*, it does seem fair to say that it anticipates the novel to the extent that it deals with the situation of a stranger who arrives in a village but is unable to find hospitality at the inn there.[1]

1916/1917 Intensive work on Schopenhauer. (See especially WV, 156 or WI, 128).[2]

1917/1918 Five instances of the image of the castle or royal palace occur in Kafka's writings.[3] Namely:

Spring 1917 In the two stories: *Ein altes Blatt (An old Leaf)* and *Eine kaiserliche Botschaft (An imperial Missive)*.

29.vii.1917 (Diary entry) The king comes into the shop where Franz is working in the darkness and summons him to move into the castle.

1917/early 1918 Two sketches for stories in the Octavo Notebooks (H, 130 and H, 160) contain references to the business of gaining entry to a Castle.

---

[1] See Max Brod, '*The Castle:* Its Genesis.' In: *Franz Kafka Today*, Angel Flores and Homer Swander (eds.), Madison, 1962, p. 161. In this essay, Brod also draws attention to similarities between *Das Schloß* and Božena Němcová's novel *Babička (The Grandmother)* which Kafka had read during his youth.

[2] See Reed, p. 168.

[3] See Reed, pp. 168–9.

March 1920 to May 1922 Kafka's affair with Milena which almost certainly had an effect upon *Das Schloß*.[4]

1921 No reference made to *Das Schloß* anywhere in Kafka's writings.

29.i.1922 (Diary entry) The mood of this entry, made in the village of Spindelmühle where he was staying for his health, is very reminiscent of the mood of *Das Schloß*.

Spring 1922 (Letter to Robert Klopstock (B, 374)) Says that he has begun to write a little in order to protect himself from 'nerves'.

15.iii.1922 Reads the first chapter of *Das Schloß* to Max Brod.

May/June 1922 (Letter to Robert Klopstock (B, 374)) Says that he would like to hide himself away with his notebooks for at least a year and speak to no one.

12.vii.1922 (Letter to Max Brod (B, 392)) *Und das Schreiben? (Das übrigens hier unter-mittelmäßig weitergeht, sonst nichts, und immerfort von Lärm gefährdet.) . . . Ich bin von zuhause fort und muß immerfort nachhause schreiben, auch wenn alles Zuhause längst fortgeschwommen sein sollte in die Ewigkeit. Dieses ganze Schreiben ist nichts als die Fahne des Robinson auf dem höchsten Punkt der Insel.*

And my writing? (while, I may add, is going forward here at a less than average rate and is continually imperilled by the noise) . . . I am away from home and have continually to write home, even if it turns out that everything resembling a home has long ago dissolved into eternity. All this writing is nothing other than the flag which Robinson has placed on the highest point of his island.

20.vii.1922 (Letter to Max Brod (B, 392)) Refers to his notebook which, he says, exists to be written—not to be read.

c.20.vii.1922 (Letter from Max Brod) Brod indicates here that he had read Chapters Eight and Nine of the novel.

---

[4] For this and the following details I am entirely indebted to Malcolm Pasley and Klaus Wagenbach, 'Versuch einer Datierung sämtlicher Texte Franz Kafkas', *DVjS*, 38, 1964, p. 159.

10.ix.1922 (Letter to Max Brod (B, 413)) Says that he has had to put down the 'castle-story', apparently for ever, as he had been unable to begin work on it again after the 'breakdown' which had begun a week before his journey to Prague.

The following stories of Kafka's were written during the period (January to September 1922) when he was working most intensively on *Das Schloß*: *Erstes Leid* (*First Sorrow*), *Ein Hungerkünstler* (*A Hunger Artist*), *Der Aufbruch* (*The Uprising*), *Fürsprecher* (*Advocates*), *Forschungen eines Hundes* (*Researches of a Dog*).[5]

3.vi.1924 Death of Kafka in a sanatorium near Vienna.
1926 First publication of the German edition of *Das Schloß*.
1930 First publication of the Muir translation of *Das Schloß*.

[5] For other possible origins of the castle image in Kafka's mind see Malcolm Pasley, 'Zur Entstehungsgeschichte von Franz Kafkas Schloß-Bild' in *Weltfreunde*, Eduard Goldstuecker (ed.), Prague, 1967, pp. 241–51. Here Mr. Pasley mentions three real castles (Friedland, Wossek and The Hradschin) which may possibly have made an impression on Kafka and draws attention to several literary castles and palaces (e.g. the two castles in Comenius' *Labyrinth der Welt*, the royal palace in *Salomon Maimons Lebensgeschichte*, the palace in Vol. II of *Sagen der Juden*, the two castles in Kleist's *Michael Kohlhaas* and the vision of the Temple in the Book of the prophet Ezekiel) which may have contributed to the development of the image in Kafka's mind.

A SELECT BIBLIOGRAPHY OF
DAS SCHLOß

(Not all the works listed below have been consulted during the preparation of this book).

A. *Books devoted entirely to Das Schloß*

GRAY, Ronald D., *Kafka's Castle*, Cambridge, 1956.

NEUMEYER, Peter F. (ed.), *Twentieth Century Interpretations of The Castle: A Collection of Critical Essays*, Prentice-Hall, Englewood Cliffs, 1969.

PHILIPPI, Klaus-Peter, *Reflexion und Wirklichkeit: Untersuchungen zu Kafkas Roman 'Das Schloß'*, Tübingen, 1966.

B. *Articles, Parts of Books and Reviews dealing with Das Schloß*

ALMÁSI, Miklós, 'Diskussion in Kafkas Schloß', *Littérature et réalité*, Budapest, 1966, pp. 204–215.

ARENDT, Hannah, *Sechs Essays*, Heidelberg, 1948, pp. 134–7.

BEST, Otto E., 'Zwei Mal Schule der Körperbeherrschung und drei Schriftsteller', *Modern Language Notes*, 85, 1970, pp. 727–41.

BRAYBROOKE, Neville, 'Celestial Castles: An Approach to Saint Teresa and Franz Kafka', *Dublin Review*, 229, 1955, pp. 427–45.

BROD, Max, 'Bemerkungen zu Kafkas "Schloß"', *Neue Züricher Zeitung*, 20 October 1951, p. 5.

———, 'Eine Bemerkung zu Kafkas "Schloß"', *Franz Kafka: Eine Biographie*, New York, Schocken Books ed., 1962, pp. 334–9.

———, '"The Castle": Its Genesis', *Franz Kafka Today*, Angel Flores and Homer Swander (eds.), Madison, 1962, pp. 161–4.

———, 'The Homeless Stranger', *The Kafka Problem*, Angel Flores (ed.), New York, 1946, pp. 179–80.

CHASTEL, André, Review of *Das Schloß*, *Cahiers du Sud*, 26–27 March 1940, pp. 193–8.

CHURCH, Margaret, 'Time and Reality in Kafka's "The Trial" and "The Castle"', *Twentieth Century Literature*, 2, July 1956, pp. 62–9.

COHN, Dorrit, 'K. enters "The Castle": On the Change of Perspective in Kafka's Manuscript', *Euphorion*, 62, 1968, pp. 28–45.

COHN, Ruby, '"Watt" in the light of "Das Schloß"', *Comparative Literature*, 13, 1961, pp. 154–66.

DANIEL-ROPS, Review of *Das Schloß*, *Nouvelle Revue Française*, 26 March 1939, pp. 526–9.

——, 'The Castle of Despair', *The Kafka Problem*, pp. 184–91.

EMRICH, Wilhelm, *Franz Kafka*, seventh ed., Frankfurt and Bonn, 1970, pp. 298–410.

FIETZ, Lothar, 'Möglichkeiten und Grenzen einer Deutung von Kafkas "Schloß"-Roman' *DVjS*, 37, 1963, pp. 71–7.

FLEISCHMANN, Ivo, 'Na cestě ka zámku' ['On the Way to the Castle.'], *Franz Kafka*, Prague, 1963, pp. 203–9.

FLORES, Angel, Review of *Das Schloß*, *Books Abroad*, 15, Autumn 1941, p. 480.

FOULKES, A. P., 'Franz Kafka: Dichtungstheorie und Romanpraxis', *Deutsche Romantheorien*, Reinhold Grimm (ed.), Frankfurt and Bonn, 1968, pp. 321–46.

——, *The Reluctant Pessimist: A Study of Franz Kafka*, Paris and The Hague, 1967, pp. 163–71.

GOLDSTUECKER, Eduard, 'Grenzland zwischen Einsamkeit und Gemeinschaft: Randbemerkungen zu Kafkas *Schloß*', *Homo Homini Homo*, Munich, 1966, pp. 65–73.

GREENBERG, Martin, *The Terror of Art: Kafka and Modern Literature*, New York and London, 1965, pp. 154–220.

HARDT, Ludwig, 'Franz Kafkas "Schloß"', *Die Weltbühne*, 23, 2, 1927, pp. 75–6.

HATA, Setsuo, 'Bürokratie und Individuum: Ein Versuch über Kafkas "Das Schloß"', *Doitsu Bungaku*, no. 27, 1961, pp. 50–7.

HELLER, Erich, 'The World of Franz Kafka', *The Disinherited Mind*, Penguin, London, 1961, pp. 175–202.

HILSBECHER, Walter, 'Kafkas *Schloß*', *Wie modern ist eine Literatur?*, Munich, 1965, pp. 113–38.

KOBS, Jörgen, *Kafka: Untersuchungen zu Bewußtsein und Sprache seiner Gestalten,* Ursula Brech (ed. posth.), Bad Homburg, 1970, pp. 200–3, 234–9 et passim.

KOMLOVSZKI, Tibor, 'Kafkas *Schloß* und das Fortuna-Schloß des Comenius: Anmerkungen zur Vorgeschichte des Kafkaschen Weltbildes', *Acta Literaria,* 10, 1968, pp. 83–93.

KRAFT, Werner, *Franz Kafka: Durchdringung und Geheimnis,* Frankfurt, 1968, pp. 97–133.

KUDSZUS, Winfried, 'Erzählhaltung und Zeitverschiebung in Kafkas "Prozeß" und "Schloß".' *DVjS,* 38, 1964, pp. 192–207.

MANN, Thomas, 'Dem Dichter zu Ehren: Franz Kafka und "Das Schloß"', *Der Monat,* 1, 8/9, 1948–49, pp. 66–70.

MARTINI, Fritz, 'Franz Kafka: *Das Schloß*', *Das Wagnis der Sprache,* Stuttgart, 1954, pp. 287–335.

NEIDER, Charles, *Kafka: His Mind and Art,* London, 1949, pp. 122–152.

ONG, Walter J., 'Kafka's Castle and the West', *Thought,* 22, September 1947, pp. 439–60.

OSBORNE, Charles, *Kafka,* Edinburgh and London, 1967, pp. 92–104.

PARRY, Idris, Review of *Das Schloß,* The London Magazine, 1, May 1954, pp. 78–81.

PASCAL, Roy, *The German Novel,* Manchester, 1956, pp. 233–57.

PASLEY, Malcolm, 'Zur äußeren Gestalt des "Schloß"-Romans', *Kafka-Symposion,* Berlin, 1965, pp. 181–8.

———, 'Zur Entstehungsgeschichte von Franz Kafkas Schloß-Bild', *Weltfreunde: Konferenz über die Prager deutsche Literatur,* Eduard Goldstuecker (ed.), Prague, 1967, pp. 241–51.

PEARCE, Donald, '*The Castle:* Kafka's Divine Comedy', *Franz Kafka Today,* pp. 165–72.

POLITZER, Heinz, *Franz Kafka: Parable and Paradox,* Ithaca, New York, 1962, pp. 218–81.

PONGS, Hermann, 'Franz Kafka: *Das Schloß*', *Das Bild in der Dichtung,* 3, 1969, pp. 435–63.

PRIESTLEY, J. B., 'Kafka: The Last Irony: *The Castle*', *The Sunday Times,* 7 February 1954.

QUENTIN, Pol, 'Adapter "Le Château".' *Cahiers de la Compagnie Madelaine Renaud—Jean-Louis Barrault*, 5, 20, October 1959, pp. 13–16.

REED, Eugene E., 'Moral Polarity in Kafka's "Der Prozeß" and "Das Schloß",' *Monatshefte*, 46, 1954, pp. 317–24.

REED, T. J., 'Kafka und Schopenhauer: Philosophisches Denken und dichterisches Bild', *Euphorion*, 59, 1965, pp. 160–72.

REISS, Hans S., *Franz Kafka: Eine Betrachtung seines Werkes*, Heidelberg, 1956, pp. 67–109.

RENDI, Aloisio, 'Influssi letterari nel "Castello" di Kafka', *Annali-Sezione Germanica*, 4, 1961, pp. 75–93.

RICHTER, Helmut, *Franz Kafka: Werke und Entwurf*, Berlin, 1962, pp. 252–86.

ROBERT, Marthe, *L'Ancien et le Nouveau*, Paris, 1963, pp. 173–311.

SAHL, Hans, Review of *Das Schloß*, *Das Tagebuch*, 8, 1927, pp. 150–2.

SARRAUTE, Nathalie, *L'Ère du Soupçon: Essais sur le Roman*, Paris, 1956, pp. 42–52.

SAURAT, Denis, 'A Note on "The Castle",' *The Kafka Problem*, pp. 181–3.

SEBALD, W. G., 'The Undiscover'd Country: The Death Motif in Kafka's "Castle",' *Journal of European Studies*, 2, March 1972, pp. 22–34.

SEIDEL, Bruno, 'Franz Kafkas Vision des Totalitarismus: Politische Gedanken zu Kafkas Roman "Das Schloß" und George Orwells Utopie "1984",' *Die Besinnung*, 6, 1951, pp. 11–14.

SEIDLER, Manfred, *Strukturanalysen der Romane 'Der Prozeß' und 'Das Schloß' von Franz Kafka*, Diss, Bonn, 1953.

SHERWOOD, R. E., Review of *Das Schloß*, *Scribner's*, December 1930, p. 21.

SOKEL, Walter H., *Franz Kafka: Tragik und Ironie*, Munich and Vienna, 1964, pp. 391–500.

——, 'Kafka und Sartres Existenzphilosophie', *Arcadia*, 5, 1970, pp. 262–77.

SORENSEN, Willy, *Kafkas Digtning*, Copenhagen, 1968, pp. 152–78.

SWANDER, Homer, 'The Castle: K.'s Village', *Franz Kafka Today*, pp. 165–72.

SWANDER, Homer, 'Zu Kafkas "Schloß"', *Interpretationen*, Vol. 3, Frankfurt, 1966, pp. 269–89.

SYKES, Gerald, Review of *Das Schloß*, *The Nation*, 15 October 1930, p. 411.

TAUBER, Herbert, *Franz Kafka*, London, 1948, pp. 131–85.

THORLBY, Anthony, *A Student's Guide to Kafka*, London, 1972, pp. 68–83.

TOMLINSON, K. C., Review of *Das Schloß*, *Nation and Athenaeum*, 10 May 1930, p. 182.

VOLKMANN-SCHLUCK, K. H., 'Bewußtsein und Dasein in Kafkas "Schloß"', *Die Neue Rundschau*, 62, 1951, pp. 38–48.

WAGENBACH, Klaus, 'Wo liegt Kafkas Schloß?', *Kafka-Symposion*, pp. 161–80.

WEBSTER, Peter Dow, 'A critical examination of Franz Kafka's "The Castle"', *American Imago*, 8, 1951, pp. 3–28.

WEINBERG, Kurt, *Kafkas Dichtungen: Die Travestien des Mythos*, Berne and Munich, 1963, pp. 438–72.

WERNER, Herbert, 'Die Gottlosen haben keinen Frieden. Zu dem Roman von Franz Kafka: *Das Schloß*', *Die Stimme*, 3, 1951, pp. 15, 389–90.

WEST, Rebecca, *The Court and The Castle*, London, 1958, pp. 221–41.

WINKLER, R. O. C., 'The Novels', *Kafka*, Ronald D. Gray (ed.), Eaglewood Cliffs, 1962, pp. 45–51.

INDEX

INDEX